Death

Other books by Herbie Brennan

The Atlantis Enigma
A Guide to Megalithic Ireland
Martian Genesis
The Secret History of Ancient Egypt
Time Travel: A New Perspective
Astral Doorways
Experimental Magic
An Occult History of the World
Occult Tibet
The Magical I Ching
The Ultimate Elsewhere

Death

The Great Mystery of Life

HERBIE BRENNAN

CARROLL & GRAF PUBLISHERS
NEW YORK

DEATH
THE GREAT MYSTERY OF LIFE

Carroll & Graf Publishers
An Imprint of Avalon Publishing Group Inc.
161 William St., 16th Floor
New York, NY 10038

First Carroll & Graf edition 2002

Designed by Simon M. Sullivan

Library of Congress Cataloging-in-Publication Data is available.

ISBN: 0-7867-1044-6

Printed in the United States of America
Distributed by Publishers Group West

For Maggie and Sophie

Table of Contents

Three Amazing Things . . .

I DISCOVERED THREE amazing things while researching this book. The first was that in culture after culture across the face of the globe, death is blamed on women.

The most familiar expression of the idea is in the Judeo-Christian tradition. Eve, the mother of us all, was supposedly seduced by the Serpent. She then persuaded Adam to eat fruit from the tree of the knowledge of good and evil, thus introducing death into the world—"for dust thou art, and unto dust shalt thou return," God remarked crossly.

But Genesis isn't the only place where the theme emerges. Polynesian myth claims that in ancient times people changed their skins instead of dying, but a woman put her old skin back on again, setting a fashion for death we've followed ever since. In Africa, it was sight of a woman half in and half out of her skin that brought death to us all. A belief prevalent in South America's Orinoco Basin suggests that when God told humans they could live forever by changing their skins, an old woman laughed at the idea and an offended deity sentenced humanity to mortality.

The Aborigines of New South Wales in Australia tell how God warned people not to go near a particular tree that had bees nesting inside. The men obeyed, but the women wanted honey. When one of them struck the tree with an ax, Death flew out and has been killing people ever since. Baganda myth suggests the first woman came from heaven, but her brother was Death, who was allowed to accompany humanity forever when the woman disobeyed God. Native American

Algonquin tribes have a legend that humanity was granted the gift of immortality by the Great Hare, but a woman disobeyed orders, opened the gift package, and immortality escaped and flew away.

And so the story goes, with variations on the theme taken up from the tropics to the icy plains of Greenland, relentlessly and ludicrously blaming women for the fact that you and I must die one day.

The second amazing thing I discovered was that one aspect of these myths is true. There really was a time when life existed on our planet but death did not.

Life's origins are something of a scientific mystery. There are lots of theories, of course: the most popular claims that organic molecules were created by the action of lightning on an atmospheric mixture of hydrogen, methane, ammonia and water vapor.[1] But wherever it came from, the earliest form of life seems to have been primeval slime mould, which reproduced, amoeba-like, by splitting. Thus, while pieces of the mould eventually wore out and disappeared, the creature as a whole survived. It may, for all I know, be with us still, lurking in some dark crevice of our planet.

Biologists assure us what brought death to our world was sex, another eerie echo of some ancient myths. Once living creatures gave up budding in favor of sexual reproduction, they could no longer be considered immortal by any interpretation of that term. But while individuals might die, the overall trade-off was good. Sexual reproduction opened the door to variety and evolution. Given world enough and time, you and I walked through that door.

The third amazing thing I discovered is that old age doesn't kill you. It certainly makes you prone to disease, which usually does, but in the absence of disease, there seems to be no good reason why you shouldn't last indefinitely . . . except, of course, you don't. This is something I'll go into rather more fully in the course of the book as part of an investigation that's less scary and more hopeful than you might imagine.

Enjoy . . .

Introduction

A dying man can do nothing easy.
Last words of Benjamin Franklin, April 17, 1790

SEVERAL MINUTES AFTER your heart has stopped beating, doctors can still record a mini-electrocardiogram by probing for signals from inside the cardiac cavity.

At this stage, are you really dead?

Three hours later, your pupils will still contract violently in reaction to pilocarpine drops exactly as they did in life. Your muscles will still shorten if someone taps them repeatedly.

At this stage, are you really dead?

Surgeons can incise a viable graft from the skin tissue anywhere on your body twenty-four hours after you expire. They can achieve a viable bone graft forty-eight hours later, a viable arterial graft even after seventy–two hours.

At what point in this process are you really dead?

Edgar Allan Poe was just one of many historical personalities obsessed by the fear of being buried alive. Given the uncertainty of death, was he right to worry? And should you be worried too?

The Bible claims God allots three score years and ten of life to members of the human race. Statistics suggests He has grown more generous in recent years. For people living in the industrial West, average life expectancy is now four years more.

Herbie Brennan

In Third World countries, by contrast, your chances of survival are considerably less. Even in a relatively developed country like Egypt, life expectancy is only fifty. In many African and Asiatic countries it is actually less than it used to be in Ancient Greece or Rome.

You are most at risk of death at birth and in old age, least at risk between the years of ten and twelve. But your appointment in Samarra is already made. Even you will die one day. [2]

And the frightening thing is, you have almost no idea what that means.

In Western culture, death is hidden. Hospitals shield us from observing the reality of dying. Undertakers are well paid to keep us from looking in the face of death. A corpse is scrubbed, sanitized, and cosmeticized in order to appear "lifelike." It is displayed in a comfortably padded casket. It is laid "to rest" in consecrated ground . . . but the grave is only filled in when the mourners have gone home. At the crematorium, velvet curtains preserve our innocence of the inevitable.

But we pay a heavy price for this protection. Death is the Great Unknown and nothing terrifies more than the unknown.

This book is an attempt to remove the curtain from the Great Unknown and examine, in stark detail, the one phenomenon that concerns us all.

Preface

THE STORY GOES that a Zen monk, Ten Yin-feng, asked his colleagues if anyone had ever died while standing on his head. When assured that no one ever had, Ten promptly stood on his head and died.

The monks at the monastery were loath to disturb the corpse and carried it upside down to his funeral pyre. This caused consternation among the pyre attendants, who were unwilling to cremate him in that position but equally unwilling to turn him right-side up.

For a time it looked as though Ten wouldn't be cremated at all. Then someone had the idea of calling for his younger sister. The girl arrived and fiercely told Ten he had been a nuisance in life and was still proving a nuisance in death—with which she poked him until he fell over with a thud and the cremation continued.

The most interesting aspect of this story is that it is told in Zen circles to illustrate how Ten achieved liberation.

1

Your Likely Way To Die

Here am I, dying of a hundred good symptoms.
—Alexander Pope on his deathbed at Twickenham,
London on May 30, 1744

IT'S A MIRACLE you're reading this at all. While there are really only two ways to get into this world—naturally or by cesarean section—the ways out are positively legion.

You might, for example, die from exposure while attempting to break into your own home wearing only underwear and socks. It happened to a woman in Dayton, Ohio, in 1988. She seems to have mislaid her keys, and rather than disturb her husband, she tried to climb in through a pantry window. Somehow the window closed and trapped her foot, leaving her dangling upside down. She was spotted by a neighbor, who mistook her for a store-window dummy and consequently failed to investigate until the snow-covered housewife had died of cold.

Or you might be killed by a soft-drink machine as happened to fifteen Americans—eleven of them servicemen—and one young Briton during the 1980s. (Some thirty-nine other victims escaped with only injuries.) The Briton was a seventeen-year-old who was staying in a London hotel in 1988 when, according to the night porter, he discovered he could get free cans by tilting the hotel's eight-hundred-pound machine. He had extracted three drinks in this way and was trying for a fourth when the machine fell on top of him, causing brain damage that led to his death after three months in a coma.

Alternatively, you might choke to death when a custard pie is pushed into your face, like one French comedian. Or you could be mistaken for a rutting stag and shot by a poacher as happened to a Yugoslav man in 1978. (He had gone into the woods to practice his rutting stag impersonation.) Or you could be killed by something falling from the sky, as was a seventy-nine-year-old woman in Essen, Germany, who in 1990 was struck by an Airedale terrier; and then there were the cows that sank a Japanese fishing boat in the Sea of Okhotsk, drowning certain of the crew.[3] Or perhaps you will simply explode like the eighty-two-year-old patient in Nottingham Hospital, England, who went out with a bang while undergoing surgery in 1988.[4]

But exits like these are frankly unlikely. If you're a resident of almost any First World country, your likeliest way to die is heart disease. It carries off some 724,859 U.S. citizens[5] every year, mainly in the over-sixty-five age group. This sort of demise has long been thought of as the prerogative of the harassed male, but statistics belie it. Substantially more American women now die from heart disease than men.[6]

The figure quoted represents a death rate of 164.4 per hundred thousand population, which is high, but no world-beater. The worst figure (409) currently comes from Russia, with other East European countries like the Czech Republic, Hungary, and Bulgaria all well ahead of the United States. Combined figures for England and Wales are higher too—197.6 per hundred thousand—and Scotland shows up with a massive 250.4. Even if you live in France, which has a remarkably low incidence of heart attacks, cardiac disease still remains the most likely way to go. Only in Japan, Spain, and Portugal is there another preference. I'll deal with the residents of those countries in a moment.

For the rest of us, this is what happens when we embark on our favourite way to die.

If you have regular medical checkups, the first sign of anything amiss may come when your doctor reports you have high blood pressure or cholesterol.

High blood pressure is exactly what it sounds like—an overall increase in the pressure your blood exerts on the inside of your arteries and veins. The actual pressure varies every minute of the day from a high point when your heart contracts to a low point when it relaxes before getting round to the next beat. Blood pressure also rises when you take exercise and falls while you're asleep. It was generally lower when you were a child than it is now that you've grown up.

But all these are natural factors. If you're a healthy, resting adult, your blood pressure will push a column of mercury to a height of about 120mm when your heart contracts. Even when it's resting between beats, the pressure will still be enough to move the mercury to the 80mm mark. Your doctor will usually express these readings as "one-twenty over eighty." So long as they stay in that neighborhood, give or take a couple of points, you don't have anything to worry about. If they drop a little, you probably don't have to worry too much either—low blood pressure can have its problems but a point or two is unlikely to be serious. [7] High blood pressure is something else. If the readings rise, you could be in trouble. You might even have heart disease.

High cholesterol is a bit more complicated. Cholesterol is a white, waxy substance that circulates in your blood. Despite the bad press it's been getting, you would not survive without it. Cholesterol is actually used to build cell membranes, bile acids necessary for digestion, certain hormones, and your personal supply of vitamin D. The substance is manufactured by your liver and taken in with the food you eat. The more you consume by mouth, the less your liver must manufacture so a healthy balance is maintained.

At least that's the theory. The reality is that sometimes the flood gets higher than the dike. High-cholesterol foods like butter, cream, chocolate bars, good red meat, and full-fat cheese are so tempting that we often eat more of them than the liver can compensate for by reducing its share of the output. Alternatively, lifestyle factors like alcohol and stress can so unbalance your liver that you overproduce cholesterol irrespective of what you eat.

Lately, you may have noticed your doctor has been talking about "good cholesterol" and "bad cholesterol." Actually there's just cholesterol, but the effect it has on your body depends entirely on what it's attached to. Substances called low-density lipoproteins—thankfully shortened to LDLs—carry cholesterol from the liver to the various cells and tissues, where it separates out and is happily used. High-density lipoproteins (HDLs) carry any excess back to the liver, where it's broken down and eventually excreted. "Good" cholesterol is carried by HDLs, since the more HDLs you have in your blood, the more likely it is your blood cholesterol levels will drop. "Bad" cholesterol is the stuff associated with LDLs. If you have an abundance of that floating around inside you, you're in big trouble—or will be if you don't get it down to manageable proportions.

The problem is, cholesterol won't dissolve in blood. Without enough HDLs to clean it up, it just keeps on circulating until it lays down a fatty deposit on the inside of your arteries and veins. After a while this thickens, calcifies, and eventually scars the vessel wall. As the walls thicken, the blood passageway narrows. You don't have to be a rocket scientist to figure out what happens next. Blood pressure tends to increase as the passage narrows, and one day the blood vessel will close off altogether, or get blocked up by a clot that would have passed freely through if things were normal.

Once that happens, you become a prime candidate for a heart attack.

If you don't believe in regular checkups, your first sign of the problem might well be angina. *Angina pectoris*, to give the condition its full name, translates as "pain of the chest" brought on by exertion in those of you with ailing arteries leading to the heart. The attack hits as a deep pain underneath the breastbone across your heart and stomach. It feels like your chest is being squeezed in a giant vise. Sometimes the pain spreads into your left shoulder or crawls down the inside of the arm. You'll often think you're suffocating, but if you pay careful attention—which may not be all that easy in the circumstances—you'll discover your breathing is actually unaffected.

Although angina can sometimes be quite mild, even a low-pain attack will fill you with dread. (Your body knows when something's seriously wrong, even if you don't.) In severe cases, you'll turn pale, your pulse will drop, and you'll convince yourself you're on the brink of death.

Fortunately this conviction is (usually) inaccurate. Angina attacks don't come out of nowhere. They arise because your narrowed arteries can't deliver enough blood to your heart to cope with whatever you're up to. So if you're walking, running, taking exercise after a heavy meal, furious with somebody, under far too much stress, or even just outside in the cold and wind, waste products build up in your heart muscle and start to irritate the nerves there, which is what causes the dreadful pain. Stop what you're doing, rest a little, and relax. In three or four minutes you'll be right as rain.

At least for the time being.

The trouble with angina is that it tends to get worse. Unless you try something drastic like a change of lifestyle, the chances are your arteries will continue to narrow. As this happens, you'll find it takes less and less exertion, less and less stress to trigger an attack. At this point, your doctor will probably prescribe nitroglycerin, an explosive substance that has the fortunate property of dilating your blood vessels. Pop a pill under your tongue and the pain goes away. It's a blessed relief, but it remains a stop-gap measure. If your arteries continue to narrow, you're going to need surgery. Sometimes this just means widening the arteries. Sometimes it means replacing them completely.[8]

You can live for quite a while with angina—my father had it for years and died from something else—but it's a warning signal that shouldn't really be ignored. It's also a warning signal that doesn't always arise. What with your smoking habit, your eating habits, your alcohol consumption, your stress levels, your high blood pressure, and your raging LDL cholesterol, you could leapfrog angina completely and go straight to the big one—*myocardial infarction,* doctor lingo for a heart attack.

You may not want to know this, but in any heart attack there's always a little bit of you that dies. The little bit is a piece of your heart muscle, which ceases to function due to an interruption of the blood flow. What causes the interruption is usually a blood clot lodged in a coronary artery narrowed by cholesterol plaque. The size of the bit that dies determines what you'll feel.

There's a small possibility you'll feel nothing at all. Some people sail through their heart attacks without pain or even much discomfort, dismissing any slight symptom as gas or indigestion. They only know they've had one if their doctor orders an electrocardiogram, which shows up the area of dead muscle.

But painless heart attacks are unusual. For most of us there's a sudden, crushing chest pain often radiating into the neck, arm(s), and back. It's very like angina, except it doesn't go away. Nitroglycerin won't help, nor will rest. If you simply sit there worrying, you'll still be in agony after thirty minutes. You could still be in agony after an hour or more. (Always assuming you haven't died, of course.) To go with the pain, you'll probably have difficulty breathing. You'll sweat. You'll feel nauseous. Your blood pressure will drop. Your heart will race, although the beat may be irregular. You'll feel a deep sense of impending doom.

That feeling is by no means misplaced. One in five of those hit by a heart attack don't even make it to hospital. You're carried from the ambulance, marked "dead on arrival" and taken to the morgue. The risk of death is highest within the first few minutes of your attack. Thus about 40 percent of those marked out by the Grim Reaper will go within an hour. Three hours later another 20 percent will have joined them.

Most of the really early deaths are directly caused by an irregular heartbeat—what the doctors call *fibrillation*.[9] Thus the first line of treatment is nearly always drugs or electric shock to get this problem under control. The whole thrust of treatment, then and thereafter, is to limit the damage to your heart muscle and stop complications. You'll probably be given morphine for the pain—a treatment that may later leave you constipated. You may get beta-blockers, which will help with pain as well and bring down your heart rate. Something like streptokinase will stop new clots from forming (and thus avoid triggering another attack). If you manage it through the next four weeks, the chances are you're going to survive.

Until the next attack, of course.

For those of you reading this in Spain, Portugal, and Japan, heart attacks are only your second favorite way to die. The number one slot is taken up by something listed as *cerebrovascular disease*—the reassuring way of describing a good old-fashioned stroke.

Curiously enough, strokes are made more likely by the same suspects you find implicated in heart disease—smoking, high cholesterol, diabetes, aging, and genetic factors. You'll even find a heart attack can play its own part in giving you a stroke. But the mechanism is a bit more complicated than heart disease.

There are four main roads you can take to reach your stroke.

First, most straightforward, and far and away the most common is the formation of a clot inside a brain blood vessel.

Second, the blood clot may form elsewhere, then travel to your brain. This is where heart attacks come in. Along with valve damage and fibrillation, heart attacks can lead to traveling clots. Once a clot forms or lodges in the brain, it reduces blood flow to surrounding tissue. In some cases it stops blood flow altogether, except for blood that sometimes oozes out of the offending blood vessel, which adds to your problems rather than reducing them.

The third cause of stroke is a narrowing of brain arteries. Even without clots forming, this can cause a sludging of the blood or a spasm of the artery wall. Either way, it cuts down or cuts off the brain's blood supply.

Finally, there's bleeding directly into the brain. High blood pressure can lead to a weakening of the artery wall, as can copper deficiency. The thinned wall can bulge or rupture.

None of these situations is good news for your well-being. Even mini-strokes can turn into big trouble in the long run. These occur when long, thin, deep-brain arteries get blocked. Deprived of blood, the surrounding tissue withers, creating a tiny hole in the brain.

That's what happens. What you experience might be no more than a temporary disturbance of your vision, a little weakness, maybe numbness, of an arm. The side of your face might feel odd or you could find yourself slurring your speech as if you've had too much alcohol. You could experience a moment of confusion. But any or all of these symptoms will pass away. You might mention to your spouse at lunchtime that you felt a bit peculiar, but it won't strike you as anything serious and you'll probably have forgotten all about it by dinner.

But while one hole may be a minor inconvenience, a succession of them over the years will riddle your brain like Swiss cheese, leaving you prey to a type of dementia not unlike Alzheimer's disease. Even if that doesn't happen, recurring little strokes will almost always lead to more widespread—and often permanent—paralysis at some point down the line.

Before you reach that stage, it can be interesting to contemplate how tiny injuries to specific parts of the brain influence particular parts of your body. If, for example, you experience paralysis on the right side of your body, it means the *left* side of your brain has been affected—nerve connections cross the center line. With a good knowledge of anatomy and an up-to-date chart of brain function, you could, if you had a mind to, go some way toward pinpointing roughly where your mini-strokes occurred while you waited for the big one to hit.

The big one, of course, will be a lot more spectacular. It can strike, without warning, at any time. From a standing start, minding your own business, perhaps strolling on the beach or sitting with your feet up watching television, you will find yourself massively paralysed and unable to speak. If the cause of your stroke is a hemorrhage, there's a likelihood you'll pass into a coma and die within days . . . or even hours; that's something that can happen with other illnesses as well.

Even following a massive stroke not everybody dies, of course. If you survive, your doctors will work very hard to find what exactly caused the problem. If it turns out to be a blood clot, they'll pump you full of anticoagulants to stop any more from forming. But that sort of treatment would finish you off if the stroke was caused by hemorrhage. Sometimes both clots and bleeding are involved, which makes you a very tricky patient. Where there's a blockage of the carotid arteries—the main blood source of the brain—you might be in for surgery to remove the problem by inserting a graft or some sort of synthetic bypass.

Should treatment save your life, you could be looking forward to another twenty years or more. To help you make the most of them, your health professionals will begin a rehabilitation regime within days. The human brain is a remarkably versatile organ so that given time and a lot of encouragement undamaged areas can sometimes be persuaded to take up the jobs once carried out by those areas that have now been damaged beyond repair. But while many strokes respond well to this sort of treatment, some don't. If you're one of the unlucky ones, you're trapped inside a useless body with very little to look forward to except visits from your loved ones and the ultimate release of death.

These, then, are your most likely ways to die in a First World country at the start of the twenty-first century. But history teaches they may not be your most likely ways tomorrow.

2

Black Death

The plague that raged all over the land . . . consumed nine parts in ten of the men through England, scarcely leaving a tenth man alive.
—Bristol and Gloucestershire Archaeological Society, 1883

SOMETIME IN 1346, a Flemish priest received a disturbing letter from a friend in the Papal Curia. It described how, over the space of just three days, an entire eastern province "hard by Greater India" had been utterly overwhelmed by a series of bizarre weather events.

The first day had seen a rain of frogs, lizards, and venomous creatures like snakes and scorpions. On the second, a massive thunderstorm produced not only lightning but sheets of fire and hailstones so enormous that they killed off almost all the population. The third day brought more fire from heaven, this time accompanied by "stinking smoke" that wiped out the few surviving pockets of humanity and all their domestic beasts. Every town and city in the province suffered.

The letter went on to say that the foul air, which seemed to have originated somewhere to the south, had poisoned not only the province in question but the seashore and neighboring lands as well. The area, it was claimed, grew more poisonous from day to day.

Medieval readers took such stories seriously, especially when they were set in the mysterious Orient. Since the venomous rain and violent thunderstorms were over and done with, speculation focused on the malodorous cloud. Some believed it was caused by a battle between the sun and the sea in the Indian Ocean. The battle resulted in so many rotting fish that the vapor they produced rolled over the land, contaminating everything it touched. The monkish author of the *Chronicon Estense*[10] claimed the cloud arose from the heavenly fire that had burned the mountains and plains. He recorded that any man or woman who saw the cloud died within half a day; and those who saw the corpses quickly died as well.

That final detail pinpoints the reality behind the whole fantastic story. When people start to die from contact with those who have already died, you can be sure the most likely cause is a contagious disease.

There really *was* a contagious disease raging through the Orient in 1346. At the time it was known as the "blue sickness." Today it is more often referred to as the Black Death, or in less emotive terms, bubonic plague.

Bubonic plague is caused by the bacterium *Yersinia pestis*, typically carried by rats. It passes to humans in a particularly unpleasant way. Fleas feed on infected rat blood. The bacteria multiply in the flea's digestive tract and eventually block it altogether. Since fleas are promiscuous creatures, their next meal may well be taken from a human. But with a blocked tract, the flea vomits undigested rat blood—with its store of plague bacteria—into the bite. Within a few heartbeats, the bacteria are circulating through the human body.

Yersina pestis is an ancient enemy of humanity—some scholars implicate it in the fall of the Roman Empire—but by the fourteenth century it had lain dormant for so long most people had forgotten its existence. One area where pockets still survived, well contained and causing little trouble to anyone, was China.

It might have stayed dormant indefinitely had it not been for an extraordinary combination of circumstances.

China has always been a disaster-prone country, but what happened in the 1330s was almost unbelievable. First came drought. The rivers Kiang and Hoai shrank to a trickle while crops withered on their flood plains. The same picture was repeated throughout China. Famine inevitably followed and huge segments of the population starved. Throughout the land, everybody prayed for rain.

In 1333, their prayers were answered with downpours of such intensity that 400,000 people died. The floods were so extensive that the foundation of Mount Tsincheou (in what is now the Ningsia Autonomous Region) was undermined. In a unique geological phenomenon, the mountain collapsed in on itself, leaving gaping chasms in the earth. The following year, drought came back to Houkouang and Honan provinces. What few crops were left were eaten by swarms of locusts. Famine returned and a depleted, weakened population fell prey to disease.

At this point, the earthquakes started. The first struck massively in the Ki-Ming-Chan Mountains, causing so much land slippage that a lake was formed more than a hundred leagues in circumference. Volcanic activity was felt in Canton.

For the next decade, earthquake followed flood, followed locusts, followed famine in a hideous procession of disasters. For China, it must have seemed like the end of the world. But worse was to come. One result of these massive upheavals was an exodus of rats. Some, it seems, were carrying bubonic plague.

In 1344, Nestorians began to die in thousands in the Semiriechinsk district of central Asia. The disease was not recognized for what it was, though even if it had been, there was no effective treatment available. Unchecked, it began to spread eastward, back into China. A major difference between China and Semi-riechinsk was population density. The newly active bacteria cut an unimaginable swathe of death across China. There were five million victims in Tche alone.

China is a huge country—at 3,696,100 square miles, it rivals the entire European continent and occupies fully one fourteenth of the land surface of the Earth. In the fourteenth century it was an isolated kingdom where for most people the fastest form of transport was their feet. Consequently, the new plague remained contained for a time. But inevitably the bacillus began to cross borders. Once that happened, its spread was terrifying.

By 1346, the year the Belgian priest received his letter, plague had laid low most of Asia and reached deep into the Middle East. Wrote J. F. C. Hecker, whose definitive work *The Epidemics of the Middle Ages* was published in London in 1859: "India was depopulated. Tartary, Mesopotamia, Syria, Armenia were covered with dead bodies; the Kurds fled in vain to the mountains. In Caramania and Caesarea, none were left alive."

The virulence of the disease was mind-bending. First signs appeared suddenly. In a few hours body temperature would rise to about 40 °C (104 °F). Victims became gravely ill, with vomiting, muscular pain, mental disorganization, and delirium. Lymph nodes throughout the body—especially those in groin and armpits—became enlarged, excruciatingly painful, and filled with pus. These were the "buboes" that gave bubonic plague its name. In anything up to 90 percent of cases, death occurred within a few days. There were contemporary accounts that claimed some victims went to bed free of symptoms and were discovered as putrefying corpses the next morning.

The priest's letter was not the only indication that something was amiss. Travelers' tales of the epidemic reached Europe and soon the great disaster in the Orient became a matter of common gossip. Incredibly, nobody seemed to think Europe itself was in any danger. But the disease began to crawl along the silk roads. It moved from Baghdad up the Tigris through Armenia. By 1346, it had reached the Italian trade stations in the Crimea. Within months the death toll had climbed to 85,000. Local Tartars decided it was all the fault of Christian merchants and mounted an attack on a Genoese trading station at the city of Tana (now Azov) in southwestern Russia. The merchants fled to their coastal redoubt of Feodosia. Pursuing Tartars settled down outside the city walls to lay siege. But before they could do much, the plague caught up with them. In days their numbers were decimated.

The Tartars decided to call off the siege, but not before giving the Christians a taste of their own medicine. They had observed that those who came close to plague victims often fell ill themselves, so they loaded the pus-filled bodies into giant catapults and flung them over the city walls.

The Genoese dumped the corpses into the sea, but the damage was already done. In carrying the Tartar corpses through their town, they actually encouraged the fleas to seek out new hosts. Within days the city was infected. As plague spread through Feodosia, its citizens quickly realized the few who were likely to survive could never defend against a renewed Tartar attack. There was a panic-stricken exodus by sea. Plague-ridden rats and fleas climbed into the ships with the fearful Genoese.

The Genoese plague ships were not the only vessels of death plying the open seas at this time. Scores of trading galleys had been calling in on Eastern ports. Now they headed for Genoa itself, for the beautiful port of Venice, for Messina and other Italian ports. By the time they arrived, their crews were dying at their oars.

Port authorities climbed on board to make what would, in normal times, have been a routine inspection. They were met with scenes reminiscent of hell. The dead and dying were everywhere. The ships were sent packing, of course, but this feeble attempt at quarantine came far too late. Even as the inspectors recoiled in horror, fleas hopped unnoticed and rats scuttled ashore. By the time the galleys left, their deadliest cargo had been unloaded. While their crews lasted, the ships themselves sought other ports, spreading the disease even further. By 1347, the plague was raging through the whole of Italy.

Toward the end of January 1348, the dreadful pattern repeated. A plague-ridden galley, banished from Italy, put in at Marseilles. Once again the port authorities came on board to inspect. Once again rats jumped ship. Several of the French inspectors were themselves infected. The ship was denied permission to stay and set sail for Spain. But for France it was all too late. The bacteria were already leaving Marseilles in search of fresh hosts on the European mainland.

Just two years later, the Black Death had continued its dreadful progress eastward into Germany. It seems to have reached Bavaria first, then traveled north along the Moselle Valley. By this time it was already well established in Cyprus, in Greece, and in Turkey. Watching its pestilential progress in Constantinople, the contemporary historian Nicephoros Gregoras wrote, "The calamity did not destroy men only, but many animals living with and domesticated by men. I speak of dogs and horses, and all the species of birds, even the rats that happened to live within the walls of houses."

From Northern Italy, plague crossed the Adriatic into Dalmatia. Dubrovnik went under in the opening weeks of 1348. When the plague reached Split two months later, wolves poured in from the neighboring forests to attack the few survivors. Piles of corpses rotted in the streets—there was no one left to bury them.

The horror reached England at about the same time. Historians are divided over where the plague struck first. Bristol and Southampton are possibilities because of their constant trading contact with the Continent, but the small Dorsetshire port of Melcombe Regis, now part of Weymouth, is considered the strongest contender. As the Bishop of Bath and Wells ordered weekly penances to beg God's protection against the pestilence sweeping France, two ships docked a few days before the Feast of St. John the Baptist[11] in 1348. A sailor on one of them was already suffering from the illness, picked up in Gascony or possibly Marseilles. God ignored the Bishop's pleas and plague began to spread through Britain.

At the time, only about 12 percent of the population lived in towns or cities. London was, of course, the largest with approximately 70,000 inhabitants. Next came Norwich, which housed some 13,000 souls, and York, which was a little smaller. The remaining 88 percent of the population lived almost entirely in villages ranging upward from a dozen families to communities of three or four hundred. It was here that the impact of the Black Death was most strongly felt. Many villages were to lose more than half their residents.

The pestilence moved swiftly up the Bristol Channel so that Bristol itself became the first major city to be hit. One contemporary chronicler recorded that "almost the whole strength of the town" was "suddenly overwhelmed by death." Few were sick more than three days before succumbing. Some died within half a day of their first symptoms. The Town Council lost almost a third of its members at a single stroke. Existing burial facilities were quickly overwhelmed. The parson of Holy Cross de la Temple, one of Bristol's largest churches, was under so much pressure for graveyard space that he seized additional land without waiting for a royal license and had to be specially pardoned by the king.

The plague spread to Exeter, where a rising death toll brought the wool trade to a halt and stopped construction work on the local cathedral. Then it turned eastward. The citizens of Gloucester tried to protect themselves by banning entry to anyone from Bristol, but the attempt at isolation proved futile. At the time no one suspected the part played by fleas and rats.

Pestilence spread rapidly into Oxfordshire, Berkshire, and Buckinghamshire, depopulating villages so savagely that many suffered complete economic collapse and disappeared within the next century. Some did not have to wait a century to disappear. After tax collectors visited Tilgarsley in 1359, they reported back to the Abbot of Eynsham that not one of his tenants was left alive.

From Southampton, *Yersina pestis* seized Wiltshire before significant numbers of deaths began to be reported in neighboring Hampshire. The Bishop of Winchester, William Edendon, decided it was "man's sensuality" that had provoked divine wrath and ordered barefoot penetential processions around market places and churchyards every Sunday, Wednesday and Friday. Despite this swift reaction, he managed to lose more of his clergy to the plague than any other diocese in England. Almost half the total city population followed them into an early grave.

Once the plague struck Surrey, it was only a matter of time before it reached London. The first cases were reported in November 1348, somewhat earlier than the outbreaks in the surrounding countryside. Soon the Prior of Canterbury was writing in alarm to the Bishop of London about the extent of the lethal incursion. Existing graveyards quickly proved too small to meet the growing demand. New ones were hurriedly consecrated at Smithfield and Spittle Croft. One historian recorded that 200 people were buried every day between February 2 and April 2. Another claimed 50,000 bodies were interred within the confines of a single monastery.

Caught up in the horror, an anonymous rhymester composed a telling little poem to the pestilence:

Ring a ring a rosies,
A pocket full of posies
Atchoo! Atchoo!!
We all fall down.

Garlands of roses and pockets stuffed with posies were the means by which the ignorant attempted to combat the Black Death, still popularly believed to be spread on the noxious smell of decaying corpses. Sneezing was often the first sign the disease had struck. And shortly afterwards those who had it fell down dead.

Having accepted the nightmare gift from Europe, England sent it on to Scandinavia. The crew of a wool ship that sailed from London in 1349 succumbed to the plague while at sea and died to a man. The vessel eventually ran aground near Bergen in Norway. Looters carried away more than they bargained from the wreck. The blue sickness spread south into Denmark and east into Sweden. King Magnus II saw it coming. In 1350 he announced to his subjects that the "great punishment of God" had killed off most of the Norwegians, that pestilence was raging in the Netherlands, and that if the Swedes did not mend their ways, they would soon be in the same boat. Penances were introduced, including fasting and more barefoot processions around churchyards, but the plague came in just the same. The king survived. Two of his brothers died.

Nowhere could doctors help. They were hampered most by lack of understanding. In her superb fictional recreation of the Black Death, *Doomsday Book*, Connie Willis describes how open sores and wounds were bandaged with filthy rags. If anything, this is an understatement. One contemporary expert, Gentile of Foligno, recommended poultices of human excrement.

Only slightly less repulsive was the practice of bloodletting. John of Burgundy convinced himself there were particular areas of the body—called emunctories—where bleeding produced specific results. The emunctory of the heart, for example, was located in the armpit, where the poison that caused the sickness could be drawn off through an appropriate vein. If the physician missed his chance here, the poison progressed to the liver and had to be released by bleeding the groin. By the time it reached the brain, only bleeding the throat or a spot beneath the ears would stop it.

Other physicians were less discriminating, and bloodletting was widely used as a preventative. It fell to the Arab doctor Ibn Khatimah to sound a warning on the practice. He believed bleeding useful only to the point where a patient lost eight pounds in weight.

To protect themselves from the noxious fumes, most doctors went well beyond the pocketfull of posies immortalized in the nursery rhyme. They wore leather masks, gauntlets, and armor over an unwashed shirt powdered with multicolored chalks. Small sponges of vinegar and rose water were often tucked into the sides of their mouths. Fevered patients watching such apparitions approaching must have felt they were being summoned to hell.

Physicians handed out pills of myrrh and saffron, and chopped up snakes to compound with treacle and wine. For the rich, powdered emerald was used—Gentile of Foligno held it was so powerful it could cause a toad's eyes to crack. Dietary restrictions forbade the use of boiled meat and boiled eggs, not to mention sleeping after a meal. Even sleeping safely at night required alternating between right and left sides, in order to maintain a steady heat in the liver.

A distorted practice of homeopathy came into play as physicians speculated that like would combat like. Since the plague was caused by fetid air, patients might protect, or even cure, themselves if they spent long enough inhaling the stench from their latrines and chamber pots.

It is important to realize these bizarre treatments did not arise from the stupidity of individual doctors. They were a direct result of orthodox medical training. Any question of experimentation was severely frowned on. Even personal experience was limited. In plague times, most doctors declined to visit their patients (for fear of infection) and those who did were usually kept at a distance by relatives who placed far greater confidence in the ministrations of a priest.

The church also interfered with medical practice at a far more profound level. Pope Boniface III, faced with a proliferating black market in religious "relics," issued a bull in 1300 forbidding the mutilation of corpses. It stopped the study of internal anatomy dead in its tracks. The pious Medical Faculty of Paris promptly declared its opposition to surgery. Montpellier Medical School, perhaps the most enlightened institution of its type in Europe, held one class in practical anatomy, by special dispensation, every *two years*.

Unchecked by the helpless physicians, the pestilence raging in the European heartland was to kill 75 million people before burning itself out. This represented somewhere between a quarter and a half of the total population of the continent. It was not the first time the bacillus had spread in pandemic proportions—it killed an estimated 100 million people in the Middle East, Europe, and Asia during the sixth century. Nor was it the last time. Outbreaks of bubonic plague continued to ravage Europe for the next two hundred years.

Of all the ways humanity may die, *Yersinia pestis* is undoubtedly the most persistent, the most horrifying, and the most difficult to treat. It manifests in three forms: bubonic, pneumonic, and septicemic. The ghastly outbreak in the fourteenth century contained all of them. Bubonic plague, spread by rats and fleas, was characterized by the lymph gland swellings known as buboes from which it got its name. Pneumonic plague, which attacked a victim's lungs, spread far more quickly, since it was carried in the water droplets of the breath. Septicemic plague, which attacked the blood, was the most deadly. It accounted for the reports of symptomless victims who died overnight.

In more recent times, smaller epidemics have occurred in Southeast Asia, India, Africa, and South America. Even in the United States, scattered cases were reported as late as 1968. None of these outbreaks turned into anything remotely resembling the great pandemics of the past. What has changed is the discovery of antibiotics. *Yersina pestis* is vulnerable to streptomycin, chloramphenicol, and tetracycline, provided they are administered within fifteen hours of the first appearance of symptoms. So we no longer have anything to fear from this ancient monster.

Or do we?

3

The Next Plague

*Which maladies seemed to set entirely at naught both the art of the
physician and the virtues of the physic.*
Boccaccio, *The Decameron.*

DEADLY EPIDEMICS HAVE not been confined to the Middle Ages.
Influenza swept the globe in 1918 and killed more people in a
year—some 21.5 million—than died throughout the First
World War that preceded and helped spread it round the world.
At the time, it was possible to catch typhoid fever in downtown
Baltimore. Although not so spectacular because it killed more
slowly, tuberculosis was an almost permanent epidemic. As late
as 1939, nursing students in Chicago were routinely tested for
TB. If they didn't have it when they entered their profession,
most of them picked it up during their first year on the city
wards. Bacterial pneumonia, the disease that killed my father,
was commonplace in winter. In America during the thirties,
two patients in every five died despite the best of hospital care.
Elsewhere, the incidence of death was even higher.

Even apparently minor problems could have profound implications. Author Laurie Garrett describes how her aunt picked
up an ear infection at the age of nine. It not only made her deaf
but attacked the mastoid bone and triggered a bout of
osteomyelitis that left one leg shorter than the other, so that she
limped for the rest of her life. My own ear infection, contracted

as a child in the same era, proved even more problematical. Inside of a day I passed from high fever to coma and was, according to the family doctor, within hours of death when medical intervention finally succeeded.

All that changed in the 1940s when penicillin became available.

The actual breakthrough was earlier. The existence of microorganisms was known since the middle of the nineteenth century, thanks to the work of Louis Pasteur. By 1865, the British Baronet Sir Joseph Lister discovered you could destroy them with carbolic acid—something until then used mainly to clean out sewers. He was particularly interested in amputation, a surgical procedure that routinely killed half its patients. With the application of Lister's discovery, the death rate dropped to 15 percent. But while substances like carbolic acid worked wonderfully as external applications, they were far too toxic to be taken into the body. A search began for some agent that could combat internal bacteria without poisoning the patient.

In 1928, a Scottish bacteriologist called Alexander Fleming finally found it.

Fleming started his search for a workable antibacterial right after taking his degree at St. Mary's Hospital Medical School, London, in 1906. He was still searching as a member of the Royal Army Medical Corps during World War I. In 1921, three years after the war ended, he finally identified an enzyme called lysozyme that was present in saliva and inhibited bacteria to some degree.[12] The antibacterial action of the enzyme was not enough to make it suitable for therapeutic use, but the discovery was clearly a step in the right direction.

The breakthrough came in 1928 when Fleming noticed one of his bacteria samples had been contaminated by a green mold. To his surprise there was a bacteria-free ring around the contamination. The mold was *Penicillium notatum*. When Fleming investigated, he found it contained a substance that stopped most common bacteria dead in their tracks. It was potent stuff. Even diluted eight hundred times, it still acted as an antibiotic. Fleming called the substance *penicillin*, after the mold itself. Experiments showed it was not toxic.

Fleming knew well what he had, but in one of the most frustrating periods of his career, he could not use it to help the patients at his hospital. Medical technology was simply not sufficiently advanced to extract enough of the purified compound. It took more than ten years and the impetus of a looming world war before the situation was rectified. Howard Florey, Ernst Chain, and their colleagues at Oxford University carried Fleming's discovery a step further when they developed the means to isolate, purify, and produce penicillin in useful quantities in the late 1930s.

All the same, it was two years into the Second World War before supplies began to filter through to the Allied forces. There was a strict army directive that the new wonder drug should be used sparingly. The recommended dosage was five thousand units. Today your doctor will routinely prescribe more than three times that amount for the most minor infection, but in 1942, a five-thousand-unit shot was capable of performing miracles. Army doctors were stunned by the results they got. So much so that until the supply situation improved, urine of treated patients was distilled and recovered penicillin crystals used to dose others.

Once the initial excitement died down, it became clear that while penicillin was the most remarkable drug ever discovered, it was not a universal panacea. One huge disappointment was that it did nothing for tuberculosis. For more than a century, the disease had been the leading cause of death for all age groups in the Western world, and while this situation was improving somewhat because of better hygiene standards, it still remained a major killer. But spurred on by Fleming's example, an American biochemist, Selman A. Waksman, and his team at Rutgers University, in New Jersey, isolated streptomycin from soil cultures and found it worked like a charm against TB. The second great antibiotic was added to the medical armory just two years after the first.

Since even penicillin and streptomycin together did not wipe out every common infection, the 1950s saw a medical gold rush as biochemists sought—successfully—to develop new antibiotics that would fill the gaps. Miracle drug followed miracle drug throughout the period and there was a huge sense of optimism abroad. A feeling grew among the general public that if medicine had not conquered disease completely, it was only a matter of time. The feeling failed to distinguish between bacteria and viruses.

A bacterium is a single-celled creature so small it can only be seen with a microscope. Its average length is no more than 0.000039 of an inch. But bacteria are giants compared to viruses. Viruses are so small they can (and sometimes do) live inside a bacterium. But despite their minute size, these specks can kill you just as effectively as any bacteria. Antibiotics have absolutely no effect on them.

If the distinction was lost on the general public, it also seems to have been lost on the medical profession. Many doctors took to prescribing antibiotics in cases of viral illness. At first, prescriptions were written in hope. The new drugs were so remarkable that they *might* just work against a virus. Then they were prescribed because patients insisted on the latest treatment— they knew miracles were afoot and wanted their share.[13] Finally they were prescribed (and are still being prescribed) as a prophylactic against "secondaries"—opportunist bacterial infections that might strike a patient weakened by a virus. Prophylactic use of antibiotics was an extraordinarily bad idea, and like so many bad ideas in the twentieth century, it became immensely popular.

In hospitals, old notions about scrupulous cleanliness were gradually displaced by antibiotic usage. Massive broad-spectrum doses scrubbed up patients *internally* before surgery. No matter that this sterilized benign bacteria throughout the body, it stopped the possibility of infection while the surgeon did his work. As the miracle drugs became cheaper and more widely available, general practitioners took to handing them out like sweets, whether the situation warranted them or not. Then farmers shrewdly concluded that it was cheaper to dose their livestock in advance of a disease than it was to treat—or slaughter—a sick beast. Antibiotics had come to be routinely added to animal feed.

Farm livestock like cattle, sheep, pigs, and chickens comprise a major part of the human food chain. For years now, healthy individuals throughout the Western world have consumed quantities of antibiotics with every steak, every pork chop, every chicken wing they ate. Many still do, although awareness of the situation has been growing in recent years and antibiotic-free foodstuffs are increasingly available, usually at a premium. This sensible development has, however, come too late.

One of the earliest straws in the wind was streptomycin, the antibiotic developed by Dr. Waksman to combat TB. While patients initially responded wonderfully well, it became evident the drug soon lost its potency. Investigation showed this had nothing to do with streptomycin itself or its manufacturing process. What was actually happening was that the tubercle bacillus was becoming resistant to the medicine.

Drug resistance is an interesting example of Darwinian

evolution. The individual bacterium does not become inured to a drug as you might become inured to muggings if you lived in a rough neighborhood. The individual bacterium, by and large, just dies. But what happens to individuals is of little consequence if there are billions of bacteria invading your body. In many cases, a potent antibiotic will kill them all. But if you keep dosing with the same antibiotic, there is an increasing statistical probability that among the billions there will be a few mutant bacteria that just happen to be immune. These bacteria will survive your treatment. Having survived, they will reproduce. Among the characteristics they will pass on to their descendants will be their immunity to the particular antibiotic. Before you know it, you have incubated a whole new resistant strain of bug, ready to pass on to your friends and loved ones when circumstances permit.

Some bacteria are better at the mutation trick than others. The tubercle bacillus was very good indeed. So scientists came up with an interesting—and effective—strategy. They figured that if streptomycin killed off most of the tubercle bacilli, maybe some other drug, *administered at the same time*, could mop up the mutated stragglers. They tried various possibilities and eventually came up with two substances—para-aminosalicylic acid and isoniazid—that worked beautifully. Combination therapy was born. Combine any two or more of streptomycin, para-aminosalicylic acid, and isoniazid and you have a treatment that will cure TB; not quite always, but nearly always.

In the heady excitement of the battle against tuberculosis, nobody seemed to absorb the basic lesson of the situation: if you keep exposing bacteria to a given substance, the average colony will eventually become immune. It may take a while and if you're clever, like the combination doctors, you can delay the day, but it's going to happen sometime, sure as sunrise.

The lesson still wasn't learned when it happened with penicillin. In just a few years, the wonderful substance discovered by Fleming—the same drug that worked miracles for soldiers in tiny five-thousand-unit doses—became increasingly ineffective. Some clinicians took the hint and stopped prescribing it so indiscriminately. Others just upped the dosage. Scientists started to look for new varieties and eventually produced semisynthetic antibiotics that worked against those inconvenient bacteria that were now immune to the original penicillin.

The worrying decline in antibiotic potency was graphically illustrated by the terrifying march of the staphylococcus bacterium—ironically the very culture Fleming was working on when he discovered penicillin. This spherical microbe is present on your skin and in your mucous membranes as you read these words. It is present in your spouse, your dog, your cat, your sheep, your goats, and just about every other warm-blooded animal on the face of the planet. Most of the time your immune system keeps it happily under control, but when certain species of staph get out of hand they can cause you problems ranging from chronic inflammation of the eyelids through septic arthritis all the way up to and including death.

In 1952, there was absolutely nothing to worry about from a staphylococcus infection. Penicillin wiped it out with a success rate that fell only just short of 100 percent. But if you contracted the same infection in 1982, the march of modern medicine ensured penicillin would fail to cure you nine times out of ten.

The mutation that produced this massive immunity took place at the DNA level and neutralized the genetic element (a beta-lactamase plasmid) that penicillin used to fight staphylococcus. When the problem first became evident in the late 1960s, physicians everywhere switched from penicillin to methicillin, which worked a different way. The move was hugely successful. Methicillin dealt with staphylococcus infections much the same way penicillin had in the good old days. There were reports of failures from hospitals in the United States, Britain, and France, but so few they could be blithely ignored.

While it took staphylococcus thirty years to beat penicillin, it overcame methicillin in less than fifteen—and developed immunities to several other antibiotics as an encore. In 1982, a staphylococcus strain turned up in San Francisco's Moffitt Hospital that was resistant to methicillin, naficillin, all the penicillins, and all the cephalosporins. This hardy little monster announced itself by killing a baby.

The San Francisco case was not particularly unusual, except in the range of resistances shown by the particular strain. Throughout the Western world, hospitals had begun to report the appearance of methicillin-resistant staphylococci by the start of the 1980s. Things got steadily worse through the decade. Outbreaks grew larger and more frequent. Resistant staphylococcus infections gradually moved out from the vulnerable city center hospital conglomerations to the smaller rural clinics. By 1992 fully 15 percent of all staphylococcus strains in the United States were methicillin resistant. In the larger hospitals, the figure was as high as 40 percent. More than 900,000 Americans fell prey to staph infections after surgery despite heavy preoperative doses of antibiotics. On the world stage, the picture was scarcely more cheerful. Even poor countries like Ethiopia where antibiotic usage was far smaller than in the United States reported the appearance of resistant strains. In Australia a variant of staph turned up that was resistant to thirty-one different drugs including penicillin, cadmium, neomycin, streptomycin, tetracycline, kanamycin, and trimethoprim.

There was only one drug left on earth that you could be

absolutely sure would kill off staphylococcus. That drug was vancomycin. As early as 1991, physicians were reporting the first indications that vancomycin was losing its original effectiveness.

Since staphylococcus is such a common organism, its mutations would still have been cause for concern had it been the only bug that developed antibiotic resistance. But it was not. By 1993, virtually every bacterium capable of causing illness in the human body was showing clinically significant signs of resistance. At least twenty-four of these newly resistant strains were perfectly capable of killing you. One of them, a mutant streptococcus, killed Jim Henson, the man who created the Muppets. At the time he succumbed, less well-known streptococcus patients were dying elsewhere in the United States, in Canada, England, Scandinavia, Germany, and New Zealand.

Just how serious the streptococcus situation has become is illustrated by the antibiotic dosages doctors now use to control it. In the early 1940s, it took just four days to cure any strep infection of the lungs. Doctors administered ten thousand units of penicillin a day. By 1992, the same condition required 24 *million* units of penicillin a day with absolutely no guarantee the infection wouldn't kill you anyway.

Some of humankind's oldest murderers have started to mutate. Among them is leprosy. This biblical bacterium (*Mycobacterium leprae*) slowly executed its victims for thousands of years until the discovery of dapsone. While it could do little to reverse the ravages leprosy wrought on a long-term victim, dapsone, a sulphone antibiotic, stopped the spread of the disease within the body, thus granting a reprieve from certain death. At least it stopped the disease until 1977, when a dapsone-resistant strain of leprosy appeared in Ethiopia. Within ten years, leprosy was resistant to dapsone in India, China, Senegal, Guadeloupe, Martinique, and New Caledonia. The situation has continued to worsen. Today there are an estimated 11 million cases of leprosy worldwide. One of them is an Ethiopian whose strain of the disease is not simply resistant but absolutely invulnerable to every known antibiotic.

Much the same pattern has become evident in the venereal disease gonorrhea. To the delight of libertines everywhere, penicillin wiped out gonorrhea quickly and easily . . . at first. Then, like so many other conditions, it became increasingly difficult to treat. By the 1970s it had developed such a widespread resistance to penicillin that doctors switched to spectinomycin as their drug of choice. By the 1980s gonorrhea was resistant to that as well, and from about 1985 onward clinicians couldn't even be sure tetracycline would work. Toward the end of the decade, the New York Academy of Medicine was recommending combination treatment—usually an injection of ceftriaxone and a doxycycline tablet. Although one in five Americans is allergic to ceftriaxone, this and other quinolone antibiotics were effective in curing gonorrhea for a period of three years. Then a ceftriaxone-resistant strain turned up in Southeast Asia, from where it spread to Australia and Great Britain.

Another ancient enemy is dysentery, a diarrheal disease that kills an estimated 3.2 million children a year in poorer countries. *Shigella dysenteriae* proved to be a fast-mutating bacterium. It became resistant to penicillin in the early 1960s but fortunately remained vulnerable to several other antibiotics. Then, in 1983, a Hopi woman came down with dysentery in Arizona. Her doctors, to their horror, found her disease was resistant to ampicillin, carbenicillin, streptomycin, sulphamethoxazole, sulfisoxazole, tetracycline, and trimethoprim. Despite the best attempts at containment modern medicine could provide, by 1987 more than a fifth of all Hopi and Navajo *Shigella* infections were of the mutant strain. The nationwide figure topped 7 percent. The strain reached Canada in 1990 and moved out to take on the world.

Other intestinal bacteria were busily following the *Shigella* example, among them *Salmonella*, which by 1993 had become virtually untreatable even in the developed countries.

Multiple studies carried out in communities as diverse as Brazil, Pakistan, Romania, South Africa, and the United States, all confirm the same thing: as bacteria mutate, the wonder drugs that medicine has relied on for the past sixty years are becoming less and less effective. As my editor Philip Turner points out, for millions of years, life on Earth was subject to the process of biological evolution through natural selection, with death a constant. At a very recent point in evolutionary time, coinciding with the advent of humanity, cultural evolution and cultural selection became operative. Now, it seems we are faced with a dangerous by-product of culture and science, which we might reasonably call bacterial evolution. In the long term, new antibiotics will simply breed new strains of superbugs. For a while there, it looked as if we might have done away with the great bacterial plagues of the past, but the golden days are almost over. Eighteen months before I started on this book, antibiotics helped contain an outbreak of the Black Death in India. But there is no doubt whatsoever that it will be back, leaner, meaner, and more deadly than it ever was in 1346.

And in this bright new millennium, the Black Death may be the least of your worries.

In August 1976, a forty-four-year-old Zairi named Antoine Lokela borrowed a Land Rover from the Yambuku Mission, where he worked, and took six of his friends on a sight-seeing tour of northern Zaire. A few days after he got back, he started to feel feverish and asked one of the Belgian Sisters for a shot. She thought he had malaria and gave him quinine.

Five days later, on September 1, Antoine turned up again complaining that the quinine hadn't worked. He was now running a fever of more than 100°F. The Yambuku hospital, established by Belgian missionaries in 1935, had no doctor. Patients—up to four hundred a day—were treated by one Zairian nurse, seven male nursing assistants, a sixty-seven-year-old priest and four Belgian nuns, a situation by no means unusual in Africa. The Sisters examined Antoine again and recommended rest. He returned home to Yalikonde, a village about a mile away from the mission, where his heavily pregnant wife, Mbuzu Sophie, undertook to look after him.

In four days Antoine stumbled back into the mission, looking like a dead man. He was agitated and confused. His fever was still running high, but now he had chest pains, a vicious headache, and acute diarrhea. His eyes were glazed and deeply sunken. The skin of his face was stretched like yellowed parchment across the bones. Most alarming of all, he was bleeding profusely from his nose and gums. There was blood in his excrement. He was vomiting blood.

The Sisters had no idea what was wrong with him, but they did everything they could. Since the diarrhea had clearly left him dehydrated, they gave him intravenous fluid, then administered massive doses of antibiotics, chloroquine, and vitamins. His condition continued to deteriorate. Three days later he was dead.

It was customary in Zaire for a man's closest female relatives to prepare his body for burial. Part of the preparation was the removal, by hand, of any excrement and undigested food from the intestines. The task was carried out by his mother; his wife, Sophie; her sister Gizi; and her mother, Ngbua. Within days, all four had succumbed to the same disease that killed Antoine. His mother died on September 20, his mother-in-law shortly after. The disease spread like wildfire. Twenty-one members of the Lokela family and their friends soon showed symptoms and eighteen of them died. Among the survivors were Sophie and her sister, but Sophie's baby was stillborn.

Unknown to the hospital authorities, several others had the mystery disease at the time Antoine first began to bleed. On August 28, a young man from the village of Yandongi turned up with a bad case of diarrhea. Soon after he was admitted, he began to bleed from the nose. He signed himself out two days later against the advice of the Sisters and was never seen again. A sixteen-year-old girl called Yombe Ngongo was hospitalized for anemia at the time and received blood transfusions. She was discharged on August 30 but came down with the fever shortly afterward. Her nine-year-old sister Euza caught it from her almost at once. A Yalaloa villager, Sebo Dombe, accompanied her husband to the hospital when he was admitted for a hernia operation and took the opportunity to ask the Sisters for some vitamin shots. The operation was successful and the pair returned home, but Sebo sank into a delirium and began to bleed. Twenty-five-year-old Lizenge Embale attended the hospital suffering from what seemed like a bout of malaria. She went home at the beginning of September, apparently on the mend, then relapsed suddenly and started to bleed. Her husband, who had looked after her in the hospital, grew feverish and began to bleed as well.

It was the initial trickle of what fast became a flood.

Villagers piled into the hospital terrified by the new illness that made people bleed to death. In many of them, symptoms were bizarre. Some failed to recognize their own children. Others lapsed into a sort of autism. Still others became violent, tore off their clothes, and ran away screaming. Hallucinations were common. Everyone bled. On September 12, the first nun succumbed. Forty-two-year-old Sister Béata woke to bleeding gums and fever, followed by nausea and diarrhea.

Five days later, the influx of new patients was so high that the hospital's supply of antibiotics ran out. It made no difference to those suffering from the mystery fever—by now it was clear antibiotics wouldn't touch it. It was also clear the disease was spreading. Reports reached Yambuku of outbreaks in no fewer than forty of the surrounding villages. On the afternoon of September 19, Sister Béata died. One of the male nursing assistants, a twenty-six-year-old named Amane Ehumba, followed suit four days later.

Sister Myriam, who'd nursed Sister Béata, fell ill as two professors from the National University of Zaire arrived to study the situation. So did Father Augustin Siegers, the Superior of the Yambuku Mission, who, disturbingly, did not work directly in the hospital. The professors took them both to Kinshasa for treatment. Sister Myriam died there on September 30.

In Yambuku itself, ten of the seventeen hospital staff were now either dead or too ill to carry out their duties. The hospital was reluctantly closed to all but the last remaining victims of the bleeding disease. Sister Romana, who had hurried from the Lisala Mission to replace Sister Béata, died in a delirium on October 2. Father Germain Lootens, a member of the medical staff, died six hours later.

The crisis had now reached such a pitch that President Mobuto was notified. Around the first week of October, he immediately issued a quarantine order not just for Yambuku but for the whole of the Bumba Zone, an area that stretched between the Ubangi and Zaire rivers and was home to more than a quarter of a million people. Martial law came into operation on every road, waterway, and airfield in the region. Inside a week, all movement of goods and people stopped.

On October 15, the World Health Organization issued an official warning about the new hemorrhagic fever that, it had now been determined, was of viral origin. By then, 137 cases and 59 deaths had been reported from the Bumba region. The bulletin revealed the virus was new to medical science. No one had the slightest idea how to treat it. A $10 million international effort was soon under way to try to find a cure.

On November 6, the Zaire Ministry of Health announced that out of 358 cases of the illness to date, 325 had proved fatal—a mind-numbing death rate of almost 91 percent. The killer had now been given a name. It was to be called *Ebola*, after a river in the region where the first outbreak had been detected.

Ebola is one of only two known filo-viruses.[14] If you look at it through a microscope, you'll see long, living filaments, some branching, some twined together. Nobody quite knows how it devastates the human body, but doctors speculate that it produces proteins that depress the immune system, allowing the virus to reproduce unchecked. When it enters the body, there's an incubation period that varies from about four to sixteen days, then the disease erupts like a volcano. Victims develop fever, loss of appetite, severe headaches, and muscle pains. Within days, the blood is simultaneously clotting and hemorrhaging. The clots tend to concentrate in the liver, spleen, and brain, causing bleeding into surrounding tissue. At this stage victims suffer a bloody diarrhea, accompanied by nausea and vomiting. Conjunctivitis and sore throat develop. A lumpy rash breaks out on the body, then spreads to arms, legs, and head. Spontaneous bleeding arises profusely from every orifice and any breaks in the skin. The only consolation at this stage is that, nine times out of ten, death will intervene within eight to seventeen days.

The virus erupted again in Zaire in 1995 with much the same results as with the first outbreak. At the time of this writing, there is still no known cure. Antibiotics combat only bacteria and there has yet to be any major breakthrough in the development of antivirals. So when Ebola strikes, doctors try to maintain fluid levels and give transfusions to compensate for the massive bleeding. Other than that, you take your chances. But if it can't be cured, we now know it can be contained. The virus proved to be contagious—that's to say it spreads through contact. Specifically, someone has to handle infected blood, tissue, or excreta in order to contract the disease. Barrier nursing (which isolates the patient), decontamination of equipment, and a lot of care will usually ensure it does not spread. But these precautions are only relevant to the virus strain we have already met. The nightmare of tropical medicine is the filo-virus that mutates.

Shortly before Christmas 1989, the American Society of Tropical Medicine held a conference in Honolulu that investigated a scenario based on the emergence in Africa of a mutant airborne strain of Ebola. What they discovered was terrifying. On best available estimates, the disease would take less than ten days to reach Bangkok, Manila, Frankfurt, Geneva, Washington, New York, and Honolulu. Within a month, a global pandemic would be well under way, and not one of the eight hundred tropical disease experts who attended the conference had the slightest idea how to stop it.

No one knows for certain where Ebola came from, but there is a scientific consensus that it is just one of several vicious killers to emerge from the world's rain forests in the closing decades of the twentieth century. In other words, Ebola may not be new at all. It could well have existed for thousands, perhaps even millions of years, safely contained in its own ecological niche until our destruction of the rain forests released it. As rain forest land is claimed (usually) for farming, humans and sometimes domestic animals come into contact with new microorganisms for the first time, some of them potent killers. These organisms are then carried out of the forest into the human community. Since destruction of the rain forests has, if anything, increased since 1976, most scientists wonder in their darker moments what else might be in there. But even if nothing else is—an unlikely scenario—there's still the worry about mutation. A sudden change could turn Ebola, or any other virus, into what microbiologists now refer to as an "Andromeda strain"[15]—the sort of microbe capable of wiping out the human race. As the Honolulu delegates discovered, airborne Ebola would fit the bill.

Since drug companies have so far produced vanishingly few antivirals,[16] we don't yet have the hothouse for mutations that antibiotics have built for bacteria. Those mutations that do occur among viruses have been triggered by the normal processes of evolution, notably environmental pressures like natural radiation. Of course, the hole we've now drilled in the ozone layer with our fluorocarbons has increased radiation levels dramatically.

It could yet be the death of us all. If a world war doesn't get us first.

4

The Great Invention

They couldn't hit an elephant at this dist—
General John Sedgwick, just before he died in battle, 1864

THE "war to end all wars" was fought between 1914 and 1918. It was a conflict of almost unimaginable scale and ferocity. Some 61,526,000 soldiers were mobilized. In just four years 8,300,000 of them were dead and 19,536,000 wounded—7 million maimed for life. Civilian casualties were almost as bad—8 million dead. By the time it ended, the First World War had cost everyone involved more than $82 billion, a sum that seems a bargain until you realize it is expressed in the monetary values of an era when some people earned an annual wage of eight dollars.

Twenty-one years later, the same major participants did it all over again with even more gruesome results. Since then, war has been a daily preoccupation of humankind. There has not been a single moment since V-Day, 1945, when some nation somewhere has not been engaged in slaughtering its neighbors.

War has long been a common cause of death. Exactly how long no one is absolutely sure, but there are clues. Archaeologists came up with an ingenious theory that linked the eruption of war with the construction of walled cities. The reasoning was persuasive. Without war, why go to the expense of building a city wall? A simple stockade would be more than enough to keep out a troublesome neighbor or animal. Only a large-scale attack warrants the erection of an actual wall.

This theory gives war a long provenance. The biblical city of Jericho on the west bank of the Jordan is one of the oldest human settlements on earth. There is archaeological evidence of walls—and massive stone walls at that—in place by about 8000 BCE. There are also remains of an enormous stone tower, quite possibly only one of several. Such fortifications certainly suggest the inhabitants of ancient Jericho did not have friendly neighbors. All the same, war itself seems to date at least fifteen hundred years earlier—a time when conventional wisdom assures us neither cities nor civilization had been invented.[17]

Somewhere in the middle of the ninth millennium BCE, a wholly new type of arrowhead makes its appearance in the archaeological record. Specialists refer to the family of weaponry as the "tanged point complex." Examples have turned up in enormous quantities along the northwest coast of Europe and in the Near East.

Nobody knows where these arrowheads came from. There is no indication that they were an indigenous development. Indeed, the whole tanged point complex is something of a mystery. The technical development offered no great advantage to hunters, so it's a puzzle why it came about in the first place, why it survived, and why it spread as widely as it did. But more and more archaeologists have now come to the conclusion that tanged points had little to do with hunting. The clue comes not from the arrowheads themselves but from contemporary burial sites.

Prior to the ninth millennium bce, prehistoric burials occasionally showed broken bones, but all of them were indicative of accidental injuries. Around 9500 BCE that picture changes. In North Africa, the Djebel Sahaba excavation unearthed fifty-nine burials with arrowheads lodged in the rib cages and spines, occasionally in other bones. Far to the north, the Dnieper River rises west of Moscow and flows through Russia, the Ukraine, and Belarus before draining into the Black Sea. No fewer than forty-four excavated graves along its banks show essentially the same pattern. Here, as elsewhere at the same period, archaeologists are clearly examining warrior graves.

In the Spanish Levant, an area of Spain that fringes the Mediterranean, there are rock paintings that may throw some light on the mystery. Their dating is controversial, largely because of their style, but at least some experts are of the opinion that they were created in the era we are examining. Interestingly, they are very unusual paintings. Earlier Magdalenian cave art in Spain, in France, and elsewhere, has always been characterized by its animal subject matter. Representations of humans do appear—the occasional hunter or shaman—but not often. There is such a preponderance of prey animals that many prehistorians have speculated the paintings were acts of sympathetic magic designed to ensure successful hunting and the fertility of the herds.

The Levant paintings are quite different. Their subject matter is exclusively human. And what they show are bowmen in the heat of battle. Put all the evidence together and it seems reasonable to suggest the first wars date back to at least 9500 BCE. We know little enough about them. There are no clues as to why they were fought or between whom or which side emerged victorious. But we can at least guess how they were conducted.

There is archaeological evidence that for thousands of years in deep prehistory much of humanity survived in hunter-gatherer communities. If modern examples are anything to go by, the women were the gatherers who produced most of the food while the men were the hunters who supplemented supplies with occasional forays for meat. Hunting produced tools with lethal military potential. Javelins, spears, spear-throwers, slings and arrows were all developed to kill game. Flint daggers skinned the beasts. Stone ax heads butchered them. But all could be turned against your fellow man once the idea occurred. By the time the great walls of Jericho went up, humanity was almost certainly using wooden clubs, ax handles and spear shafts . . . and carrying them to war on a fairly regular basis.

But it was the early Bronze Age before a weapon was specifically designed for military use. That weapon was the mace.

In its simplest form, a mace is a rock about the size of your hand to which you've attached a wooden handle. You can bash people fairly effectively with a hand-held rock, but the handle gives much more force to the blow and saves the hand from injury. As a technological development, it doesn't sound like much, but it was. There are real problems in attaching a rock to a handle, as you'll quickly discover if you try it. Attaching it firmly enough to withstand a battle is more tricky still—so much so, in fact, that most historians believe early use of the mace was confined to royalty and people's champions. There's a depiction of this—the earliest known—on the Palette of Narmer. The Palette, a small piece of carved green slate, shows the Egyptian pharaoh Narmer about to use the royal mace on the head of an enemy. The artifact dates to about 3100 BCE.

Once people got the idea that they could design a special weapon for war, it was only a matter of time before they figured how to improve it. By the middle of the third millennium bce, the Mesopotamians had begun to cast mace heads in copper. These were easier to attach to the haft and, though you might not think it, did more damage than stone. The idea was such a good one that it quickly spread to neighboring Syria, Palestine, and eventually Egypt—the first time metal had been used for anything other than ornament.

Copper is a soft metal, but other examples of early weaponry were made from metals that were softer still—gold, silver, and electrum (a natural gold/silver alloy)—and consequently less effective. With low melting points, they were easier to work than copper, but that doesn't seem to be the reason why they became popular. My best guess is that soldiers believed the precious metals had some special magic and held on to them, even for armor, well into the second millennium BCE. There may have been some psychological advantage as well. A gold-clad warrior glinting in the sun must have been an impressive sight. But eventually experience triumphed over belief and precious metal weaponry was relegated to ceremonial use: the killer mace became the scepter of kings.

Although bronze was worked with increasing skill and sophistication, the use of iron weaponry was widespread by the rise of the Roman Empire. From then until the Dark Ages, what you really needed to wage war was plenty of muscle. Infantry dominated tactics throughout the entire period. There were horse archers on the Eurasian Steppe at the time, and Alexander the Great used shock cavalry to great effect, as did his father, but cavalry never became a generally dominant factor until as late as the fourth century AD. Until then, almost the whole of the fighting fell to the grunt on the ground.

The grunt on the ground even carried his own load. A well-muscled man is just as efficient a pack animal per calorie consumed as a horse, although he obviously can't transport as much. But then again, horses couldn't transport as much at that time either. The problem was harness. Throat and girth bridles choked the poor beasts and cut down on the blood supply to their brains. As a result, their pulling power was limited. Mules and donkeys were in the same boat. Oxen fared a bit better—their yoke and pole harness was less problematical—but oxen are far too slow for warfare. For most armies, a minimal number of animals carried the really bulky items. The foot soldier carried all his own equipment and part of his rations.

But while most early battles were won by big sweating men hacking at each other with swords, there were signs of changes to come when the first example of military artillery was developed by the ancient Greeks. Missiles had always been a part of warfare. A rock thrown in anger is a missile—and a fairly deadly one if hurled from a sling. So is the arrow shot from a bow. But the Sicilian tyrant Dionysius the Elder had something a bit better in mind when he prepared to go to war with Carthage in 399 BCE. He instructed his engineers to prepare military machines that would give his army an edge and enable his soldiers to kill the enemy without getting close enough to be killed themselves. His engineers responded by designing a "belly shooter." This device, which sounds far more dignified under its original Greek name *gastrophetes*, was the world's first known crossbow. And a large one it was: you had to brace the stock against your belly before you could draw the bowcord.

The gastrophetes made military tacticians sit up and take notice. They could see the potential, but also the limitations. With a mind-set that has remained unchanged over the centuries, they called for more power, heavier missiles, greater range. By the middle of the third century BCE, the bow part of the crossbow had been replaced by boxed-up wooden arms so heavy that they could only be drawn by torsion applied to great bundles of hair or sinew. No silly little arrows for this monster. It could hurl a javelin a good eight hundred yards. The device was known, with good reason, as a "shield piercer"—in Greek, *kata* (to pierce) *pelte* (a shield), from which we derive our own word "catapult."

Since torsion worked so much better than tension, catapults

quickly caught on and it wasn't long before they were shooting something other than a single javelin. Josephus records that by 70 AD the Romans were routinely hurling fifty-five-pound rocks four hundred yards or more during the siege of Jerusalem.

The Romans actually brought catapult engineering to a peak of perfection that lasted right up into the Middle Ages. They developed two main types—a single up-and-over arm that threw things in the manner of an English cricket bowler and a pair of matching arms that spun to throw things like an Olympic discus champion. Both machines used torsion. The former was called an *onager* (which means "wild ass") because of its hefty kick. The latter was a *ballistae*. Both were handy as siege engines—an answer at last to all those walls. Smaller, wheel-mounted *carroballistae* using much the same principles could cause chaos in a tightly packed opposing army.

The speed of warfare improved dramatically in 378 AD when Gothic horsemen put to rout the Roman legions of Emperor Valens at the Battle of Adrianople. Horse-drawn chariots had been used in battle by the Sumerians as long ago as 2500 BCE and the Iranians introduced warhorses nine hundred years later. But by the end of the second millennium BCE, both these promising approaches had more or less died out, probably due to the difficulty of breeding horses suited to carrying an armed man. But horses were back with a vengeance from about 400 AD onward.

Knights in shining armor gradually came to be the order of the day. Although less welcome to maidens than mythology attests—they ravaged far more women than dragons ever did—knights were impressive fighting machines. With fortresses behind them for rest, replenishment, and recreation, this tiny but heavily armored mounted elite came to dominate the whole of feudal Europe. But they weren't what you would think of as a disciplined cavalry. Those closed helmets meant they couldn't see very well and they certainly couldn't communicate easily with their comrades. As a result, they tended to be solitary fighters and that made them vulnerable to group attack, even when their opponents were less well-armed. All the same, they dominated the scene for centuries. What eventually provided their downfall was gunpowder.

Like so many other life-changing developments, gunpowder was invented in China. Chinese alchemists of the ninth century AD discovered that if you mixed potassium nitrate, sulphur, and charcoal in just the right proportions, it behaved quite differently than any other substance known. Set light to it and you got a flash, a bang, dense white smoke, and a distinctive smell. You also got surprising quantities of superheated gas.

Gunpowder really fascinated the Chinese. They realized that once you contained it, at least partially, the explosion could drive a projectile. With enormous ingenuity, they began to construct rockets (where the projectile was the container itself), Roman candles, cannon and even, some scholars believe, bombs. This was military technology that would have allowed China to take over the world, but in one of history's mysteries, development stagnated. The Middle Kingdom turned in on itself and fell to dreaming. It was not until Europeans got hold of some black powder from the Mongols[18] in the thirteenth century that its real potential began to be exploited.

There were problems at first. Gunpowder mixed dry, known as serpentine, proved dangerously unpredictable. It was quite capable of exploding spontaneously. Conversely, it might just fizzle when something nasty was running at you with a lance. It also had a hugely irritating habit of separating out in transport. But shortly after 1400 AD, weaponsmiths found that if you mixed the ingredients as slurry in water, the end result was far more stable when it dried out. One day a smith ran out of water and improvised by pissing in the pot. He discovered that the resultant gunpowder was a higher quality than the stuff made with ordinary water.[19] In time it was also discovered that charcoal made from willow produced the best gunpowder for use in cannon while dogwood charcoal was better for powder used in small arms. Improvements in gunpowder drove parallel improvements in weaponry. The older guns tended to explode when used with the later powder.

Projectile weapons powered by gunpowder changed the face of war completely. It became apparent that lancers, swordsmen, archers, and even cavalry stood no chance at all against musketeers, especially when the old single-shot breech loaders were later replaced by repeating weapons. The lesson was learned slowly, as shown by the ludicrous charge of the British Light Brigade at the Battle of Balaclava in 1854 during the Crimean War, but eventually it became clear to even the most entrenched traditionalist. By the outbreak of the First World War, armies of all the major powers were using smokeless, bolt-action, magazine-fed repeating rifles.

Defensive measures had to take the development into account. Cavalry mercifully became obsolete, so that fine horses no longer had to die in humanity's quarrels. They were replaced, by and large, by tanks, which were introduced in the First World War but not pressed into really widespread service until the Second.

It was in the Second World War (1939–1945) that things began to get particularly nasty. The old-style gunpowder had been replaced by more powerful nitrocellulose (gun-cotton) propellants by then and the conduct of war was almost entirely mechanized. Light tanks and armored cars were multi-terrain vehicles capable of tackling desert or swamp. Amphibians—the British Tommies called them "ducks"—could carry you to be killed across land or water. But the biggest change was the use of aircraft. Manfred von Richthofen, Germany's famous Red Baron, might have cut a heroic figure in his biplane during World War One, but aerial war was very much a sideshow to the main event. Just twenty-one years later it had moved center stage, and by 1999 NATO strikes on Yugoslavia demonstrated some wars could be won with aircraft alone, without sending in a single foot soldier.

The increasing emphasis on air power called for bigger and better bombs, which in turn killed more civilians than the warrior tradition. In 1945, America rolled out the biggest bomb ever, then dropped it on Hiroshima. It killed more people (66,000) instantly than any other weapon in the entire history of humanity. President Truman claimed the city was a military target[20] and dropped another one on Nagasaki three days later, killing a further 39,000.

The atomic bomb worked differently than all the other explosive devices. Substances like gunpowder blow up simply because they burn fast—a principle that allows hooligans and freedom fighters to use petrol bombs. High explosives like TNT or dynamite blow up because they decompose rapidly, developing high pressures in the process. But atomic bombs used a whole new principle. They exploded because the atoms of certain elements can be persuaded to split, releasing vast quantities of energy. The process is known as atomic fission.

It's actually fairly easy to make an A-bomb once you get the hang of it. (The problem is finding the right materials.) Heavy elements like uranium or plutonium are in a state of atomic decay. The condition makes them emit natural energy, called radioactivity, as they lose particles. Certain rare types of these elements lose particles faster than others and hence generate more energy. If you collect enough of the substance together—usually referred to as a "critical mass"—the process goes rogue and you get a massive explosion. To build an A-bomb, you need two quantities of fissionable material that would exceed critical mass if you added them together. Naturally you take great care not to add them together until you're ready. You put them well apart in a bomb case, then add some conventional explosive that will send them smashing into one another when it goes off. You stand well clear, detonate the conventional explosive to create critical mass, and nature does the rest.

The principle was tested at Alamogordo, New Mexico, in July 1945, using plutonium. The Hiroshima bomb was packed with uranium, while for Nagasaki, America switched back to plutonium. Either way, the material used was radioactive, a radiation that quietly does dreadful things to the human body. So the area of an atomic blast remains polluted for years and radioactivity adds steadily to the original death toll. Which is, of course, what happened in Japan. There is no real way of knowing exactly how many people those two bombs killed, except that it was well in excess of the 105,000 victims who died immediately.

Since humanity has long believed you can't murder too many of your enemies, America decided atom bombs just weren't good enough and pressed ahead to develop something that would do *real* damage. The goal was achieved in the fall of 1952 when a bright U.S. physicist named Edward Teller and a team of fellow scientists exploded the world's first H-bomb.

H-bombs (the "H" stands for "hydrogen") not only work differently from high explosives, they also work differently from A-bombs, although there is a certain mechanical similarity. The explosive release of an H-bomb comes from fusing two light elements together to form one heavy one. But you can't achieve this fusion without high temperatures. Indeed, you can't achieve this fusion without such high temperatures that the only thing capable of providing them is an atomic bomb. So while an atomic bomb needs a high explosive charge to set it off, a hydrogen bomb needs an atomic bomb to do the same job. Once you do set it off, however, an H-bomb gives you very high-class killing power. The explosive force of an atomic bomb is measured in kilotons, each one equivalent to a thousand tons of TNT. H-bombs are routinely measured in megatons, each one equivalent to one million tons of TNT.

At the time Dr. Teller cracked off the first of these brutes, Americans believed most of their enemies lived in Russia. Since Russians believed much the same thing about America, they had to match the firepower and did so just over nine months later. The government of Her Britannic Majesty decided to join in the fun and funded H-bomb research that bore fruit (in the form of another big test bang) in May 1957. China joined the club ten years later, France two years after that.

This was about the time people began to realize there might be a downside to bigger and better weaponry. An H-bomb, even a little H-bomb, will destroy all life for miles. It will level buildings for miles. If the buildings are burnable, it will start firestorms for miles. The flash alone will permanently blind people and animals for miles. But the radioactive fallout is in a different league from the central explosion. The radioactive fallout distributes worldwide.

It took time and lots of test explosions to establish this disturbing little fact, but no time at all to realize the implications. If you hurled too many H-bombs at your enemies, you didn't just kill them, you killed your own people as well. It mightn't happen quickly and there weren't so many fireworks, but radioactive fallout meant it would happen eventually.

Herbie Brennan

There were two happy results of the realization. The first was a treaty to stop H-tests in the open air. The second was a desperate attempt by the five nuclear powers to make sure nobody else got this deadly technology. The first was more or less successful. The great outdoor test programs of the fifties and sixties that raised worldwide radiation levels appreciably are now largely over. But the second wasn't successful at all. At the time I write, India and Pakistan are both officially nuclear powers, while many knowledgeable politicians are convinced South Africa and Israel both have covert nuclear weapons. The breakup of the old Soviet Union means several other countries—like Ukraine—have an independent arsenal of old stock.

By any rational criterion this is a worrying situation. If a kindly old Democrat like Harry S. Truman could bring himself to nuke Japan (twice) and lie about it afterward, it makes you wonder how far the real nutters might go. Pessimistic governments have pressed their scientists—with some success—to come up with low-fallout bombs so they can raze several million acres of enemy land without taking out the whole planet. But scientists like the late Carl Sagan have long since decided even clean bombs won't hack it. Their calculations show an all-out nuclear exchange will throw so much dust into the atmosphere that it will block out the sun and lead to a worldwide nuclear winter. A nuclear winter breaks the food chain. Everybody starves to death.

In some ways it's similar to what many scientists now believe once happened to the dinosaurs.

5

Death from Heaven

Even the curass of the sky, which encompasses the world, is not proof against . . . invasion . . . from without.
—Roman poet Lucretius, 95–55 BCE

ON MAY 15, 1996, two American astronomers, Tim Spahr and Carl Hergenrother, detected a massive asteroid approaching Earth. With the sole exception of our own moon, it was the largest object to come this close to our planet since modern astronomical record-keeping began in 1833. Spahr and Hergenrother alerted NASA and their sighting was quickly confirmed. NASA didn't call Bruce Willis or any other team of astronaut heroes to save Earth from the impending collision. Outside of Hollywood fantasies, a situation like this was quite beyond remedy.

If there was an official announcement of disaster, I missed it; and I suspect you may have too. For four days, the giant body continued to hurtle toward Earth until, just seven hours from impact, it swung away again. It had passed within 400,000 miles of our planet—an astronomical whisker.

In March 1998, it looked as if another one was on the way, although this time there *was* an official announcement. The asteroid, called 1997 XF11, had been discovered a few months earlier and recognized at once as "potentially hazardous to Earth." But that only meant its orbit could take it within a few million miles of Earth and it was big enough (roughly a mile and a quarter in diameter) to do serious damage if it hit. Initial calculations showed a close pass in 2028, but not too much to worry about in the short term.

It was Dr. Brian G. Marsden, director of the Planetary Sciences Division of the Harvard-Smithsonian Center for Astrophysics, who sounded the first serious note of alarm. What concerned him was new data on the asteroid released by the McDonald Observatory in Texas. Using this data, his calculations showed the close pass in 2028 would not be a few million miles away, but only some tens of thousands. That would bring it closer than the moon. It would also mean if there was even a tiny margin of error, the asteroid could come crashing into the Earth, either on a direct collision course or reeled in by Earth's gravity.

Dr. Marsden realized he needed to do something about that margin of error and the only way was to gather more information. He issued a request to the international community of astronomers for follow-up observations with emphasis on determining the asteroid's size. Within hours of the request being issued, other scientists announced categorically that even on the basis of existing information, the Earth was in no danger of a collision in 2028.

Dr. Marsden would not accept what he judged could be false reassurances. He remembered the first appearance of the Shoemaker-Levy comet. Back in 1992, this astronomical body hurtled toward Jupiter . . . and missed. It was a close call, so close that Jupiter's massive gravity broke the comet into pieces, but a miss, as we all know, is as good as a mile. Except that in this case it wasn't. Inside two years, the fragmented Shoemaker-Levy was back and this time it *did* collide with Jupiter, providing one of the most spectacular astronomical displays in history. What happened if 1997 XF11 did the same to Earth? What happened if it missed in 2028, but came back later on an exact collision course? When he ran the figures again, Dr. Marsden discovered there were certain situations that would allow for a partial impact on October 27, 2037, or a full, catastrophic impact on October 26, 2040. He desperately needed the additional data to confirm, or, he hoped, to refute, his calculations.

When the additional data came in, the astronomical community heaved a collective sigh of relief. New measurements showed the 2028 pass would not be so close after all—and there was no chance of a comeback impact on the later dates. But just as the thought of hanging concentrates the mind, Dr. Marsden's theoretical impact calculations switched on an important spotlight. Suddenly both the scientific community and a worried public began to take seriously the possibility that the Earth might well be under threat from space.

In point of fact, Earth is bombarded by space rocks every day of the week. Every time you see a so-called shooting star, you aren't observing a star at all—you're watching a meteor, a lump of something from space that enters the Earth's atmosphere and heats up to a pretty glow because of friction. On any night of the year, something around fifteen of these visitors appear in the sky every hour. (The same happens every day as well, only you can't see them.) On some nights, the number jumps to about seventy-five an hour, the result of what's known as a meteor shower.

You can make a wish without worrying too much. Most meteors are no larger than a pea, little pieces of rock and ice that burn up completely moments after they enter the atmosphere. But you do need to worry a little. A few meteors are so big our atmosphere won't burn them up completely and their remnants reach the ground, at which point they become known as meteorites. The largest meteorite ever found turned up near Grootfontein, Namibia, in 1920 and weighed more than sixty tons.

Rather more recently, a meteor with a diameter of thirty meters caused a spectacular daytime display over the United States. On August 10, 1972, it was possible to track the monster with the naked eye across Montana, Wyoming, and Utah, moving at an estimated 33,500 miles an hour. It was the brightest meteor ever recorded, but since it only grazed the upper atmosphere, it did no damage to our planet. But had it fallen on, say, Salt Lake City, the impact would have been equivalent to a nuclear explosion.

On the whole, though, meteors pose little threat to our planet. Astronomers are far more concerned about comets and asteroids.

There have been 810 comets to visit our solar system in the past 2,200 years, but since some of them return again and again, the total number of sightings rises to 1,292. New ones are discovered regularly, although not all come close enough to be seen with the naked eye. One that did was a comet first observed by Alan Hale and Thomas Bopp on July 23, 1995. Two years later, everybody was watching it. Hale–Bopp, as the comet was officially named, came closest to Earth on March 22, 1997 and could be clearly seen in the night sky until the beginning of May. It was no danger to Earth, but comets on a collision course would be an unmitigated disaster. One of the giant supercomets now discovered in deep space could destroy our planet completely.

But comets, by and large, are seen as an outside chance. Asteroids are the most pressing concern.

Asteroids are actually planetary bodies, albeit small. The largest yet observed is Ceres, with a diameter of about 640 miles. Two other giants are Pallas and Vesta, both with diameters of about 341 miles. There are another two hundred or so with diameters more than sixty miles and several thousand smaller examples of the breed. Almost all of them form a cluster circling the sun in a broad but clearly defined band of orbits—called the Asteroid Belt—between Mars and Jupiter. When first discovered, many astronomers thought the belt was the remains of a shattered planet. Some still do, but the majority now believe it to be debris left over from the formation of the solar system.

You may have noted the word "almost" in that last paragraph. While most asteroids are confined to the Asteroid Belt, a number pass outside the orbit of Mars. Astronomers classify these as "near-Earth asteroids" since Earth is the sunside planetary neighbor of Mars. Until 1932, nobody suspected "near-Earth" could mean very near indeed. In that year a German astronomer named Karl Wilhelm Reinmuth found a cluster of near-Earth asteroids that actually crossed our planet's orbit.

It was a disturbing discovery made positively nerve-racking by the fact that Reinmuth lost his cluster almost as soon as he found them. There had been no time to calculate whether the asteroids posed a threat to our planet, no time to determine their size accurately. Astronomers just knew there were things out there that were far too close for comfort and bent their best efforts toward finding them again. Unfortunately asteroids are dark bodies that reflect light poorly, and more than forty years went by without another sign.

In 1976, American's Eleanor F. Helin became the second astronomer in history to report asteroids crossing Earth's orbit. Two years later, Reinmuth's original group was rediscovered. Astronomers began to wonder just how many dangerous objects were orbiting out there and set up a dedicated study. By the end of the 1970s, it was clear that asteroids of this type were far from rare. A total of twenty-five were discovered.

Observations continued and the news got worse. During the 1980s, a further eighty turned up. The total jumped again to 154 in the early 1990s. Today[21] astronomers estimate that between

1,800 and 2,000 asteroids more than half a mile in diameter regularly cross the orbit of Earth.[22] With all this debris, it comes as no surprise that there has already been at least one near miss. The brave new year of 1991 saw an asteroid with an estimated diameter of nearly thirty-three feet approach Earth to within less than half the distance of the moon. We also know collisions are entirely possible. In March, 1996, NASA's Jet Propulsion Laboratory at Pasadena, California, announced the discovery of ancient impact craters in Chad, central Africa. Each one was between seven and ten miles across, indicating they had been made by objects almost a mile in diameter. They seem to have been the result of asteroid bombardment or possibly even an impact with a shattered comet like Shoemaker-Levy.

Is any of this really worth worrying about? Scientists assure us that every year of our life, more than forty tons of space debris has slammed into our planet. Chances are you never even noticed. But that debris—mostly meteorites—came down in bite-sized chunks. Unless you have the vast misfortune to be standing directly underneath one, the damage it will do to you is minimal. Unfortunately the same can't be said about larger pieces.

Our first, and indeed only, line of defense against a space rock is air. Once the object hits the atmosphere, friction causes it to heat up. It quickly becomes incandescent and its outer layers begin burning off. In most instances, as we've already noted, the object will burn up completely long before it hits the ground. Only three factors are involved in this process—the size of the object, its composition, and its speed. Some objects are big enough, hard enough or slow enough to survive all or most of the atmospheric trip with something of themselves left. This is where the situation gets worrisome.

A meteorite no larger than a baseball will release energy equivalent to the Hiroshima atomic bomb if it strikes our planet with sufficient speed. There's no radioactive fallout, of course,[23] but you'll recall that blast alone killed 66,000 people in Japan. Such impacts are not just theoretical possibilities. America's nuclear early-warning system has already detected more than 250 explosions of this magnitude in a single decade. Fortunately all of them have been pre-impact bursts in the upper atmosphere, but it would be naive to suppose our luck will hold out forever.

Once the killer baseball gets through the atmospheric shield, what happens next will depend entirely on where it lands. The earth is a big place and despite the astonishing spread of humanity, much of it is still empty. An impact in the ocean or the Arctic tundra might cause a scientific stir, but damage would be localized and loss of human life small, if, indeed, there was any at all. In May 1931, for example, a sizeable body entered the Earth's atmosphere and split into three before impacting in the Brazilian jungle with a force equivalent to half a dozen Hiroshima bombs. Some five hundred square miles of rainforest was destroyed, many animals perished, but no human life was lost. But if the baseball comes down on some densely packed population center—Calcutta, perhaps, or Tokyo, or New York— it will take months to count the dead. There is no known way to stop impacts of this type. With the best technology in the world, you can't even see them coming.

Bigger rocks cause more damage and don't even have to reach ground zero.

In 1786, a French scientist, Pierre Méchain, made the first observation of a new, though faint, comet in our solar system. Thirty-three years later a German astronomer named Johann Franz Encke managed to calculate its orbital period—the time it takes to circle back into our area of space—and found it was only 3.3 years, the shortest of any comet known. For this work he had the comet named after him.

Comet Encke, like most of its breed, is engaged in a long, slow period of disintegration. In so doing, it has created what astronomers call the Beta-Taurid complex of asteroids, an area of space debris through which the Earth travels every June and November. In June 1908, a date within my father's lifetime, scientists believe a piece of this debris, between fifty and one hundred yards across, moved onto a collision course with the Earth.

A rock this size is potentially big enough to survive the journey through our atmosphere, but given our present state of knowledge about comets, the chances are this was not a solid rock. It seems far more likely it was an aggregate of ice and dust. It entered our upper atmosphere travelling at an estimated speed of 62,000 miles an hour and began immediately to burn up. But this thing was huge. Most astronomers believe it weighed at least 100,000 tons and some estimates put it at well over a million. It entered the atmosphere at a shallow fifteen-degree angle on the morning of June 30 and cut a fiery swathe across the sky. It was still about five miles up when it exploded in midair.

So enormous was the explosion that the flash could be seen five hundred miles away. Eyewitnesses on the ground described how a massive fireball lit up the horizon. Shortly afterward the ground began to tremble and hot winds sprang up strong enough to throw people off their feet. Buildings shook as if caught in an earthquake. Seismograph needles throughout western Europe jerked violently. For months afterward there were abnormally bright nighttime skies across the continent: you could read a newspaper at midnight.

Clearly something extraordinary had occurred. But it happened in an extremely remote location, somewhere over a huge sweep of inaccessible pine forest that grew near the Podkamennaya Tunguska River in the central Siberian region of Russia. So it was not until 1927, nearly two decades after the event, that the first of a series of expeditions led by the scientist Leonid Alekseyevich Kulik arrived on the scene.

What Kulik found was astonishing. Even after twenty-nine years, the scene of the explosion was one of massive devastation. Trees lay shattered and splintered over a distance of more than eighteen miles. Everything was so scorched that only a few patches of tough scrub had begun to grow again. Subsequent expeditions revealed the full extent of the damage. A forest area of some two thousand square miles had been flattened. Experts calculated the force of the initial blast at somewhere between ten and fifteen megatons—well into the H-bomb class. Had it occurred over Moscow—only a three-hour time difference—an estimated 10 million people would have died and world history would have changed completely.[24]

The larger (and faster) the intruder, the bigger the bang. A comet no more than half a mile in diameter, which is small as comets go, would generate the energy equivalent of 300,000 tons of high explosive in an ocean impact. When you remember Hiroshima was destroyed by the atomic equivalent of just 12,000 tons it puts the problem into perspective. Lockheed Martin's Sandia Energy Laboratory has computer-modeled the result of an Atlantic impact by a mile-sized comet weighing 1,000 million tons and travelling at 37 miles a second. If you live in New York, you might want to skip the next few paragraphs.

According to the Sandia simulation, the impact releases the energy equivalent to 300 gigatons of high explosive. That's *gigatons*, (1 billion tons) not the kilotons (1,000 tons) used to measure atomic blasts or the megatons (1 million tons) that refer to H-bomb explosions. With a mile-sized comet, we're in a whole different league. The energy release is equivalent to exploding the world's entire stock of nuclear weapons all at once . . . then multiplying the result by ten.

The first thing such an explosion would do is vaporize sea-water: some 500 cubic kilometers of it. Even though the (simulated) impact site is fully twenty-five miles south of New York, it takes just five seconds before a plume of superheated steam and seabed debris scorches the residents of Long Island. Six seconds later, the entire New York shoreline will have been swamped. Within minutes the city is on fire.

The bad news is it's no use moving to Philadelphia. The heat generated at point of impact is in the region of 5,000 °C (9032 °F) and the rubbish thrown up will have a global spread. For mile upon mile from the epicenter, superheated fallout will set forest fires and burn urban properties. On a wider scale, the temperature will actually plummet as the debris cloud obscures the sun. Weather predictions are for worldwide snowstorms and temperature drops over a period of weeks.

But all this is a minor inconvenience (except for New Yorkers, of course) when compared to the results of a collision with a really massive intruder—something, let's say, three times larger than Sandia's simulated comet. Dr. Monica Grady of the Natural History Museum in London, England, has already done the sums. Her calculations show immediate aftereffects like giant tidal waves and massive earthquakes. Superheated debris would be scattered for thousands of miles, causing widespread fires. The smoke from these fires, combined with millions of tons of dust spewed into our atmosphere would reflect back sunlight to create an "impact winter" similar to the nuclear winter mentioned in the last chapter. But before that happened, humanity might have to suffer the effects of corrosive rain, poison gases, and ozone depletion, depending on the chemical composition of the intruder and the area it struck.

Once the impact winter began to bite, all our troubles would be over. With a perpetual dust cloud blocking out the sun, plants could no longer engage in the business of photosynthesis, the process by which sunlight is converted into sugar for energy. Without photosynthesis, vegetation would die. Without vegetation, oxygen would cease to be produced, herbivores would have nothing to eat, nor would the animals who ate the herbivores. In short, as in a nuclear winter, the human species would slide hungrily into extinction.

Species extinction in an impact winter is something that's happened before, at least according to the American geologist Walter Alvarez.

At the end of the Mesozoic Era, some 66.4 million years ago, there was a mass extinction of a range of creatures that included ammonites, belemnites, and certain bivalves, bryozoans, crinoids, and a number of plankton species. The most famous animals to go were the dinosaurs.

What caused this global disaster has long been an intriguing mystery and to some extent remains so today. But in the 1970s, Dr. Alvarez discovered a clay layer with a high iridium content that dated to the time of the extinctions. Investigation showed this layer seemed to be virtually worldwide—it appeared at excavations in country after country. This got him thinking. Iridium is a metal that exists in only tiny quantities in the Earth's crust. (It's heavy and consequently sinks down into the molten depths of our planet's interior.) So why such a high concentration at this particular level? Dr. Alvarez decided the metal had been carried by an asteroid or comet—where iridium tends to be plentiful—and spread across the face of the globe as the result of a massive impact.

It was a theory that also solved the problem of the extinctions. An impact of that magnitude would certainly produce an impact winter, and as food became increasingly scarce, big eaters like the dinosaurs would go down fast.

Although evidence for the Alvarez theory continues to mount—including the discovery of a massive prehistoric impact crater on the Yucatán Peninsula in Central America—his ideas remain controversial. But *something* killed off the dinosaurs, a species that dominated the Earth for nearly 180 million years.

If it could happen to them, it could happen to us.

6

The Mystery of Death

*. . . and behold, he was an old man, a hundred years of age, with
hair frosted, forehead drooping, eyebrows mangy, ears slitten, beard and
mustachios stained and dyed, eyes red and goggle, cheeks bleached and
hollow, flabby nose like a brinjall or eggplant, face like a cobbler's
apron, teeth overlapping and lips like camel's kidneys, loose and
pendulous—in brief, a terror, a horror, a monster.*
The Arabian Nights, trans. Sir Richard Burton, 1850

THE DEPRESSING THING is that even if you avoid the heart
attacks and cancers, the bacteria and viruses, the nuclear wars
and impact winters, the famines like that which killed off 20
million Chinese between 1969 and 1971, the road accidents
that claimed their millionth American as long ago as 1973,
the murderers who annually dispatch 300,000 victims worldwide, the floods, the earthquakes, the volcanic eruptions, and
the urge to suicide, you're *still* going to die one day. What will
get you is old age.

I discovered more than twenty years ago that there are doctors who don't believe old age kills anybody. I was taking an
insurance physical at the time. Among the questions on the
form were: *Mother's age at death* and *Cause of mother's death*. I
answered "86" to the first and "old age" to the second, but the
doctor told me it wouldn't do. "We need an *actual* cause of
death," he said. "I'll put down 'heart failure.' "

As a layman, I assumed heart failure would be taken as evidence of a heart defect. Since I had enough problems getting
insurance, I didn't want that sort of genetic inheritance on my
documentation. "Put down 'old age,'" I told him firmly.

He shrugged philosophically. "I will if you say so, but they won't accept it."

The exchange intrigued me so much that I checked the situation with friends in the medical profession. Without exception they confirmed that "old age" was quite unacceptable as the cause on a death certificate. What did they put down when there was no specific illness present? Most, like my insurance medic, plumped for "heart failure," which, I was assured, simply meant the heart had stopped, not that there was necessarily anything wrong with it. [25] In modern America, I've since discovered, the favored term is "myocardial degeneration," which means that the heart has worn out, again without necessarily carrying the suggestion of a defect.

Curiously, a somewhat similar idea occurred to my mother when, as a child, I discovered that an elderly uncle was in the process of dying. "What's wrong with him?" I asked.

"He's just worn out," my mother told me.

Clearly a lot of people "just wear out" but there is a massive denial of the fact in the World Health Organization and the United States government, both of which decline absolutely to list it in their mortality statistics. This may be because my mother's view of death as "wearing out" has its problems.

You may be surprised to learn the projected life span of our species is around 115 years. And there are specimens who manage to live longer, like Jeanne Calment, of Arles in France. She was 122 years old when she died in August 1997 and seems to have been the oldest human being ever. (I know there are stories of older people, particularly in places like Georgia, Russia, where residents are reputed to reach 140 or even more. But I mistrust Russian record-keeping and human memory. Mme Calment's claim to extreme longevity is firmly based on an official French birth certificate, still in existence and dated February 21, 1876.)

Life span, unfortunately, is very different from life ex_
Living longer is something the Japanese do better than any
other nation on the planet, but even if you're Japanese, life
expectancy at birth falls far short of life span—76.2 years for a
man, 82.5 for a woman. As a newborn American these days, you
can expect 71.6 years if you're a boy, 78.6 if you're a girl. It
wasn't always so. Throughout all but a tiny fragment of history,
life expectancy was somewhere between eighteen and twenty
years. It only rose to 33.5 years as late as the seventeenth century; and then only in Europe. Immediately after the Second
World War, the average U.S. citizen did not even make the biblical promise of three score years and ten: life expectancy at
birth was just 66.7.

What generally makes the difference is mishap. Although you
could theoretically live as long as Mme Calment, there is an
excellent chance that disease, accident, malnutrition, overeating or
some other misdemeanor will get you long before you manage
to approach her years. Nonetheless, approximately one-third of all
deaths after the age of 80 have no known cause. However much
my insurance company dislikes it, they must be put down to old
age. But nobody quite knows how old age kills you.

There are plenty of observable changes. Pull the skin on the
back of your hand, then let go. If you're a sprightly thirty-
something, it will snap back like elastic. But if you're over sixty, it
will return to its original position at a noticeably more stately
pace. The skin itself will be thinner too, although you would
need a specialist's measurements to confirm it. You've probably
already noticed the gray hairs, a loss of pigment that is one of
the most widely discussed and commonly disguised signs of
aging.[26] What you may not have noticed is that even without
baldness (a genetic and/or hormonal condition that isn't necessarily age-dependant) you have fewer hairs on your head than

you used to. As against that, ladies past the menopause grow more facial hair, while elderly gentlemen often have extra on their ears, eyebrows and nostrils.

But that's just for starters. The second most discussed sign of aging is middle-aged spread, a tendency for fat deposits to settle on the thighs and hips. How much fat depends on your diet—there are plenty of skinny old people—but where it goes depends on your age.

If you're old, I can also confidently predict you're shorter than you used to be. The process started quite early, somewhere around the age of thirty, when the discs that keep your vertebrae apart began to thin. Thirty was also the age when your fingernail growth started to slow. Twenty years later, your bones began to get lighter, a process that affects both sexes but is far more noticeable in women. The main cause is hormonal changes, although diet and a tendency to take less exercise both play a part. Oddly enough, your brain is noticeably lighter by this time as well. As early as twenty-five, nerve cells started to disintegrate so that by the time you're seventy, you've lost 100 grams weight of them. That loss is not without its price. Your memory for names goes to pot, and given time, much of your short-term memory gradually follows. You have perfectly adequate—indeed often vivid—recall of things that happened to you in your teens, but can't remember the appointment you made last week. Timothy Leary, the LSD guru of the 1960s, loved it. He said senility was the best trip he'd ever had.

Your senses aren't doing so well by this stage either. Only the pure in heart can hear a bat squeak, according to folklore. The bat squeaks in a high register that's perfectly discernable to children, but becomes ultrasonic by middle age. After seventy the problem expands to take in most high range tones. You'll notice you have trouble following conversations during noisy cocktail parties, as the doctors discovered of President Clinton while he was still in office. It's not exactly deafness in the classical sense. Consonants take their distinctive audibility from the high tones. Once those go, speech begins to fuzz. At the same time—and this is really odd—you'll find you don't notice really loud noises as much as younger people.

Hearing is only the start. In three-quarters of the over-sixty-fives and all but 10 percent of the over-seventy-fives, the lens of the eye has thickened so you become far-sighted and have to hold text at arm's length to read it without glasses.[27] With old age, your sense of smell also deteriorates, which may possibly have something to do with the fact that you begin to eat less—although a lowered metabolic rate may be a factor in that too.

Your reaction time slows, making it more difficult for you to drive safely. You don't cope so well with extremes of heat and cold. You don't sleep as much, and when you do, you don't dream as much. You're prey to aches and pains. It takes you longer to get over illness. This is particularly true of chest complaints, since your lungs don't work the way they used to. To tell the truth, a bout of flu you'd have thrown off in a week during your forties could kill you in your seventies. Cuts and bruises take longer to heal. Inside, your arteries are hardening and may be building up those cholesterol deposits we talked about earlier. (Although the good news here is that if you get *really* old, cholesterol deposits stop forming, possibly because your liver is quietly packing up.)

There will be some unfortunate sexual changes. Many of us men can look forward to an enlarged prostate and all of us will produce fewer and less mobile sperm, weaker ejaculation, and worst of all, far less pleasurable orgasmic buildup. Arousal becomes more of a hassle and fully two–thirds of all males over seventy have erection problems. They're usually treatable, but will you go see your doctor? Most men won't. By this time, the whole sex business that so preoccupied your early years hardly seems worth the trouble.

This is particularly bad news for old women, who don't, by and large, lose the urge, although they do experience considerable sexual changes. The most notable is, of course, menopause, when menstruation reluctantly ceases and infertility sets in. When this actually occurs varies greatly and often seems to be related to the onset of menstruation—early starters tend to finish late. Once menopause is over, you can count on reduced sex hormones, reduced fat in the pubic pad, a reduced clitoral hood, and a thinner, less elastic vagina. Since none of this adds up to reduced sexual appetite and the old fellow you married would now rather prune his roses, the growing popularity of boy toys becomes completely understandable.

But while most or all these signs are typically present in old age and some may leave you increasingly vulnerable to illness, not one *in itself* seems to be a lethal factor. Indeed, while everything I've just described is generally accepted as a sign of aging, it does not necessarily require the passage of time to bring such signs about. Progeria and Werner's syndrome, two rare genetic conditions, can age you so prematurely that (in the case of progeria) children have died of age-related illnesses before their thirteenth birthday. This leads to the bizarre conclusion that while old age often precedes death, it does not, in the absence of illness, seem to cause it. My mother's intuition about wearing out has an instinctive appeal yet does not quite appear to fit the facts. Suddenly death, the most common thing in the world, takes on an aura of mystery.

The mystery deepens when you realize there are people who have died and then returned to life. A case in point is that of a Canadian girl called Erika Nordby.

On the night of February 25, 2001, Erika felt restless. She was in strange surroundings and wasn't finding it particularly easy to sleep. Eventually she decided to take a little stroll. She climbed out of bed and, without bothering to dress, headed for the back door. It was bitterly cold outside—Canadian winters can be brutal and the temperature in Edmonton that night had fallen to -30 °C (-22 °F)—but one-year-old Erika was too young to understand her danger. Dressed only in a lightweight T-shirt and diaper, she toddled barefoot out into the snow.

Within minutes, her toes, fingers, ears, and the tip of her nose fell victim to frostbite. The condition occurs when extreme heat loss from living tissue allows ice to form inside the cells. The frozen crystals cut through the cellular membranes, causing damage that can be irreversible in severe cases.

Erika continued to loose heat dramatically. The skin is the first thing to shut down when a human being is exposed to extremes of cold. This is a survival mechanism that allows body heat to withdraw inward, protecting the vital organs. But it also allowed the frostbite to spread rapidly across her exposed arms and legs. The toddler felt no pain. Her skin surface was becoming hard, white and bloodless. Erika pressed on regardless.

In a twenty-five-pound child, heat loss is terrifyingly swift. Her total body temperature began to plummet like a stone. Erika struggled on through a garden gate and across a yard. Degree by degree her temperature dropped. As it did so, she began to feel sleepy. When it reached 24 °C (75.2 °F), some 13 °C below normal, her heart stopped. No more than thirty feet from the house, Erika collapsed face forward in the snow and died.

Time crept by in the darkness. The little body continued to chill. The toes froze together. A bubble of saliva turned to ice and sealed her lips. Blood pooled in the stomach and facial tissue. Core temperature dropped to 16 °C (60.8 °F). Skin surface hardened. Internal organs began to freeze. Dr. Allan De Caen of the Stollery Children's Health Center at the University of Edmonton Hospital remarked later that "by every textbook definition she was dead."

At 3 A.M., Erika's mother, Leyla Nordby, woke to discover her little daughter was no longer sharing her bed. She got up to find out where on earth the toddler might have got to. At first, the thought that Erika could be outside simply did not occur to her. She began, with increasing panic, to search the house. Then, after nearly an hour, she noticed the back door was ajar. Tiny footprints led her directly to Erika's body.

Less than ten minutes later an ambulance arrived. Among its crew was Krista Rempel, a paramedic who had been on call seven years previously when another little girl froze so completely that hypodermic needles broke on her skin. Krista forced a breathing tube between Erika's frozen lips and wrapped her in a blanket. The ambulance team alerted the Stollery clinic.

Shortly after 4 A.M., Erika's body arrived at Stollery. Standard treatment for frostbite is a rapid thawing of the hands or feet in warm water baths, but Erika was well beyond this. Doctors wheeled in a heart-lung machine and prepared her for an urgent blood transfusion which, it was hoped, might warm the body.

Then something absolutely unpredictable occurred. Before she could be attached to the machine, Erika came back to life. Her heart began spontaneously to beat again. Her temperature began to climb. Within days she was sitting up in bed complaining because her nurses wouldn't let her watch *Barney* on TV.

At least one doctor[28] was reported to have described Erika's resurrection as a miracle. Maybe so, but it's a miracle that has occurred before. In 1994, a two-year-old named Karlee

Kosolofsky wandered off into the night during a heavy snow-storm. She was slightly better dressed than Erika—boots and a coat thrown over her pajamas—but not enough to save her when the door slammed shut, trapping her outside. She died at some stage over the next six hours in Saskatchewan temperatures that ranged below -22 °C (-7.6 °F) . . . and was subsequently revived by a Canadian medical team.

With far less body mass than an adult, a young child's blood and body organs freeze faster. This clearly means the child will die more quickly but, ironically, raises the chances of a successful resurrection. Fast freezing means less tissue damage. All the same, it's not just children who return from an icy grave.

In 1999, a trainee surgeon from Gothenburg in Sweden was on a skiing holiday in neighboring Norway when she fell through the ice on a frozen river near Narvik. Friends watched in horror as Dr. Anna Bagenholm struggled beneath the ice, then gradually grew still. She was in the freezing water for an hour and twenty minutes before paramedics managed to cut a hole in the ice and free her. She was long dead when they pulled her out.

The corpse was taken to Tromso Hospital, where doctors discovered a body temperature of just 13 °C (55.4 °F), well beyond any possibility of survival, but the medical team decided to try anyway. They attached Dr. Bagenholm to a heart bypass machine and used it to circulate warmed, highly oxygenated blood through her body. Within an hour, her heart started to beat again. Within nine, she was awake. In a matter of months, she was back on the ski slopes.

Some doctors believe the key factor in this and similar cases may be the speed at which the brain freezes. If it freezes fast, as can happen in certain conditions, it may reach a sort of hibernatory shutdown *before* the heart stops beating. This prevents the sort of permanent brain damage that would occur at higher temperatures—indeed, seems to prevent any short-term brain damage at all. Other, less delicate, organs are preserved in their turn by the cold, allowing successful revival to take place over a far longer period than would normally be the case. Some victims suffer a degree of damage. Others, astonishingly, come through unscathed.

All this indicates that dying may not be as straightforward as you might imagine. Since it's something you will have to do someday, it may be worth examining a little more closely.

7

Under the Microscope

Once the life of an animal ends, the life-sustaining processes slowly cease, causing significant changes in the postmortem muscle. These changes represent the conversion of muscle to meat.
Encyclopedia Britannica, 1998

LIKE SO MANY other things, death was far more simple years ago.

Since people who died clearly stopped breathing, generations of doctors sought to determine death by the mirror test. You held a looking glass to the mouth of the corpse and waited patiently to see if it would cloud. If it didn't, you knew breathing had actually stopped, not simply become too shallow to be noticeable. From earliest times, most doctors realized corpses had no heartbeat. An ear to the chest or a finger on the pulse was often enough to determine the state of the organ, but until the invention of the stethoscope in 1816, it was all too easy to make mistakes,[29] so the breath test was considered more definitive.

But not, unfortunately, definitive enough. There were so many stories of premature burial in circulation by 1792 that Duke Ferdinand of Brunswick ordered himself a special casket with a window and an air hole. He also specified that instead of nailing down the coffin lid, as was the near-universal custom, his casket should simply be lockable . . . and the keys buried with him.

There is nothing to suggest Ferdinand was still alive when the time came to use his casket, but airhole or not, he would have

75

suffocated within an hour of his grave being filled in. Germany's Dr. Adolf Gutsmith had a rather better idea. In 1822 he designed a coffin with a breathing tube that would extend beyond the surface of the grave and allow the dear not-quite-departed to call for help if he found himself in unfortunate circumstances. Another German, Johann Taberger, improved the design by attaching wires to the hands and feet of the corpse. These were linked to a bell above ground that would ring if there was movement. Russia's Count Michel de Karnice-Karnicki went one better. His coffins contained an ingenious mechanism that would raise a warning flag if the sleeper awoke.[30]

Although devices of this type continue to be made to the present day—one offered for sale in Italy contains a beeper, a telephone, an electric torch, an oxygen tube, and a heart stimulator—the real thrust of medical research has been to make sure patients really are dead before you bury them in the conventional way. One result is the recognition that death is not an event but a process.

Assuming absence of illness, which can often complicate matters, death is most likely to occur in the wee small hours of the morning when your body's biological processes are at their lowest ebb. You may be asleep at the time and hardly notice, or you may wake up for the great event. Either way, your breathing becomes shallow and labored. There could be a few facial twitches, a few muscle spasms. You could even produce the world-famous death rattle, a curious gurgling in the back of the throat, as you draw your last breath. All these are preliminaries. The death process really starts when your heart stops.

But even though your heart has stopped, you aren't exactly dead. Nowadays, death is frequently defined as "irreversible cardiac arrest." The key word is "irreversible." A stopped heart can often start again, sometimes spontaneously, sometimes as the result of medical intervention. You've seen the movie a hundred times. The handsome young doctor first thumps the patient's sternum (breastbone) in the hope sudden shock will get the organ moving. If that doesn't work, he injects a stimulant directly into the heart muscle. And if that doesn't work either, he reaches for those wonderful electrical paddles and snaps sternly, "Clear!" Nurses and assorted lackeys step back, frowning. The paddles are applied firmly to the patient's chest and someone hits the juice. In the best movies, the corpse arches convulsively. In the very best it sparks to life after the third hit.

Should the corpse fail to respond, someone drags away the weeping doctor and the patient is pronounced dead. It's a moot point whether this pronouncement is correct. Certainly irreversible cardiac arrest has occurred and the patient is now almost certainly on a one-way trip, but the final moment of death is still a little way off.

Biologists have long noted that the body seems to function as a support system for the brain.[31] Lungs oxygenate blood, digestive system fills it with glucose, heart pumps the nutrient-rich mixture to the brain, which uses up fully one fifth of your entire oxygen intake. Once the heart stops, blood no longer circulates. Without fresh blood, the brain may be in trouble, but it's not dead yet. For anything up to three minutes, your brain still functions wonderfully well, and probes will show continued electrical activity. But somewhere between three and four minutes, the nerve cells of the cerebral cortex begin to die. After seven or eight minutes the damage is irreversible . . . but there's still electrical activity. The brain stem, which doesn't need nearly so much oxygen, can hang in there a few minutes longer. This is one of death's little ironies. These longest-lasting of the brain cells are precisely those that control your breathing and heartbeat—the very things that shut down and caused all the trouble.

But however tenaciously the brain stem clings to life, it will starve eventually. The electroencephalograph goes flatline. You're now brain dead and most of us would assume you've joined the dodo. Yet there are still things going on in your body.

At the moment your heart ceases to beat, your pupils dilate and stay that way. Your muscles relax completely, possibly for the first time in months. Your whole body begins to cool. While you are alive (and remember full death comes in stages) a whole series of interrelated controls keep your body temperature in or around 98.6 °F (37 °C). Now those inner mechanisms will cease to function. Like any other inanimate object, you lose heat to your environment until you achieve thermodynamic equilibrium. So your body temperature continues to drop until it is exactly that of your surroundings. Your loved ones will find you cold to the touch, but that's only because they're so used to finding you warm. At worst you'll be no colder than the air in the room.

The loss of heat happens from the outside in, with core temperature dropping last. This allows forensic experts to determine roughly (very roughly) how long the cadaver has been dead. A temperature gradient forms between the exterior and the core, after which heat loss is constant and predictable. What isn't so predictable is how long it takes for the temperature gradient to become established. Without that information, time of death can only be an estimate, whatever the thriller writers tell you. A further complication arises from the fact that, having cooled, the body will start to warm up again if left too long, something we'll deal with, in all its gory details, presently.

If, like the biblical Esau, you are a hairy man, your beard will quickly start to look more prominent as the little muscles around the follicles begin to contract. The hair itself stops growing. I know you believe that hair and fingernails continue to grow long after a corpse is buried, but I'm assured by experts it's an old wives' tale.

At this stage, your kidneys and liver are still alive at the cellular level and while they aren't doing very much, they'll stay alive for a good half hour. So will your heart. It seems my insurance doctor was quite right when he assured me heart failure didn't always signify a defect. You can remove a corpse's heart thirty minutes after it has stopped beating and still have an excellent chance of a successful transplant. The corneas of your eyes last even longer—they're still viable for anything up to twelve hours, as is your skin. Although your blood has ceased to move, its white cells are still swimming, mindlessly seeking to protect you against microbial invasion for the next six hours.

And not all life signs are at this hidden, microscopic level. You can still get a knee-jerk reflex out of a corpse for up to twenty minutes after you've cut off its head, a ghoulish tidbit of useless information confirmed by medical examination of French guillotine victims in the nineteenth century. Muscles generally will contract under electrical stimulation for some hours, but there are changes going on that will put a stop to this eventually. With your breathing ceased and your blood no longer circulating, oxygen is unavailable to muscle cells, which cleverly try to compensate by producing energy through a process called anaerobic glycolysis—a fancy way of saying that even without air, the cells can still use stored carbohydrate. But the conversion of glycogen produces lactic acid that builds up in the muscle tissue, turning it increasingly acidic. Since much the same process occurs during vigorous exercise or prolonged manual labor, you can guess what this means—your muscles become stiff.[32]

The stiffening process manifests between one and six hours

after death[33] and begins at the jaw. It progresses downward from the head, affecting all the major muscle groups until it eventually locks up the legs and feet. You have entered the condition so beloved of crime writers. You are suffering from *rigor mortis*. The good news is it doesn't last. Enzymes eventually eat the proteins that hold muscle fibers together and the rigor breaks, a process that can start fairly quickly but is unlikely to be completed in much less than thirty-six hours.

Another hearty sign of death is *livor mortis*, a condition that, while less well known than *rigor mortis*, is almost as interesting. *Livor* arises because once your heart stops beating your blood becomes subject to gravity and begins to pool in various low-lying areas. Somewhere between half an hour and two hours, the results show on your skin in the form of dark-colored spots. Things get worse for about eight to twelve hours, at which time the process peaks.

Without your immune system to hold them in check, *Escherishia coli* bacteria begin to multiply in your intestine. Within two days—unless somebody has been kind enough to refrigerate or embalm you—they will have spread so much that there is a measurable rise in your body temperature. Decomposition has begun.

This unhappy process starts, naturally enough, in the intestine as the bacteria begin to eat their former home. They release copious quantities of gas, as many of us do after a full meal, and eventually the pressure reaches such a peak that the intestine ruptures, allowing the bacteria to enter the blood and attack the other organs. What happens can be divided into a number of increasingly unappealing stages.

At first the corpse looks fresh enough, but this is purely superficial. Regardless of the outside, the interior has started to decay because of the bacteria, protozoa, and nematodes swarming around in there even before death occurred. Next, the cadaver begins to swell, due to the bacterial release of gases. By now it's started to smell, that unmistakable sickly-sweet odor of decomposing flesh.

How long the process takes—if not interfered with by embalmers or other busybodies—depends largely on the ambient temperature. But whatever the temperature, things can only get worse. Give the corpse a week or two and hair, fingernails, and teeth become detachable. After about a month, tissues begin to liquefy. Initial putrefaction transforms into black putrefaction. Covered flesh, by contrast, takes on a creamy consistency. It's at this stage that quantities of noxious gases escape so that the body begins to collapse in on itself, ringing bells in the graveyard if it's rigged up in one of those fancy coffins. The smell is now just about as bad as it's going to get. A colorless, syrupy organic liquid called butyric acid begins a process of fermentation.

By now—thankfully—the corpse is beginning to dry out, but some flesh remains and the smell turns cheesy. The skin cracks like old paint. Mould begins to form on the abdominal surfaces. Pressure helps the process of decomposition for some reason, so those parts of the body in immediate contact with the coffin—back of the skull, for example, or the shoulder blades—are the first to expose bone. Some body parts prove remarkably resilient. If you have a uterus, it will be the last organ to rot. In a man, incredibly, the prostate outlasts everything else. Tendons and ligaments resist rot too, although everything breaks down eventually. In a few more months, the cadaver dries out more or less completely. Decay continues, but only slowly and without the worst of that appalling smell. In time, there will be nothing left but bones. Bacterial action will have all but ceased.

The bones themselves disappear as well, given enough time.

In acidic, warm, wet soil, "enough" could be as little as twenty-five years. In cool, dry soil it could be as much as five hundred. In *really* dry areas such as the Egyptian desert, bones can survive for thousands of years, as indeed can flesh if you don't mind a leathery complexion. Egypt's climate gave its famous mummification techniques a substantial head start.

All this will happen if you leave a body inside, protected from insects, and let bacterial decomposition take its course. If you dump it outside, particularly in the tropics, it will be a mass of maggots inside a day. In more temperate climates, just a few days in the open will have much the same result—the average American or British bluebottle fly lays two-thousand eggs at a sitting. But even the most callous of your relatives is unlikely to do that to you. Chances are that long before the bony stage, somebody will have placed you in the gentle care of a professional undertaker.

Historically speaking, undertaking is a recent profession. There were, of course, embalmers and affiliated professionals all the way back in pre-dynastic Egypt, but undertakers as we know and respect them date only to 1675, when William Boyce hung out a sign at Newgate, London (conveniently close to the gallows), advertising coffins, shrouds, and "all other conveniences relating to funerals."

Mr. Boyce didn't know what he was starting. From those simple beginnings sprang an industry that has reached its peak in modern-day America, where disposal of the Loved One is a procedure as elaborate as a society wedding and as costly as medical care. According to Jessica Mitford, whose witty investigation of U.S. funeral customs[34] sent her to the top of the *New York Times* best-seller list, the average mortuary bill in the late 1990s was $7,800 including cemetery charges. In the United Kingom at about the same time, you could get away with £1,000 as long as you were cremated. If you wanted to be buried, the price went up. A cemetery plot was at least £500, although that did include the digging, and there were various extras like the "grave right"—a payment that ensured nobody would dig you up again for at least fifty years.[35] All in all, you'd probably have been lucky to get away with £2,000, and I'm confident the price will have gone up by the time you read this.

What the undertaker actually does for his money is something few people care to inquire about too closely, which may be as good a reason as any for going into it here.

Part of the job is what used to be considered women's work—the laying out of the corpse that was once done by the deceased's female relatives. This begins with the closure of the eyes—assuming they're open—and the shutting of the mouth. The latter is necessary since the jaw has an untidy habit of dropping at the point of death as if the dear departed was surprised to meet his maker. Then the corpse must be cleaned out, with bowel and stomach residues disposed of. The penultimate stage of laying out is the washing of the body.

At this point there is a cultural divergence between European and American practice. In Britain, Ireland, and much of Continental Europe, the body is simply dressed again, usually in new clothes, and laid on its back in a velvet-lined wooden casket. Some undertakers apply a little powder to the face to hide the pallor that comes with being dead. Then a second cultural divide occurs.

In Ireland, the corpse is returned home for the wake, a day-long[36] drinking session staged around the open coffin. Among the older generation, it remains common for a spouse to sleep in the same bed as the corpse until burial. The younger generation, by and large, wouldn't be seen dead sleeping with a corpse.

Within the Jewish community, in whatever country, it is

considered a *mitzvah* (good deed) to stay with a body until burial. Family and friends first wash the corpse, then sit with it and read Psalms and prayers throughout a single night. Burial takes place the next day. The custom seems to have deep historical roots. Some authorities date it to Old Testament times when early Hebrews watched to ensure the body was not taken by wild beasts. Over time, the practice took on a spiritual dimension.

In Europe there is country by country variation on whether the body is put on display or quietly buried. The choice is sometimes determined by the status of the individual, as witness the fate of Lenin in Russia, who was exhibited in Red Square, Moscow, for more than sixty years. If you want to see him now—and you still can, despite the fall of Communism—you have to go to the Kremlin Mausoleum, where his face is treated with preservative twice a week and he gets a fourteen-day chemical bath every second year. (Not to mention a new suit and tie.) In the little principality of Monaco, Grace Kelly lies in state, wonderfully well preserved, in the Palatine Chapel.

The British are much more reticent about showcasing corpses, however famous or important. Viewing of the body, usually in a mortuary on the morning of the funeral, used to be a fairly common practice, but it has fallen somewhat out of fashion now.

In America, by contrast, your dead bodies get more focused short-term attention from friends and relatives than most of us enjoyed during life. The corpse is the center of a funeral pageant as somberly spectacular as money can buy. Among the things that hike the price is the near-universal practice of embalming.

Many Americans believe embalming of a body is a legal requirement. Not so, Ms. Mitford has assured us. But legal or not, it is widely welcomed by families convinced that the process preserves the body of their loved one in perpetuity.[37] They might be less enthusiastic if they knew exactly what happens.

First, the undertaker inserts a tube into the large blood vessel leading into the heart, or into the heart itself. Then, using a suction apparatus, he draws off as much blood as possible. Draining a corpse is no easy job, even with mechanical help. To facilitate the process, a heady chemical mixture of formaldehyde, glycerin, borax, phenol, potassium nitrate, acetate, saffranin, methyl red, and water is pumped into the body under pressure via a vein in the armpit.

This mixture is commonly called embalming fluid and each ingredient has a specific purpose. Formaldehyde preserves the tissues. Glycerin stops dehydration. Borax liquefies the blood. Phenol, potassium nitrate, and acetate are all disinfectants. Saffranin and methyl red are dyes. They effect skin tone and give the cadaver a pleasingly lifelike appearance.

As much as two gallons of embalming fluid is introduced into the body at this initial stage. Jessica Mitford reports that there are cost-conscious funeral directors in the United States who embalm only enough to ensure the body doesn't begin to rot during the handful of viewing days before disposal. If, however, longer term preservation is needed, more fluid is pumped into arteries in the arm, thigh, and neck.

A mixture of diluted blood and embalming fluid is drawn off and more embalming fluid pumped in until, eventually, all the blood has been replaced. The major body cavities are then pumped full of fluid. At the undertaker's discretion, more may be injected directly into the skin, or anywhere else that's not already saturated.

If rigor mortis hasn't already broken, the undertaker forcibly moves the various joints to counteract it. Cotton wool is placed inside the cheeks to stop that unflattering look of emaciation that so often follows death. Then the mouth is sewn shut to prevent any further dropping of the jaw. Finally there is a general tidy-up of face, hair, and fingernails and a makeup job that will routinely include rouge, foundation cream, and lipstick.

How this work of art is finally disposed of depends largely on where you live. In Britain (where you probably wouldn't be embalmed in the first place) some 70 percent of all funerals end at the crematorium. The majority are cremated in Switzerland as well, while in the Netherlands the figure is now approaching 50 percent. The process takes about an hour at temperatures varying between 800 and 1,000 °C and at the end there's nothing left but ashes and a few scraps of metal. (The artificial hip you had put in, tooth fillings, coffin nails, that sort of thing.) These are removed by electromagnet and any bits of bone that survived the fires are pulverized. If you ever wanted to lose weight during your lifetime, you've certainly succeeded now. Your remains will tip the scales around five pounds.

In Canada, less than a third of all corpses are cremated. In the United States, the figure is about 15 percent. Catholic countries tend to be even lower—the Roman Catholic church didn't approve of cremation at all before 1963[38] and in Italy to this day only 1 percent of bodies are finished off in the oven. So, unless they make alternative arrangements, North Americans are most likely to end up in the cold, cold ground, or, in some American states, inside a sealed concrete vault to prevent contamination of the water table. But while vault burial, like embalming, slows the process of decomposition, nature will eventually take its toll.

And that's the end of that.

Or is it?

And now the good news . . .

8

Freezing to Life

The graves stood tenantless and the sheeted dead
Did squeak and gibber in the Roman streets.
William Shakespeare's *Hamlet*

IN 1735, SIR Hans Sloane, a British antiquarian and book collector, received a letter from the Hague offering him a rare copy of the *Catholicon Joannis Januensis,* one of the earliest books ever printed using moveable type. The letter was signed "P. M. de St. Germain." It is the first known reference to one of history's more mysterious and intriguing personalities.

St. Germain appeared again in correspondence ten years later. Horace Walpole, son of the British Prime Minister, Parliamentarian in his own right, father of the Gothic romance, and eventually to be the 4th Earl of Oxford, was a prolific letter writer. His appetite for gossip was insatiable. In 1745, he dispatched a missive to a friend in which he mentioned that the Provost of Edinburgh had taken into custody a multitalented musician who not only called himself the Comte de St. Germain, but freely admitted this was not really who he was. The provost had his own suspicions. He thought St. Germain might be a spy.

According to Walpole, the mystery man had been in Britain for the past two years and attracted the attention of the Prince of Wales, who had not, however, been able to find out very much about him. Rumor had it the Comte was mad, but he nonetheless had considerable talent with the violin and as a composer. He was variously believed to come from Spain, Poland, and Italy. People had widely differing ideas about his profession. One story had it that he was married to a Mexican heiress, but had stolen her jewels and run away to Constantinople.

Apparently the count remained in custody until he revealed his real identity—whatever it was—to the king. A year later, 1746, music written by St. Germain was performed in London. But the composer himself dropped out of sight for more than a decade. He turned up again in 1758 at the Court of Louis XV in Versailles.

For the next two years the count became a familiar figure in the fashionable salons of France. He was a generous man, prone to handing out gemstones to anyone who took his fancy. As in London, he demonstrated his musical talent and spoke of his interest in dyestuffs. He had an extraordinary knowledge of history and an impressive grasp of languages. He was extremely popular at court. Several titled ladies are known to have sought him out for advice on diet and accepted gifts of a mysterious elixir he concocted.

The Comte de St. Germain seems to have had the ear of the king as well. Louis sent him on a mission to Holland. But the French Minister of State Choiseul disagreed with his Sovereign's assessment of the man and issued orders for his arrest, apparently on suspicion of espionage. St. Germain only escaped by fleeing to England.

St. Germain returned to the Continent, spending time in Holland, Russia, and Belgium. His interest in chemistry and alchemy—the two were much the same thing at that time—is confirmed by a report from Belgian minister Karl Cobenzl, who witnessed him change iron into gold . . . or a yellow metal of some sort.

Once again the Comte de St. Germain dropped out of sight for more than a decade. In 1774, he reappeared in Bavaria under the name of Count Tsarogy. By 1776 he was in Germany, where he met with Prince Karl of Hesse-Kassel, who was governor of Schleswig-Holstein. The two hit it off to such an extent that St. Germain moved in as a permanent houseguest and stayed for five years, until his death from pneumonia on February 27, 1784.

That, at least, is the official story. An Internet search will quickly confirm there are still people convinced the Compte de St. Germain never died at all. They believe he discovered the secret of eternal youth and exists, under a new identity, to this day. He had a similar reputation in his own time. Even Voltaire referred to him as "the man who never dies."

The idea that it might be possible to live forever is an old one. It appears in the *Epic of Gilgamesh*, a fragmentary Babylonian tale dating to the third millennium BCE. In the story, the hero Gilgamesh visits a remote island to consult with the last of the immortals, Utnapishtim, in the hope of learning how to avoid death[39]

The belief in immortality is also widespread. Many years ago, while researching a novel to be set partly in Tibet, I came across a fascinating travel account of a visit to a Taoist monastery. While walking in the monastery grounds, the author spied a delightful miniature garden—complete with a tiny pagoda—planted in a stone basin. His guide told him this was now the home of a former abbot, who had achieved physical immortality but was shrunk to the size of a dragonfly and seldom ventured out anymore.

A revival of alchemy in the twelfth century carried the belief into Europe, where even the better educated were convinced the indefinite extension of life was possible if you could only distill the relevant potion. To this day, Christians worldwide pay at least lip service to a similar conviction. Although largely unrecognized even among believers, Christian dogma does not promise a spiritual eternity in heaven or hell after death, but rather a Judgment Day resurrection of the physical body by God.

In 1962, a Michigan physics teacher decided to give God a helping hand.

Like many another good mid-twentieth-century American, Robert C. W. Ettinger was brought up on a diet of Hugo Gernsback's pulp magazine *Amazing Stories*, reading matter with a tendency to expand the mind. He took it for granted that biologists would soon discover a means of prolonging human life, perhaps indefinitely. One day he read a story[40] that suggested how to do it.

In this story, a science professor arranged to have his body sent into Earth's orbit, where, in the absolute cold of space, it would be preserved forever.[41] Several million years later, long after humanity became extinct, an alien race of cyborgs came upon the corpse and revived the brain, which they installed in a robot body, effectively returning the professor to life.

Far-fetched though it seemed, the tale set Robert Ettinger thinking. It struck him that you really didn't need aliens to revive a frozen corpse—a future generation of humans might be able to do the trick. He was aware of reports like those described in chapter 6 and argued that if a living person could be revived after freezing, why not a "slightly" dead one? Curing the disease or healing the injuries that led to death might be beyond the skills of present-day doctors, but well within the capability of some future medical technology. In 1948, he published a short story based on the concept. [42] Nobody took any notice.

The idea continued to intrigue Robert Ettinger and in 1960 he wrote a brief synopsis that he sent unsolicited to two hundred celebrities selected from *Who's Who In America*. Faced with a minimal response, he decided a longer exposition was needed and paid to have one printed and distributed in 1962. Two years later, Doubleday published his book on the subject, *The Prospect of Immortality.*

The first chapter of Ettinger's book began with a simple, striking assertion: "Most of us now living have a chance for personal, physical immortality." He justified his optimism before the end of the first page. First he pointed out that technology *already* allowed corpses to be preserved indefinitely without deterioration, then argued that medical science would eventually learn how to repair virtually any damage to the human body, including that caused by illness, old age, and the effects of freezing itself. It was essentially the same concept that appeared in his earlier short story, but now it was no longer presented as fiction. Ettinger claimed that his readers had only to arrange to have their corpses stored in suitable freezers and "sooner or later our friends of the future should be equal to the task of reviving and curing us."

Ettinger confidently predicted that

> *the tired old man . . . will close his eyes, and he can think of his impending temporary death as another period under anesthesia in the hospital. Centuries may pass, but to him there will be only a moment of sleep without dreams. After awakening, he may already be again young and virile, having been rejuvenated while unconscious; or he may be gradually renovated through treatment after awakening. In any case, he will have the physique of a Charles Atlas if he wants it, and his weary and faded wife, if she chooses, may rival Miss Universe. Much more important, they will be gradually improved in mentality and personality. They will not find themselves idiot strangers in a lonely and baffling world, but will be made fully educable and integrable.* [43]

* * *

It bordered on a poetic vision (despite the Charles Atlas and Miss Universe references) and clearly touched something of a chord. Within a few years the term *cryonics* had entered the language and the seeds of an international movement had been sown. The Cryonics Society of Michigan, which later became the Cryonics Association, was formed in 1967. In 1976 the Cryonics Institute came into being, offering commercial cryostasis services. Today there are cryonics societies in Canada, Germany, Australia, Japan and many other countries as well as several of the earliest organizations established in the United States.

On January 12, 1967, the late Dr. James Bedford became the first human to enter cryonic suspension in the hope of a scientific resurrection. He was frozen by the Cryonics Society of California. The body was seventy-three years old. Others slowly began to follow suit. By 1992, some sixty individuals had been deep frozen, although twenty of the earliest patients thawed early when the organizations that suspended them went into (financial) liquidation.

Despite such early troubles, cryonics continued to gather momentum. ABC News was able to report that ninety Americans had been frozen by the start of 2001, with a definite upsurge of interest during the previous three years. One center had ten cats and six dogs in the deep freeze as well, its clients hopeful of a future reunion with their pets.

At time of writing,[44] you can have your body frozen in the United States for about $28,000, plus transportation, provided you've been prudent enough to make arrangements in advance. Emergency freezing costs more. One facility is quoting $35,000 to individuals who call on their services without prior warning and prices do vary from organization to organization. This, again with some variations facility to facility, is what you get for your money:

First, you receive a list of detailed instructions to be passed on to your hospital or funeral parlor immediately when you die. These urge the relevant authorities to cool down your body as soon as possible and inject an anticoagulant—the chemical of choice is usually heparin—to stop your blood from clotting. Your corpse is then shipped to the cryonics facility by the fastest available means of transportation.

Once there, you are immediately packed in ice—if the hospital or mortuary hasn't already done so—and your blood is replaced by a glycerin solution that minimizes tissue damage due to freezing. (The ice is necessary since the blood-replacement procedure takes some hours.) Next, you are put into a sleeping bag and placed, bag and all, in an insulated wooden box lined with fiberglass. For the next week, dry ice (frozen carbon dioxide) is added to a fabric platform above your box so that chill vapors gradually cool your body to a target temperature of -40 °F, the slow process designed to avoid cellular damage.

This done, you are taken to an insulated container full of liquid nitrogen. Over the course of another week, you are slowly lowered until your body is completely submerged in it. This process takes body temperature down to a mind-numbing -320 °F and prepares you for long-term storage in something called a cryostat.

You may not be alone. Cryostats are containers made from fiberglass and perlite, a high-insulation mineral. They can hold up to fourteen corpses. They too are filled with liquid nitrogen, the level of which is checked daily. Most facilities allow your relatives to visit, although if the truth be told, they can't actually see you in the box. Which is possibly just as well. There are also facilities that freeze only your head; by prior arrangement, of course, and at a reduced fee.

How viable is the procedure? It's difficult to say for sure

since, to the best of my knowledge, no cryonic corpse has yet been resuscitated. But there are scientists who take the basic principles quite seriously. NASA, for example, sponsored suspended animation research at the University of Louisville, Kentucky, until 1979, although not in the hope of achieving immortality. (The agency was more interested in the possibility of freezing living astronauts for prolonged space flights, something envisioned more than a decade earlier by Arthur C. Clarke in *2001: A Space Odyssey.*) In Europe, according to Dr. Jean Rostand of the Academy Français, sperm have survived immersion in liquid nitrogen for several months and regained their motility when thawed. Large tissue samples and even whole organs have also been successfully frozen and revived to normal function: one experiment involved a chicken heart that beat just as well after thawing as ever it did before it was frozen.

The process seems to work equally well for some seeds, certain bacteria, and various microscopic creatures like rotifera, tardigrada, and anguilla. With their life signs eliminated at temperatures close to absolute zero, they can nonetheless be revived to normal function. Two leading American cryonic facilities have gone even further by freezing and reviving dogs. The animals were anesthetized, transfused with a blood substitute, then frozen at temperatures only slightly above absolute zero for several hours. When thawed out and their original blood replaced, the dogs revived without any apparent brain damage. EEG measurements of cat brains suffused with a 15 percent glycerol solution and frozen to -20 °C for five days returned a normal EEG trace when the glycerol was replaced with fresh blood and the organs warmed up.

In 1992, another facility conducted a similar experiment on one of humanity's nearest relatives—a baboon. The creature was anesthetized and immersed in ice, bringing its core body temperature below 2 °C (35.6 °F), at which point its blood was replaced by a specially developed substitute solution. It remained frozen and bloodless for just short of an hour before being successfully revived.

Although animals apparently regain normal function after freezing and revival, cryonics facilities have been at pains to show specifically that their memories have been retained. One experiment involved tiny roundworms called nematodes. These threadlike creatures are among the simplest life-forms on our planet, but they do have a complete nervous system that carries memories of the environment in which they were raised. It is a peculiarity of the breed that if a nematode is brought up in a warm environment, it will prefer warmth for the rest of its life, while just the reverse holds good for nematodes born into chillier surroundings.

In the experiment, several nematodes were immersed in a protective solution then frozen to -80 °C (-112 °F) for a period of two hours. When revived, the worms "remembered" their original environmental preferences.

Although clearly in the interest of the cryonics industry to promote and publicize experiments of this type, they are largely superfluous. It has been known for some time that human memory will survive interruption of brain processes by anesthesia, deficiency of oxygen, reduction of blood supply . . . and freezing. EEG examinations of some accidentally frozen patients (like Erika Nordby) have shown no brain electrical activity at all, yet doctors have confirmed intact memories by the simple expedient of asking "Who are you?" once the patient revived.

If those who have frozen to death (by all clinical signs) can sometimes be revived—and clearly they can—then the basic premise of cryonics appears sound, however odd it might seem at first glance.[45] In modern hospitals, there are routine resuscitations of scores of patients who would certainly have been buried in the nineteenth century. Curative techniques have improved markedly over the last generation and the trend may well continue. So the idea of suspending physical processes—including the process of death itself—to await medical developments is by no means ridiculous.

That said, there are obvious problems. While a future generation of doctors may learn how to resurrect the dead, it hasn't happened yet; and until it does, there's always the pessimistic possibility it will never happen at all. Even if it does, you can't automatically assume all injuries, illnesses, and syndromes could be cured as well. It's easy enough to imagine the development of a vaccine against Alzheimer's, for example, or even a drug that would stop the disease dead in its tracks. But how do you recover the lost memories? The process would be difficult enough with a living patient whose relatives and friends are at hand to help fill in the gaps. With a revived corpse, perhaps centuries old, the situation would seem virtually impossible.

A brain tumor could present similar difficulties. If the cancer had destroyed enough of the brain before death, revival would hardly seem worth the trouble. And what of frozen bomb victims, missing limbs or vital organs? Could anything really be done to provide them with a viable lifestyle?

Curiously enough, the answer—a guarded *yes*—is based not on some hypothetical future development but on a technology that exists today. That technology is cloning.

9

Heirs and Spares

*Federal legislation should be enacted to prohibit anyone from
attempting, whether in a research or clinical setting, to create a child
through somatic cell nuclear transfer cloning. It is critical, however, that
such legislation include a sunset clause . . .*
Recommendation of the National Bioethics
Advisory Commission

IF YOU'RE A gardener, chances are you've created a few clones in
your lifetime. Cutting an earthworm in half with your spade
produces two segments that are each capable of regenerating
into complete worms. But both new worms are genetically
identical. They are, in a word, clones.[46]

Strictly speaking, a clone is any group of genetically identical
cells. By this definition, cancerous tumors are clone collections,
since they consist of multiple copies of a single (mutated) cell.
But these days, the term usually refers to two or more living
organisms that are genetically identical. Despite vaguely sci-fi
connotations, such clones are far more common than you might
imagine. Although sexuality is surprisingly rife in the vegetable
kingdom, many plants don't bother with it at all and reproduce
by budding. The resultant offspring are clones of the original.
Yeasts reproduce by cloning, as do bacteria. A species of shrimp
called *Artemia perthenogenetica* has successfully cloned itself for
more than 30 million years. Aphids clone themselves as well but
introduce a little genetic diversity by experiments with sexual
reproduction every few generations. Identical twins are clones,
as are identical examples of any multiple birth. Nature has been

creating clones for aeons. What has been causing some concern of late is that scientists have now got in on the act.

The commercial implications of cloning animals have been apparent since long before cloning itself became a feasible procedure. Any superior cow could be turned into a valuable herd, any desirable sheep into a valuable flock. The horse-breeding industry, which has worked for generations to breed faster and faster Thoroughbreds, could duplicate the best of them in a production line that carried few of the usual uncertainties of sexual reproduction. Rare species could be cloned for collectors and zoos. Animals with certain characteristics could be cloned for research. The applications seemed endless, if perhaps a little heartless. The problem was that nobody could quite figure out how to do it.

Back in 1938, a German scientist, Herr Dr. Hans Spemann, suggested an interesting possibility. His idea was that you started by removing the nucleus from an egg cell. (The nucleus is the bit that controls growth and development.) Then you replaced that nucleus with a new nucleus taken from a body cell of the organism you wanted to clone—which would naturally have to be of the same species. You then placed the reconstructed egg cell back in the womb.

Dr. Spemann figured the enucleated[47] egg cell would nurture its new nucleus and an embryo would form. If you could persuade the embryo to grow to term, the resultant birth would be a clone of the body cell donor. It would have to be. The only genes in the embryo were those donated by the body cell.

It was the sort of idea you just knew would have to work—the logic seemed unassailable—and it caused considerable excitement among biologists, particularly those of the Nazi regime, which had an unhealthy interest in eugenics and saw cloning as one possible route to the propagation of a master race. But fortunately there turned out to be a problem. While Dr. Spemann's idea sounded great in theory, nobody could actually put it into practice. The technology that would make it possible simply did not exist at the time.

This sort of dilemma is not uncommon in science. In 1974, for example, a physicist named Frank Tipler, then associated with the University of Maryland, published plans for a time machine. Even his most conservative colleagues accepted that the machine would work, making time travel a practical possibility. But the device, which can only be created by moving neutron stars together, is far beyond current technology and may never be constructed.

And yet, in the case of Dr. Spemann's idea, only fourteen years elapsed until it was actually implemented. In 1952, two American biologists, Robert Briggs and Thomas King of the Institute for Cancer Research in Philadelphia[48] managed to transfer body cells from frog embryos into enucleated eggs, and several tadpoles resulted.

A few tadpoles might seem little enough to write home about, but it was a result where all previous attempts had failed. The key seemed to be the use of embryonic cells. Briggs and King used very young embryos indeed—no more than a few thousand cells each—because their cellular structures were still unspecialized. As embryos grow, the level of specialization increases dramatically. Some cells become brain cells, some skin, some blood, some bone. Transplant one of those to replace a missing nucleus and the best you'll get is a bit of skin or bone. Only by transplanting an undifferentiated cell could you expect to grow an entire body. Or so it was believed at the time.

Encouraged by the work of Briggs and King, a molecular biologist named John Gurdon carried the torch forward. Working out of Oxford University in England, he managed in

1996 to produce adult frogs cloned from tadpole intestines. The experiment was even more important than you might imagine. Apart from the gratification of producing proper clones (somehow tadpoles hardly seem to hack it) the method used turned the old thinking upside down. If you could clone from an intestine, it showed that even adult cells were capable of growing a whole body. Maybe it wasn't as easy as working with unspecialized cells, but it was still possible. A new buzzword emerged—totipotency; the ability of any old cell to produce a functioning clone.

Totipotency had an interesting implication. It meant that every cell in your body carried DNA instructions for rebuilding you completely. When a cell specialized, certain genes were switched off, but they weren't dumped altogether. Under just the right circumstances, they could be switched on again.

All the same, biologists found it impossible to build on Dr. Gurdon's results. Most nuclear transplants from adult vertebrates stubbornly refused to grow. And in the few cases where an embryo came to term, the young never survived to become adult animals.

In their frustration, biologists came up with a new cloning method in the 1980s. What they did was to take an already formed embryo, created sexually in the old-fashioned way, and split it into several cellular groups or, if they were feeling particularly brave, all the way down to individual cells. Each split could be carefully nurtured until it developed into an embryo in its own right. Once transplanted into the womb of a surrogate mother, it proved relatively easy to bring these embryos to term and the result was often a healthy animal that survived to adulthood.

Every creature produced by this method was an exact clone of all the others; and of the original embryo from which cells were split. In the whole procedure, scientists were aping nature when it produces identical twins, triplets and other multiple births in essentially the same way. But there was an obvious drawback. By splitting a natural embryo, you ran the risk of copying something with all sorts of potential defects. If you could somehow clone from an adult, however difficult that might be, at least you knew what you were getting.

On July 5, 1996, Ian Wilmut got a sheep.

Ian Wilmut was a scientist at the Roslin Institute in Edinburgh, Scotland. He and his colleagues were working in the tired old area of nuclear transplantation. Many attempts had already been made to clone mice, rabbits, cows, pigs, and sheep in this way. Some were disastrous, some promising, but all were ultimately unsuccessful. Yet Wilmut and his team succeeded where all others failed. The lamb dropped in the summer of 1996 was fated to grow into the world's most famous sheep. The scientists named her Dolly.

It was not an easy delivery. The Edinburgh team tried 277 times before they managed to clone Dolly. They had been heartened the previous year by the successful births of Megan and Morag, two clones derived from a nine-day-old embryo. But Dolly was different. Dolly was cloned from an adult ewe. Dr Wilmut later described how the miracle was achieved.

First, an unfertilized ovum was taken from a sheep soon after ovulation. (Eggs of this sort can often be triggered into development with a little stimulus.) Working under a high-powered microscope, one of the research team held the egg by suction using a fine pipette, then, with the aid of a micropipette[49] sucked out its chromosomes. This was not exactly enucleation— at such an early stage of the egg's life a distinct nucleus hadn't actually formed—but the principle was much the same. Chromosomes are tiny sausages that contain the DNA. Remove them and you've got the exact equivalent of an enucleated egg.

With the recipient prepared, cells were taken from the udder of Dolly's clone mother,[50] who was three and a half months pregnant at the time and consequently growing mammary cells at a furious rate. These cells were put into a culture medium and starved for a while to stop them from dividing. Once they went quiet, they were transferred to the waiting egg, which was then zapped with a tiny jolt of electricity to encourage the cells to fuse and provide the sort of excitement that normally arises on the arrival of a sperm.

Finally the fused egg was transplanted into the womb of Dolly's birth mother[51] and the research team waited to see what would happen. Since this was the 278th time the procedure had been tried, I don't suppose many of them were holding their breath, but this time it worked. The egg developed and the resulting embryo was carried to term. A rather large, but essentially healthy, lamb was born.[52]

While the birth was clearly good news, the whole experiment was still capable of crashing. It could only really be deemed successful if the lamb survived to become an adult sheep. The team continued to wait and this time my guess is they really *were* holding their collective breath.

Six months later, with Dolly still alive and grazing, the Roslin team were seriously considering a press release when Britain's *Observer* newspaper beat them to it by announcing the (forthcoming) announcement. Tipped off about the *Observer* scoop, the *Sunday Telegraph* ran the story as well. It was equally promptly picked up by the Press Association, who wired it across the world. Within hours it was on television everywhere.

It is no exaggeration to suggest the news caused political consternation. For years, politicians had been assured by their advisors that serious cloning was science fiction and unlikely ever to become an issue. Now, suddenly, it had happened. The problem was not, of course, one rather sweet-looking sheep, nor even the healthy mice and cattle clones that soon followed her. The problem was that if you could clone an adult sheep, there was a good chance you could clone a human being.

Bill Clinton was the American president of the day. He took the news so seriously he actually moved faster than one of his predecessors did when Saddam Hussein invaded Kuwait. Within forty-eight hours he banned federal funding of any scientific project dedicated to human cloning. Then he gave a newly appointed commission just ninety days to report on the ethical and legal implications. Other countries reacted just as quickly. Norway took steps similar to those of the United States, and the entire European Community considered an immediate response.

If they hadn't known it already, America's National Bioethics Advisory Commission members quickly discovered there was considerable public unease about the prospect of human cloning. A clone of this type is not an alien being. What emerges from the womb is a baby who will hopefully grow into a healthy human. But it is a baby without parents in any normal sense of that term. It is a child with no clearly defined legal status. It is an individual deprived of anything resembling a normal upbringing or family life.

Against a background of historical prejudices based on nothing more substantial than skin coloring, economic status, or religious beliefs, it was easy to imagine potential reactions to a new and different type of human. There were also substantial worries about the psychological welfare of the cloned children themselves. Were they not likely to develop doubts about their individuality or even about their ability to function as a fully autonomous member of our species?

When the commission sought guidance from America's religious communities, the reaction was almost universally negative.

Some authorities argued that human cloning was immoral under any circumstances. Others were prepared to allow it might be permissible in very limited situations but required strict regulation. Everyone emphasized the opportunities for abuse presented by the new technique.

But on the other side of the coin, you had concerns about choice, individual and scientific freedom, and the heady possibility that human cloning might lead to medical breakthroughs of incalculable value to the race as a whole. To clone or not to clone was by no means a clear-cut question.

In the event, the commission decided on a wait-and-see policy. They concluded human cloning was morally unacceptable at the time, largely due to the level of risk to embryo, fetus, and child. The current state of scientific techniques meant there was a real possibility of monstrous births. It was also clear that there were a great many ethical considerations requiring careful public deliberation before even a risk-free technique might be permitted. The official recommendations were that

a) The ban on federal funding of human clone research should continue.

b) All relevant bodies, whether federally funded or not, should be immediately requested to impose their own voluntary moratorium on human cloning.

But these were only holding strategies. What the commission really wanted—and said so clearly—was federal legislation banning human nuclear transfer cloning outright. There was, however, one proviso. Any legislation should include a "sunset clause" to ensure that the legislation was reviewed after three to five years to see if it was still needed.

There were a number of other recommendations—debate on the issues should be encouraged, international cooperation should be sought, and so on—but fundamentally the commission was calling for an immediate ban on any American attempt to create human Dollies. And while this might be reviewed in a few years' time, it should continue until cloning techniques were safer and the American electorate was made fully aware of the issues.

President Clinton bought the thinking. In May 1997, he announced that human nuclear transfer cloning would be banned for five years but fell short of forbidding research, although the ban on federal funding would continue. Congress went along with the federal funding bit but threw out his proposal for an outright ban.

Four years later, in January 2001, the United Kingdom legalized human cloning, provided the embryos were created for research purposes and destroyed before implantation in a surrogate womb. It was a law with a loophole. Implantation is a simple procedure taking up no more than an hour of your time. It could be done in a hotel room anywhere in the world. Thus, while I would not wish to suggest any British biologist would dream of such a thing, it remained possible—and legal—to develop a cloned embryo in Britain and implant it in any one of the scores of countries where the legislation has not caught up with the techniques.

Meanwhile the techniques themselves continued to improve. Dolly firmly established her viability as a clone by giving birth to a healthy lamb.[53] Toward the end of 1998, Japanese scientists cloned cows using cells taken from their milk. A cloned mouse was created in Hawaii and, inevitably, named Mickey. Notably fewer unsuccessful attempts were now being made before viable clones were produced. We can even say with some certainty that human cloning really is possible. In 1995, scientists in Massachusetts successfully fused a human nucleus with an enucliated cow's egg. The genes activated and cellular division began, but the resultant embryo was deliberately destroyed at a very early stage, leaving one to wonder what sort of creature might have resulted.

Despite worldwide concern about cloning, the current state (or lack) of legislation suggests the first human clone is only a matter of time. It may even be old news by the time you read this—I've just seen[54] a report that Professor Severino Antionori of Italy plans to implant cloned embryos into some two hundred volunteer women in a few months' time. Indeed, it may already have occurred at the time of publication. Persistent rumors and at least one book claim human cloning has taken place in secret. Certainly there are scientists who make no bones about their interest in experimenting. America's well-named Dr. Richard Seed has said that if outright anti-cloning legislation is ever introduced in his native country, he will move to Mexico to continue his work. There is no lack of nongovernmental funding for human clone research. Some $15 million was recently raised to set up a laboratory in Japan. A CNN survey showed that already six Americans in every hundred think human cloning might be a good idea. (Many more, of course, have no views on the matter at all.) It is easily predictable that once clones can be safely produced to order, the fun will really start.

The good people who sat on President Clinton's advisory commission pinpointed the problem. Clones are as human as your identical twin, but any student of human history can confirm there's an excellent chance you won't see it that way. In discussion after discussion, the question of spare parts arises.

Transplant surgery currently saves thousands of lives every year using organs extracted from voluntary donors. But the process is blighted by the dilemma of rejection. You survive in a world awash with bacteria, thanks to a finely honed immune system programmed to attack any foreign invader that enters your body. It's a great system, but it's not a smart system. It can't tell the difference between a virus out to kill you and the donor heart that saves your life. Thus, when an organ is transplanted, your immune system mobilizes to attack the invader. Doctors cope by giving you drugs that suppress the response, but nobody pretends this is anything more than a makeshift solution. Far better to find organs your body will accept as its own. And where better to find them than in your genetically identical clone?

At the level of tissue transplants, the process is fairly simple, assuming you are able to ignore all moral and ethical concerns. You simply duplicate yourself, harvest the particular tissue you need—bone marrow, skin, or what have you—then put the baby up for adoption. For basic harvests of this type, you don't want to be bothered bringing up a child. If you need more bone marrow, you can always clone yourself again.

Once the principle of clone harvesting is established, it could become routine for every embryo to be cloned, one twin allowed to develop in the normal way while the other was frozen as insurance for the future. If the living child developed a problem like leukemia, the embryo could then be implanted and allowed to develop until a cull of spare parts became feasible.

Organ transplants would be a little more troublesome. A baby's heart is not sufficiently developed to pump blood around an adult body. Here you would have to clone yourself and allow your duplicate to develop to a healthy age—say eighteen years—after which you'd have it[55] frozen. When years of sybaritic living took their toll, your heart clogged with cholesterol and your liver succumbing to sclerosis, brand-new replacements would be ready and waiting with absolutely no problem of rejection. Your body will accept cloned replacements as if they were its own. Given good transplantation technique, the doctors could keep you going for a very long time indeed.

And even if they didn't, immortality of a sort might still beckon. The British futurist Dr. Patrick Dixon has coped with a multitude of e-mails about cloning since he began to feature it on his Web site.[56] In one of his papers, he suggests that even before the Roslin announcement about Dolly a young woman had asked him if it was possible to clone her dead father and have him as her baby. Dr. Dixon himself has no doubt we will "almost certainly" be able to clone the dead. The procedure is really no different from cloning the living if you harvest a few cells before death and keep them alive in a culture, or freeze them carefully. After all, the wonderful Dolly was created using frozen cells.

Quite a few biologists will assure you it might be possible to clone the dead even if you neglected to preserve their cells in advance. So long as the corpse yields viable DNA, the procedure has a chance of working. Since DNA has been detected in Egyptian mummies several thousand years old, this opens up a lot of possibilities.[57] Perhaps Dr. Dixon's young woman really will be able to give birth to her father one day, provided he has not completely decomposed before the cloning process begins.

Even though you might recoil from the thought of hacking up your twin for spare parts, there is something strangely appealing about the prospect of another "you" emerging from a friendly womb when the present "you" is dead. Since the new "you" could also preserve cells, the duplication might go on indefinitely, with a chain of perfect copies stretching like a hall of mirrors down the ages. Future generations could enjoy your smile, admire your ready wit. You would become an everlasting tribute to your initial set of genes.

Would it really *be* you? So long as you consider only your body and brain, the likely answer is yes. We may be talking of carbon copies here, but each copy is genetically identical to the last. A forensic scientist who found your DNA at a murder scene would be quite unable to swear which of your many clones had actually done the deed. But our experience of natural twins must give us pause. Although they too are genetically identical, may look alike, sound alike, and even think alike in many situations, nobody would ever suggest they were one and the same person. Twins separated at birth have demonstrated how far their genetic inheritance may affect them. There are well-documented instances of their finding identical jobs, living in similar houses, marrying spouses with the same first names—even, in some instances, marrying another set of identical twins. But never do twins see themselves as interchangeable. That takes genetics a step too far.

The difficulty, of course, is that cloning duplicates your body, not your mind. Thought processes, character, emotional response, and personality are all modified by environment, upbringing, and experience. However similar they may be in appearance, the inner worlds of clones will always differ from the inner world of their original . . . and themselves. Perhaps most importantly, each clone has its own distinct and separate set of memories. Without your memories, your clone can never be you—not even a modified you. The clone chain we envisaged reaching down the ages is not the endless wheel of reincarnations postulated by Eastern religions. For what reincarnates in religious theory is the individual essence. Cloning only duplicates the outward appearance.

There may be a way around this. Colleagues in information technology assure me it's only a matter of time before the human persona—including memories—is captured and encoded as computer data. If what they say is true, and I frankly don't believe a word of it, your mind and memories might one day be downloaded into a computer just before your death, then transferred to the brain of your clone afterward. Such a process, repeated ad nauseam, would, barring accidents, permit you to live forever.

But a safer bet for immortality might be another form of applied science, less immediate than cryonics or cloning, which seems far more likely to emerge in the next decade than persona storage. Already a buzzword in the cryonics industry, which sees it as the possible answer to all uncertainties related to freezing, nanotechnology may be just the thing you need to keep you fit and healthy forever . . . and with little or no ethical downside.

10

Body Building

ATOMIC THEORY WAS explained to me vividly at the age of twelve with the aid of a brick. You take the brick, my science teacher said, and cut it in two. Then you take half and cut that in two as well. If you keep repeating the process, you eventually end up with a piece of brick so small you can't cut it in two any more. At that point you're left holding an atom, the basic building block of our physical world.

Today, the brick business sounds a little crude, but in fairness to my science teacher, his approach differed very little from that of the fifth century BCE Greek philosophers Leucippus and Democritus, who postulated the existence of atoms in the first place. They decided that if you cut something into smaller and smaller pieces, you will eventually produce a piece so small you can't cut it any more. They called this tiny piece *atomos,* which means "indivisible."

In the twentieth century, scientists confirmed the reality of atoms. Everything you see around you, from your slippers to your spouse, from a railway engine to a rubber plant, is made up of them. In the most fundamental sense, what makes spouse and slippers different is the *arrangement* of atoms.

If you could snap atoms together like Lego blocks, my science teacher told us, you could make absolutely anything. Not that it occurred to a class of twelve-year-olds, but "anything" in this context includes body parts. If you could manipulate individual atoms, you could, in theory, build yourself a replacement heart, liver, pancreas, brain, or anything else that looked in danger of wearing out. You could replace your entire body if necessary and keep replacing it indefinitely. If you could manipulate individual atoms, you could defeat death.

When I was twelve, nobody could manipulate individual atoms and the technical problems of ever doing so appeared quite insurmountable. Yet only nine years later, one of the world's most distinguished physicists was seriously suggesting scientists should try.

Richard Feynman was born in Far Rockaway, New York City, in 1918 and studied physics at MIT. There were signs of things to come when he produced an undergraduate thesis proposing a method of molecule force measurement that's still in use today. After picking up his PhD at Princeton, he went on to develop a whole new approach to particle physics. He was recruited for the U.S. atomic bomb project during World War Two and became its youngest group leader. After the war ended, he spent five years as an associate professor at Cornell then joined Caltech as professor of theoretical physics. In 1965, he was awarded a Nobel Prize for physics.

None of it went to his head. He remained a colorful, tough-talking New Yorker to the day he died, intellectually sparky, impatient with mediocrity, suspicious of authority, and wholly lacking any sense of self-importance. As a result his lectures were packed. The one just before Christmas 1959 was no exception.

Feynman was guest speaker at the American Physical Society. The title of his talk was puzzling— "There's Plenty of Room at the Bottom"—but when he got started, the content was fascinating. The first thing he asked was why nobody had ever engraved the whole twelve thousand pages of the *Encyclopedia Britannica* on the head of a pin.

The three hundred physicists attending the after-dinner gathering laughed at the question. But Feynman was serious. A pinhead is about one sixteenth of an inch across. Magnify it by 25,000 diameters and you have a surface area equivalent to all the pages in the encyclopedia put together. When you start to think about it (which his audience clearly hadn't) that's another way of saying that if you shrink the *Britannica* typeface 25,000 times, the whole work should fit on a pinhead.

Was such a shrinkage possible? Well yes, at least in theory. The result would still be measurable—hence readable—letters, although each one would only be about ten atoms wide.

Mind-boggling though the vision was, Feynman hadn't finished. The pinhead *Britannica* could be created with a conventional alphabet. But if you coded each letter as a series of dots and dashes, then used not just the surface area but each stratified molecular layer, you could fit all the information from *every book ever written* into a pinhead ... with a load of space left over.

Feynman pointed out that equivalent information storage had already been achieved by nature. DNA molecules coded their data in fifty-atom chunks. If nature could do it, what was stopping scientists? And if you could manipulate information at atomic levels, what was there to stop you from manipulating *individual atoms*?

It was the first time an eminent scientist had suggested such a thing in public. Feynman even proposed a technique by which it might be accomplished, a "weird possibility" in his own words. You would construct a machine designed to duplicate an exact miniature of itself, scaled down by, say, 50 percent. Then the miniature duplicated itself, again half size. Clearly, if you kept the machines running, you'd eventually get something that was manipulating individual atoms.

Feynman began to talk about some of the possibilities. Although defeating death had not occurred to him, he did foresee some very interesting applications of his proposed new technology. You could, for example, build microscopic factories that would manufacture microscopic computers with wiring just a handful of atoms in diameter and circuit boards a few thousand angstroms[58] across. By moving atoms around, you could build anything, then copy it *exactly*. This meant mass production at a level of precision quite impossible in the world we inhabit day by day. What, he asked again, was there to stop you?

The physicists listening knew full well what there was to stop them. Atoms do not stand still. Where there's heat—and there's always *some* heat anywhere that's useful to humans—atoms jiggle about in a process known as Brownian Motion. Worse still, they collide. Feynman's theory sounded fine, but when you got down to practicalities, how could you move around something you couldn't see that never stayed in the same place one moment to the next?

Maybe Feynman himself half suspected it would never really happen, because he finished his talk by doing something incredibly stupid for such an intelligent man. He offered two prizes of one thousand dollars each,[59] payable out of his own pocket, to the first engineers to produce specific examples of his proposed think-small technology. Winning the first prize would be the page of a book reduced by a factor of 25,000 and displayed so it could be read using an electron microscope. (In other words, proof positive that *Britannica* on a pinhead was actually feasible.) The other prize would be for a working electric motor that would fit into a 1/64-inch cube.

Feynman's talk made news. As a result, quite a few engineers decided to have a go at building the miniature motor. (The book page reduction seemed just too silly to attract much attention.) In November 1960, nearly a full year after the original talk, Bill McLellan, an engineer at the Electro-Optical Systems Corporation in Pasadena, California, walked into Feynman's office and unpacked not a motor but a microscope.

When everything was set up and Feynman looked through the scope, there was the motor he had specified. The rotor was 1/10,000th of an inch in diameter, and it used insulated wire just 1/2000th of an inch thick wound around four tiny iron pins. Inserted between them was a miniature magnetized disc attached to a near-invisible metal shaft. There were thirteen separate parts that together weighed 250 micrograms and fitted into the specified 1/64-inch cube. With the electricity turned on, the drive shaft spun at 2,000 RPM. Feynman paid out the thousand-dollar prize.

Twenty-three years later, Feynman gave another "Room at the Bottom" lecture, this time at Caltech's Jet Propulsion Laboratory. The talk wasn't simply a rehash of the original. He'd been asked for an update. The scientific community wanted to know if things had changed since 1959.

Many things had, of course. The most noticeable miniaturization was in the field of computers. Something with wires and valves that took up a whole room in the late fifties could now be printed on a silicon chip that wouldn't cover the tip of your finger. Feynman was confident the trend would spread, certain that it *could spread*. He claimed that using the technology available in 1983, it would be possible to construct a motor 64,000 times smaller than the one McLellan made to win the prize.

Feynman did not mention the other prize he'd offered in 1959—the one for reducing type size 25,000 times—but it came back to haunt him just the same. Two years after the Caltech lecture, a graduate student named Tom Newman was working on his doctorate thesis at Stanford when a friend from the electrical engineering department handed him a copy of Feynman's 1959 lecture with the bit about the competition highlighted.

It was right up Newman's street. He was well used to working on a microscopic scale and all the necessary equipment was right there at Stanford. More to the point, he was already experienced in electron beam lithography, an engraving technology that produces results so tiny you need a microscope to see them. Newman had already engraved 25,000 near-invisible transistors on a single chip and was pushing the limits of his craft to such an extent that he was approaching the realm of quantum effects. He started to calculate just how small a text page would have to be in order to fit the Feynman criterion. It turned out the page would be the size of one of his transistors. That made each letter of type just fifty atoms wide—five times bigger than Feynman had estimated, but still far smaller than anyone had ever attempted before.

The picture looked daunting, but it was actually well within the technology available in 1985. The trick was computerization. Computers already directed electron beams to etch the patterns on integrated circuits, which then inhabited electronics gear, including other computers. All you really needed to do was install the software that would make them etch letters instead. Newman wrote it himself.

The page he elected to shrink was the famous opening of Dickens' *A Tale of Two Cities*: "It was the best of times, it was the worst of times." It took him a while to set things up, but when he switched on, the page was scanned in only sixty seconds. Once shrunk, the problem was finding the engraving. Compared to the surface it was written on, the page was tiny. Newman had to make himself a road map of sorts with the aid

of his microscope, marking out the landmarks of the territory—
a speck of dust here, a little scratch there—until he finally
reached his destination. But once he spotted the page under his
microscope, he saw to his delight that it was legible.

Etching letters fifty atoms wide still does not involve manipulating individual atoms and is a long way from building body
parts, but it demonstrated that twentieth century technology
was at least moving in the right direction. Besides, while all this
was going on, another player was entering the game.

Eric Drexler arrived as a freshman at MIT in 1973 with his
head full of *Star Trek* ideas about exploring the galaxy and col-
onizing distant planets. His first scientific paper was entitled
"Space Colony Supply from Asteroidal Materials," and he taught
an informal course on space colonization and even founded his
own space society at the Institute. But his nighttime reading at
the MIT Library was something else entirely. He became fascinated by developments in a brand-new scientific discipline, the
emerging field of genetic engineering.

At the time, biologists were exploring wild theoretical possibilities like reprogramming bacteria to excrete insulin. Drexler
had a wild notion of his own. He reckoned that if you repro-
grammed DNA just right, you should be able to grow yourself
a small computer. He put serious thought into the technology
of microscopic engineering. He had a vision of a nanometric
computer built from the sort of components you find in biological systems, although the computer itself wouldn't be a
biological system by any current definition.

By 1977, Drexler had taken a critical step forward. He hadn't
abandoned his idea of a tiny computer, but he was starting to
imagine gadgets that would be a lot more useful. Why not build
a molecular machine that created better molecular machines, for
example, the way computers can now be persuaded to build

more intelligent computers than themselves? That way, your second and subsequent generation molecular technology improved progressively. Pretty soon you would have very efficient little machines.

His next step was to imagine self-replicating machines, as a route to microscopic manufacturing. Once you have enough microscopic machinery (the result of self-replication) whatever those machines are making will begin to show up in the Big World. As he approached the end of his student days, Drexler realized that if you could create a machine that would stack one molecule on top of another, maybe even shove single atoms around, then replicate enough copies, you could literally manufacture *anything*.

Run that by your own imagination for a moment, starting from the basic fact that everything on earth is made up of atoms. When you set up a factory stocked with Drexler's self-replicated atom-stackers, you can create anything your mind can conceive . . . building materials stronger than steel and lighter than feathers . . . a banana-shaped apple that tastes like an orange . . . a car you can fold up and put in your pocket . . . a puppy that never grows into a dog. . . . Whatever you want depends entirely on how you put your basic raw material (the atoms) together. And that raw material can literally come from anything.

Drexler started to think in terms of nano-factories that take the molecules from toxic waste and process them into wholesome food. You could start with rusty old tin cans and create nonpolluting fuel for your car. You could turn water into whiskey, rock into rubber, sand into a submarine. You could create *fois gras* without killing a single goose. You could wipe out hunger and poverty forever. In just one generation you could build a world in which everyone could have as much as they wanted of anything they desired.

More to the point (of this book at least), you could repair any damage to the human body, including the ravages of age. You could cure any disease. You could expand the human lifespan by several centuries. There was a fighting chance you could keep people going, fit and healthy, indefinitely. You could populate our planet with a race of gods.

Drexler, now Dr. Drexler, expounded his vision in a book called *Engines of Creation*, published in 1986. By then he was already well known in scientific circles for his small-world ideas, but the book expanded his reputation considerably. In 1992, he received an invitation to testify on nanotechnology at a Senate Subcommittee on Science, Technology and Space. He told them nanotechnology held the promise of "complete control of the structure of matter."

The chairman of the subcommittee, Senator Al Gore, asked the obvious question: How far off was this miracle, given a level of federal and private funding equivalent to that received by biotechnology over the previous decade? Drexler walked around it for a moment, as scientists will often do when someone tries to pin them down, then said quietly, "I commonly answer that fifteen years would not be surprising for major, large-scale applications."

What he was saying was that with the money you could be walking down the road to immortality in half a generation.

You have to ask yourself how realistic this prediction may turn out to be. The answer is actually a little scary. In 1989, three years before Dr. Drexler spoke to the Senate subcommittee and thirty years after Feynman started the ball rolling, individual atoms were actually moved about by scientists at IBM's Almaden Research Centre in San Jose, California. In the first practical example of nanotechnology in action, they pushed thirty-five xenon atoms around until they had them placed exactly where they wanted them. When you looked down the electron microscope, those atoms spelled out "IBM." Within months, other researchers in the United States, Germany, and Japan were using atoms to make portrait sketches of Albert Einstein.

Drexler himself had moved things along even further by the time he talked to the Senate subcommittee. Working with Ralph Merkle of the Xerox Palo Alto Research Center, he actually managed to create an atomic-level machine part, a planetary gearing built from 3,557 individual atoms.[60]

After machine parts one might reasonably expect machines. A developed nanotechnology promises that you can make anything out of anything. You might, for example, begin with sand, one of the most common and cheapest substances on the planet. Nanotechnology could take the atoms locked up in that sand, rearrange them cleverly, and make you a car. After which a little more of the same sand could be turned into the gasoline to fuel it and a hamburger to keep you going on the journey. The end result depends on how you rearrange the atoms, and if you happen to live somewhere that's a little short on sand, you can draw your basic raw materials from anything else that's handy.

Drexler thinks it's all a matter of funding, a proposition that is already being put to the test as more and more people—including a very high percentage of those involved in the cryonics industry—take nanotechnology seriously. So are we headed toward a world of peace and plenty, peopled by immortals fixed forever at their healthy prime? Perhaps . . . but there are problems.

As Drexler worked on *Engines of Creation*, the downside of nanotechnology began to dawn on him. Microscopic factories might be all very well, but what about their existing *macroscopic* counterparts? Once nanotechnology starts churning out consumer goods and fuel at a fraction of their traditional cost, the world economy is clearly headed into meltdown. Not one of our existing manufacturing industries could hope to compete with nanotechnology. Nor could fundamental giants like the fossil fuel industry.

This may be less of a disaster than a revolution. Long term, everyone would be better off, but in the interim we'd have economic chaos. And those who survive will still face some serious problems of their own. In a world where all your physical needs are met and all your material desires fulfilled for an affordable outlay, what is there to strive for? The struggle for survival is so deeply ingrained in our genes, we may not be able to cope emotionally when it's suddenly taken away.

But this risk, global though it is, pales to insignificance when compared with the *real* downside of nanotechnology—what Drexler poetically labelled the Grey Goo Effect.

Remember Drexler's insight that nano-machines must first of all be made to reproduce? A single nano-machine may be capable of moving individual atoms around any way you want them to go, but you can run it day and night for the next five hundred years without making any difference in the real world. But if one nano-machine gets you nowhere, a few thousand billion of them might be capable of fixing your baldness or building you a television set. To get those few thousand billion in your lifetime, the only practical course is to persuade the first one to reproduce and its offspring to reproduce until geometrical progression takes care of the numbers problem.

But suppose the reproduction process should get out of hand.

There is no doubt at all that nano-engineers will attempt to make the duplication of nano-machines self-limiting. (Drexler had the idea of creating nano-killers that would attack groups of nano-machines once they reached a certain size, rather like the way white corpuscles of your immune system attack bacteria.) But any engineer will remind you of Murphy's Law, which states absolutely that if anything can go wrong it will. What happens when the replication of nano-machines goes wrong scarcely bears thinking about, which is an excellent reason for thinking about it here.

When a nano-machine builds anything, including a replica of itself, it draws on the raw materials—molecules and atoms—it finds in its immediate environment. In other words, it eats up tiny pieces of the world. That's no problem if you're just building a few thousand copies or even a few million—they'd scarcely make a dent in a grain of sand. The trouble arises when the reproductive process is open-ended; and it arises faster than you'd ever believe possible.

Assume for a moment it takes you a conservative twenty-five years to build your first self-replicating nano-machine. Most of that time will be occupied with experimentation, ironing out the bugs, making prototypes, and so on. But once you have your little machine, it will not take it another twenty-five years to replicate itself—it will take something in the region of fifteen minutes.

So fifteen minutes from setting your first machine in motion, you have two little machines: the original and the duplicate. Both are programmed to replicate themselves, so in half an hour you have four. By the time an hour goes by, your original nano-assembler has turned into sixteen. Unless you're a mathematician, none of this sounds scary. If, on the other hand, you are, you've probably broken a sweat by now. Because at the rate we've postulated, ten hours will find you surrounded by 68 billion nano-machines, every one hell-bent on copying itself.

By the end of the day, the bulk of your microscopic engineering will be clearly visible—it will weigh more than a ton. There will probably be a gaping hole in your laboratory wall, since all those atoms have to come from somewhere. By the end of the *second* day, your busy little machines will have eaten your family, your friends, your good self (since people, of course, are made from atoms like everything else), your home, your street, your town, your country, and, indeed, your entire planet. If the replication controls fail, it takes just forty-eight hours to turn our whole world, atmosphere to core, into a seething mass of hungry little replicating machines—gray goo.

In another four hours, they'll eat the entire solar system.

This is quite a risk to run for the possibility of endless consumer goods and perfect health, but I have very little doubt nanotechnology experiments will continue and, assuming the fail-safes work, may well lead to the possibility of immortality. But even a best-case scenario produces its own problems. For while physical immortality may be desirable from a personal point of view, for society as a whole it's a nightmare. A generation that ceases to die (or is promptly revived and repaired if the cryogenic lobby has its way) must also cease to breed, otherwise global overpopulation—a serious enough problem even today—would spiral out of control in a matter of years.

Yet if immortality is matched by a corresponding reduction in the birth rate, widespread cultural stagnation, and ultimately cultural degeneration, is the predictable outcome. Any viable society requires young blood as a stimulus to change. It is an ironic fact that should a technology of physical immortality ever emerge, society's response may well be to ban it.

The question is, would the loss of *physical* immortality really matter? There are many who believe that physical death is not the end and never has been.

11

History of the Afterlife (1)

And God shall wipe away all tears from their eyes; and there shall be
no more death . . . for the former things are passed away.
Revelation 21:4

NOT FAR FROM Dusseldorf, Germany, lies the Neander Valley, an
area that owes its scientific fame to a wholly accidental discovery. In 1856, a team of quarrymen working in a cave above
the valley unearthed sixteen pieces of a human skeleton. The
fragments were clearly very old, so the quarrymen turned them
over to their superiors, who in turn forwarded them to experts
for identification. Thus was triggered one of the most heated
academic controversies of the era.

The bones were curiously formed. Some seemed too big, too
heavy. A skull fragment showed a prominent brow ridge. It was
all too easy to imagine a glowering, apelike primitive, with
deep-set eyes and massive jaw. But did the find really represent
an archaic, extinct branch of the human species, or was it simply
some early equivalent of the Elephant Man, a member of our
own line hideously distorted by disease? Even something as
commonplace as arthritis can dramatically deform bone.

The controversy raged for thirty years. Then, in 1886, two
more skeletons with the same characteristics were discovered in
a cave at Spy, in Belgium. Near them were tools and fossils of
extinct subarctic fauna originating from the Middle Stone Age.

Since the German find was now no longer unique, the theory of diseased bones weakened and in the years ahead would collapse altogether. From 1886 up to about 1910, a whole series of similar skeletons were discovered throughout western and central Europe. It was no longer possible to postulate disease as a reasonable explanation. Scholars decided they had found a whole new type of human being. In deference to the siting of the original finds, he was dubbed Homo *neanderthalensis*, Neanderthal man.

Archaeologists now believe Neanderthal man appeared around 100,000 BP in Europe, and perhaps as much as 30,000 years earlier in southern Africa and Java. When the first finds were made, scholars rushed to reconstruct this curious creature as, not so many years before, scholars had rushed to reconstruct dragons from dinosaur bones. The result was not dissimilar. What emerged was a picture of a shambling semi-human, without intelligence or language and unable to walk fully upright. Neanderthal man was seized on as the "Missing Link," an intermediary between apes and humanity who conversed in grunts and was lucky to find his backside in a fog.

The picture has been modified since then, but Neanderthals remain an early example of primitive humanity. Yet for all that, they buried their dead with floral wreaths, facing east toward the rising sun and sometimes carefully trussed so as to have the appearance of a fetus. From these facts, archaeologists deduce Neanderthals practiced religion and seem to have believed in life after death.

This ancient idea—the last Neanderthal died some 35,000 years ago—has proven tenacious. Ancestor worship has been prevalent throughout the world for tens of thousands of years—so prevalent, indeed, that it still seems to be humanity's most common form of religious expression. Virtually every tribal community on the planet honors its ancestors. There are ancestor shrines in Japan and China. Offerings to the ancestors are made in India (despite widespread belief in reincarnation). A logical corollary to ancestor worship is ancestor survival and the belief that you too will become a helpful ancestor when you die.

The development of urban communities actually enhanced the concept of an afterlife. Archaeologists have found grave goods in the royal tombs of humankind's earliest civilizations. Close to five thousand years ago, Mesopotamian kings were buried with furniture, musical instruments, and gambling gear for use in the next life. Soldiers and servants were also buried with their masters, apparently to continue their faithful service beyond the grave.

Studies of Sumero-Akkadian mythology indicate a prevalent and widespread belief in an afterlife, although not one you might look forward to with any great enthusiasm. The dead rested—if that is the word—in a realm called *kur-nu-gi-a,* the Land of No Return. They lived in darkness, ate clay, and, according to one myth, were "clothed like birds with wings." When the Goddess Ishtar decided to pay a visit, she threatened the gatekeeper that if he refused to let her in she would smash the doorpost and lead the dead up out of their gloomy underworld so they could eat the living. This hint of postmortem cannibalism reflected common attitudes toward the dead throughout the Fertile Crescent. When you were gone, you might survive, but changed for the worse in an unpleasant environment.

The picture was a lot brighter in Ancient Egypt. Sometime before 2300 BCE, masons cut hieroglyphic texts into the walls of the pyramid of Unas, the last of Egypt's 5th Dynasty Pharaohs. They consisted of prayers, rituals, and magical spells dating to an even earlier time, all designed to guarantee the dead king a comfortable life in the afterworld. Earlier still, Egyptian beliefs postulated a continued existence in the *Sekhet-Aaru* (Field of Reeds) a curious environment possibly based on the Nile marshland inhabited by the primitive hunters of predynastic times.

But the Field of Reeds seems to have been reserved for commoners. Pharaohs, by and large, were supposed to ascend to the heavens and become stars. Later, Egypt became a culture obsessed with death and evolved a complex picture of the human soul. According to this doctrine, the physical body or *khat* was linked with a *ka* or double, created at the moment of conception, which remained an exact, if invisible, replica of the *khat* throughout life. It's not altogether clear where the *ka* resided, but if you "went to your *ka* ," it meant you'd died. The *ka* itself seems to have incorporated all your talents, faults, and failings, but it survived physical death and could continue to eat, drink, and enjoy the smell of incense. It was also believed to offer you comfort after death, which suggests the Egyptians didn't think of it as your essential self.

With the *ka* were several more inner aspects. One of these was the *ba* or bird-soul, which, while associated with the individual, had a life of its own and would sometimes prompt actions you might not otherwise have thought of. During your life, the *ba* could enter or leave your body at will, but after death it was unable to survive without some physical foundation— hence the Egyptian obsession with preserving the corpse.

Other inner aspects included a spiritual intelligence called the *khu*, a sort of life-force or power known as *sekhem*, a shadow (*khaibit*) and a name (*ren*). But perhaps the most important of all was the *ib*, or heart which didn't seem to have much to do with the physical heart, but was actually a god within whose destiny it was to witness your conduct and take on the weight of your sins.

On death, it was important that due provision be made for them all. Your physical body had to be embalmed in a wrapping of bitter aloes and placed in a secret (or at least well-fortified) tomb, safe from desecration. Inside this tomb you had a special statue that would serve as the new dwelling place of your *ka*; and also a perch on which your bird soul might rest between visits to your mummy.

When a noble (and particularly a Pharaoh) died, there had to be arrangements for the journey of the *ib*. Depending on rank, this might include such things as chariots for travel, grain, and other foodstuffs for the journey; servants, slaves, and advisers in the form of statues (with a contingent of armed guards in the case of a Pharaoh); anointing oils, incense, gemstones, gold, and artifacts for use as payments or gifts to the gods; and personal equipment such as the deceased found useful or pleasurable in life. Everything was buried with the corpse.

The enormous rock-cut tombs in the Valley of the Kings were designed to provide their occupants with postmortem accommodation throughout eternity. When the tomb was sealed, the jackal-headed god Anubis entered to conduct the *ib* to a subterranean realm of the dead, situated somewhere beneath the western horizon. There were twelve gates dividing the realm, and the journey through them was not without its perils. Many strange and hideous monsters were said to inhabit this place and fearsome obstacles had to be overcome in order to proceed. But the *ib* would eventually reach the Hall of Judgment, where it was weighed against a single feather. When the heart was lighter than the feather, the gods knew you were free from grievous sin and worthy to remain with them. If, conversely, the *ib* was too heavy, it was promptly destroyed, taking everything else—*ka*, *ba*, *khu*, and *ren*—with it, carrying you into oblivion.

An inscription in the tomb of the 6th Dynasty pharaoh Pepi describes what happened when Judgment was favourable: "[The King] walked through the iron which is the ceiling of heaven. With his panther skin upon him, Pepi passeth with his flesh, he is happy with his name and he liveth with his double." That curious expression "happy with his name" was more important than you might imagine. If an individual was successfully deprived of his name, the Egyptians believed he was destroyed forever. This belief underlay the widespread, if incomplete, obliteration of monuments to the heretic king Akhenaten and seems to have survived until modern times, to judge from the fate of politicians like Stalin in the Soviet Union.

The concept of an afterlife also emerged in the later civilizations of Greece and Rome. For the early Greeks, life after death was an unedifying existence as an insubstantial shadow inhabiting a gloomy underworld where bloodless shades lacked power and longed for their lost life. This was not Hell (in the common understanding of the term) but rather an eternity of boredom and mediocrity from which only the greatest heroes escaped. Mighty men of renown were believed to avoid death altogether, despite the noticeable fact that most of them met sticky ends on bloody battlefields: they celebrated their victories as immortals in Elysium.

(Much the same theme is seen in the old Norse idea that heroes might sometimes cross the Rainbow Bridge and spend eternity in Valhalla. There they had Odin and his fellow gods for company, fought cheerfully among themselves by day, and joined together for a pork and mead feast by night ... an idealized vision of a warrior's life if ever there was one.)

By the sixth century BCE, a more optimistic note had crept

into Greek thought with the development of the various mystery religions, initiate groups characterized by secret doctrines and ritual dramas. The Eleusinian Mysteries[61] in particular held out the promise of a blissful afterlife to its members, while the hoi polloi were, as usual, condemned to the same old gloomy underworld.

The Ancient Romans held ideas of an afterlife similar to those of the early Greeks, conceiving of a gloomy shadow realm accessible by means of a one-way boat trip across the River Styx. Ever practical, the Romans realized the ferryman would want payment and placed a coin under the tongue of the corpse for this purpose. The later custom, widespread throughout Europe, of placing coins on the eyes of the dead may be a distorted survival.

Classical Judaism wasn't so sure about an afterlife . . . at least not at first. *Ecclesiastes* (9:5) said it all: "The dead know nothing and they have no more reward." All turned to dust again and a living dog was better than a dead lion. All the same, whatever the official position, belief in some sort of existence after physical death crept in. How else could you explain the story of the Witch of Endor? According to the Old Testament account, the prophet Samuel was dead and buried in Ramah when the Philistine armies threatened Israel. Desperate for advice, King Saul asked a witch to call up the prophet's spirit, which she successfully did.[62]

The appearance of Samuel—whose first words were "Why has thou disquieted me to bring me up?"—suggests his post-mortem survival in some realm. That many Israelites believed in such survival is attested by the fact that Saul was forced to ban necromancy in the days before he felt the need of it himself. The practice, it seems, had become widespread throughout his kingdom.

Where Samuel rested before he was "brought up" seems to have been Sheol, an area of shades very similar to the Babylonian underworld. Unlike in Egypt, there was no Judgment. Good, bad, or indifferent, everyone shared the same fate—survival in a dimly lit realm of grinding boredom where nothing ever happened, except, apparently, the occasional call from a necromancer.

What exactly survived is another historical problem. The Hebrew term *nefesh*, which today is usually translated as "soul" or "vital spirit" and associated with the heart, which the Israelites believed to be the seat of consciousness, originally meant neck or throat. When the transition to soul came about is difficult to determine, as, indeed, is how and why. The word *ruach*, again translated as "soul" or sometimes "ghost" in its modern usage, is a little easier to pin down. It originally meant "wind," which expanded into "breath," as in Genesis I, where it is Jehovah's *ruach*/breath that hovers over the deep. Many cultures (rightly) equate breath with life and hence the essence of life—spirit.

Sometime in or around the fifth century BCE, an extraordinary development occurred. The Book of Isaiah, a compilation of sayings attributed to the eighth century BCE prophet of that name, announced that "the dead shall live, their bodies shall rise"—the first recorded example of a belief in physical resurrection. There seems little doubt that physical resurrection is what was meant. Isaiah spoke of corpses as the "dwellers in the dust" and forecast they would "awake and sing."

Physical resurrection soon became linked to the idea of judgment. While the good, the bad and the ugly were all scheduled for a rude awakening, only some would achieve a pleasurable immortality. The rest were condemned to shame and everlasting contempt, although exactly where was by no means clear, at least at first. But judgment proved a popular concept, so that by the end of the second century BCE, Sheol had been divided in three, with separate compartments for the good, the bad, and the indeterminately mediocre. The compartment for the bad was known as Gehenna.

It is a biblical claim that the Valley of Hinnom (*Ge Hinnom* in Hebrew) was the site of child sacrifice to a devouring deity called Moloch during the time of the biblical monarchy. Later, as Jerusalem grew, somewhere had to be found to burn the rubbish and *Ge Hinnom* was deemed suitable. The valley became a smoldering wasteland of stench, smoke, and flame, a perfect model for Gehenna, where the wicked were tortured endlessly by fire.

By the time the *Wisdom of Solomon* came to be written during the first century BCE, the idea had emerged that the soul might actually predate the physical body, which it entered at birth. (The same notion had occurred to Plato some centuries earlier.) Although traditional Judaism held firm to earlier teachings, the Pharisees concluded the soul was immortal and fated by the individual's behavior either for damnation or resurrection.

Time passed, but the idea of resurrection simply would not go away. The Roman emperor Hadrian, who ruled from 117 to 138 CE, is reputed to have quizzed Rabbi Joshua ben Chanin about how exactly Jews believed God would resurrect the faithful in the world to come. Rabbi Joshua assured him God would make use of a "bone called *Luz*" located in the spinal column. This bone was indestructible. When the rabbi produced a sample and pounded it with a blacksmith's hammer, the anvil shattered but the bone remained intact.

In 210 CE, another distinguished scholar, Rabbi Oshaia, committed the story to writing. The bone, he said, was located below the eighteenth vertebrae and had proved immune to fire, water, or anything else used against it. Whatever you did, it could be neither broken nor bruised, let alone destroyed. Belief in the *Luz* survived as late as the sixteenth century. The idea of the bone was only decently buried in 1543 when the Flemish physician Andries Van Wesel (Andreas Vesalius) proved conclusively it didn't exist.

But with or without the marvelous bone, resurrection was to remain an article of faith. In the Eighteen Benedictions recited daily, God was addressed as "the One who resurrects the dead" while the Sanhedrin warned that anyone claiming there was no resurrection would be debarred from the world to come. As we shall see, the concept of resurrection was taken up by Christianity, where it remains an article of faith to this day.

Christianity is, in fact, a death-centred religion. Its central focus is the death (and resurrection) of its founder, its central symbol the cross used by the Romans as an instrument of death. It accepts—at least symbolically—the ancient Hebrew idea that Adam and Eve forfeited a natural immortality by their behavior in the Garden of Eden. "The wages of sin is death," thunders *Romans* 6:23. Nonetheless, belief in immortality remains, linked to the concept of salvation through Christ, resurrection of the physical body, and a mass judgment designed to sort out the good, who by definition accept Christ, from the bad, who do not.

Christian ideas about life after death were greatly influenced by a wholly separate doctrine—the Second Coming of Christ. According to the central Christian mythos, Jesus of Nazareth was crucified to death by the Romans but rose from the dead three days later and appeared briefly to some of his disciples before ascending to heaven. As St. Paul told the story, the historical event had a profound spiritual significance. Like those of

Osiris and several god-kings before him, Jesus' death was a sacrifice that cleansed humanity of its sins—or at least that portion of humanity who fervently believed it did.

The original expectation was that Jesus, having personally conquered death, would return in glory during the lifetime of his surviving disciples. When the last of them died, the hope was that the return would happen soon, which gradually transformed into confidence that it would happen someday. Since a thousand years seemed like a nice round figure, a millennial belief emerged. There were frissons of popular excitement—not to say outright terror—at the approach of the year 1000 CE and again, more recently, the year 2000 CE. The problem was that Christ's reappearance was supposed to herald a final judgment of everybody everywhere. Fortunately for sinners and the faithless, nothing untoward occurred on either date.

Against this suspenseful background, early Christians became increasingly preoccupied with the question of what happened to the dead while they waited for Christ's return. One theory advanced was that there had to be an immediate individual judgment, an interesting echo of the much earlier Egyptian belief. According to this view, you died, and were judged at once by God and dispatched to heaven or hell according to your just desserts.

Although this idea has proven remarkably tenacious—many Christians think in just such terms today—there were those who disagreed with it. An alternative viewpoint was that the dead were in some sense only sleeping as they awaited fulfilment of the prophesied mass resurrection that would mark Judgment Day on a heroic scale.

The idea of a mass Judgment Day had considerable emotional appeal since it tied in nicely with the vision of King Jesus returning in glory to rule our entire planet. But as a theory, it had its problems. One was that it seemed terribly unfair to postpone a true believer's well-earned trip to Paradise, and even more so to postpone the equally well-earned punishments that should surely be meted out by a loving God to sinners at the earliest possible opportunity.

The church father Tertullian bent his considerable intellect to the problem and came up with a solution of sorts. He put forward a "spacial concept"—which he suggested might be called "Abraham's Bosom"—that lay somewhat below heaven but definitely above hell. There the souls of the dead could rest and the just refresh themselves until the final resolution of their fate in a forthcoming Judgment Day. The Byzantine church liked the idea so much that they formally endorsed it as part of Christian doctrine.

The Roman Catholic Church embraced a different version of the idea in the Middle Ages with the introduction of limbo. The term means "border" and limbo was conceived of as existing on the border between heaven and hell. Here souls remained awaiting Judgment Day but with less emphasis on refreshment than in Abraham's Bosom. Long convinced that just about everybody is a sinner, Catholicism suggested penances in limbo might usefully cleanse the soul before the Final Judgment. In the thirteenth century the Church released another interesting detail about the afterlife state. Unbaptized infants, burdened only by original sin, went to hell but were given lighter punishments than the rest of us.

The seventh century CE saw the beginnings of fresh and highly graphic insights into death with the foundation of Islam by the Prophet Muhammad. According to the Qur'an, humans are animated by a vital spirit called *nafs*, which is the seat of your rational consciousness and associated with your individuality. It is also associated with Allah himself, who "breathed his spirit" into a humanity made from molded mud. This soul is taken away during sleep[63] but returned by God to those destined to survive the night.

On death, the soul rises to the throat before leaving the body altogether, then meets with *Malak al-Mawt*, the Angel of Death, who instructs the wicked to depart to the wrath of God. Many nervously attempt to disobey the order and seek refuge back in the body from whence they have to be extricated "like the dragging of an iron skewer through moist wool." Once evicted out in this way, the soul is placed by angels in a malodorous hair cloth and its sins carefully recorded before it is returned to the corpse in the grave.

The righteous have it altogether easier. They are told by the Angel of Death to depart to the mercy of God and flow gracefully from the body to be wrapped by angels in a perfumed shroud and taken to the Seventh Heaven, where their virtues are recorded. But these souls too are returned to the body in the grave.

At this point, the *Fitnat al-Qabr* begins. This graveside trial is conducted by two angels, Munkar and Nakir, who question the deceased about the tenets of Islam. Those who fail the test discover that their tomb contracts violently, crushing them so that their ribs pile up on top of one another. A mystical door opens and the smoke and heat of hell pours in. By contrast, those who pass the test have their graves expanded as far as the eye can see.

But this state of affairs is temporary in both cases. After a period known as *al-barzakh*, good and bad alike are resurrected in physical bodies to face *Yaum al-Hisab*, the Final Judgment. This sends believers to well-stocked "gardens in which rivers flow" where they will abide forever, while the wicked are condemned to hell, where they don garments of fire and have boiling water poured over their heads. New skin is substituted for the old that burns away so the damned can continue to feel their punishment.

Islamic martyrs are excused from the judgment process altogether. Those killed in a holy war or who suffered harm in the defense of their beliefs are forgiven any sins they might have committed and are sent directly to the paradise gardens.

A more recent religious view of the afterlife is rooted in the vision of an American farmer's son. In 1827, Joseph Smith, Jr, a resident of western New York State, unexpectedly encountered an angel named Moroni, who gave him a set of gold plates enscribed with mysterious writing. Smith managed to translate the plates, which he believed had been prepared by an ancient American prophet called Mormon, drawing for his source on earlier plates of the same type. They presented a history of Israelite tribes who migrated to America centuries before the birth of Christ and underwent religious experiences there.

After three years, Smith published his translation as the *Book of Mormon* and founded his own church on the basis of its doctrines. Today the principle body of that church—the Church of Jesus Christ of Latter-Day Saints—has more than 10 million members, about half of whom live in the United States, with the remainder scattered across Latin America, Canada, Europe, and parts of Oceania. The Reorganized Church of Latter-Day Saints, the next largest Mormon denomination, has a membership measured in the hundreds of thousands.

Although Mormons are Christians, as the name of their church would imply, their doctrines diverge considerably from the mainstream. One interesting idea is that God actually evolved from humanity and human beings have the potential to evolve into gods. Another is that there will be two resurrections, a thousand years apart. The first of these will be triggered by the Second Coming of Christ, the second by the completion of a millennium of temple work largely concerned with baptising the dead. As a result, faithful church members become gods blessed with eternal life, as will, apparently, just about everybody else, since following the second resurrection the world is scheduled to become a heavenly sphere.

A direct consequence of this doctrine is the Mormon fascination for genealogy. Huge efforts are made by members of the church—aided by a considerable investment in computer systems—to ensure the salvation of dead ancestors through secret temple ceremonies.

What are we to make of all this? It is clear that virtually every culture in the Western world has harbored beliefs about an afterlife. In earliest times, these seem to have been confined to an immaterial existence in some sort of alternative dimension, but later the idea of immortality in a specially resurrected (physical) body became widespread.

Widespread but by no means universal. Some Eastern religions have a wholly different view of what happens to us when we die.

12

History of the Afterlife (2)

Death was not there, nor was there aught immortal . . .
Rigveda

WESTERN MISUNDERSTANDING OF Hinduism starts with the word "Hindu." The term is not indigenous to any language of India. It was carried there by early Persian invaders and meant nothing more than "Indian"—that's to say, a native of the country with no reference to any religion he or she might hold. The British were the first to use "Hinduism" to describe the predominant religious practices of India in the nineteenth century. Indians themselves avoid it. To them, their religion is the *sanatana dharma*, an almost untranslatable phrase that carries the sense of eternal (religious) law inherent in Nature.

Against this morsel of historical background, it may come as no surprise to discover the practice of Hinduism[64] is diverse, fragmented, and sometimes even contradictory. There is no ultimate authority equivalent to a Christian Pope or Tibetan Dalai Lama. Hinduism welcomes new spiritual ideas and swallows them whole: so much so, in fact, that it is possible for a Hindu to practice another religion without abandoning his or her Hinduism. There is no founder, no Western-style revelation, no single Bible or Koran. But all Hindus revere the *Vedas*.

Western scholars, who dislike untidiness, recognize only four

Vedas—the *Rig Veda*, the *Yajur Veda*, the *Sama Veda*, and the *Atharva Veda*. Indian tradition is broader. It also includes archaic cosmological accounts called the *Puranas* and historical epics known as the *Itihasas*. Together they form a body of sacred literature that purports to describe India's ancient past and the development of her philosophical thought.

There are also differences of opinion between West and East as to the age of the Vedic literature. Western scholars assign much of it to relatively recent times. The *Bhagavata Purana* is supposed to have been written in the ninth century CE, while *Itihasa* works like the *Mahabharata* and the *Ramayana* are dated to perhaps the sixth century BCE. Even the very oldest, the *Rig Veda*, is believed to date no further back than 1500 BCE, with conservative scholars arguing that it may be much more recent. To the academic tradition of India, all this is occidental nonsense. The very word "purana" means "ancient" and many texts are dated by Indian scholars to at least 3000 BCE, possibly very much earlier.

But whenever written, the *Vedas* propose a worldview very different to the one we embrace in the West today. Epics like the *Ramayana* describe a prehistoric age when aircraft (called *vimanas*) plied the skies of India, interstellar travel was possible, and inter-dimensional contact with alien beings commonplace. According to the *Puranas*, there are some 400,000 humanoid races inhabiting various planets, not to mention 8 million other life-forms, including animals and plants. All are subject (whether they realize it or not) to a cosmic hierarchy.

Here things get difficult, since there are contradictions in Hinduism about the nature of the Being at the head of the hierarchy. Some sources see the entity as a personal God, others, equally revered, as an immanent and transcendent mystic principle. The paradox seems to be historical. The earliest texts present a polytheistic picture with a hierarchy of gods not unlike the sort of deities the Greeks once believed lived on top of Mount Olympus. Indians sacrificed to their gods in order to curry favor and obtain benefits, with the added bonus that sacrifice mysteriously placed them in communion with the divine so that they absorbed a little of its essence.

In later texts, the act of sacrifice was seen as part of a cosmic process, important in its own right and not just for what it might get you. Later still, the emphasis turned inward, as Vedic philosophers, disenchanted with the old beliefs, sought to find the eternal principle that sustained the whole universe, gods and all. This proved a turning point in Indian thought. Polytheism was replaced by something closer to pantheism, the notion that a divine principle permeates everything there is. The gods survived, but only as living entities of immense power and longevity. They no longer had the final say on how the universe was run. Like humanity they were subject to the spiritual law embodied in an Ultimate Being.

The Ultimate Being was named *Brahman*, a term that originally meant something like "sacred action." An alternative name was *Atman*, which started out meaning "breath" (hence possibly "life") but is now generally taken as "Self." Although *Brahman* could be experienced in certain ecstatic mystical states, it was not all that easy to describe. But whatever its manifestation, it was the timeless, spaceless principle of eternal Existence that at once inhabits, envelops, and ultimately transcends the entire physical universe.

It also dwells in the heart of every human.

That last belief is the key to understanding what Hindus think happens to us after death. Although there are some differences of opinion about the process, Vedic thought generally postulates that all living beings—human, nonhuman, gods, and demons—were brought into manifestation by a twin process of creation and emanation. Creation was concerned with the various bodily forms, predominantly humanoid, composed of subtle energy and brought into being by the mental action of the Creator. Once created, these forms reproduced sexually but diversified and changed, rather as living beings are thought to diversify and change through the process of Darwinian evolution.

Unlike the bodies, individual souls were *not* created. Rather they were emanated by the Supreme Being itself and are thus particles of that great cosmic principle. To the thoughtful Hindu, your innermost essence (*atman*) is not individual, however much it may appear so. Rather it is a wave on the cosmic ocean, or a small quantity of air caught in an earthen jar that shares its nature with the endless space outside.

Before reaching this insight in the depths of their history, Indians believed with most of their Indo-European neighbors that we only live once but survive physical death and go to join the gods in paradise if our moral status warrants it, or plunged into the punishment of hell if it does not. Afterward, however, the viewpoint changed. Life came to be seen as an unbroken pilgrimage through aeons of time, starting as a spark from the divine that gathers experience of every age, culture, custom, and civilization in a journey back to its original Source. The mechanism of this pilgrimage was reincarnation.

Today, the concept of reincarnation so pervades Indian thought that it is no more questioned than the fact that sunrise marks the morning. You leave this world predestined by your past actions to face a chain of future births, deaths, and rebirths. Although Hindus commonly hold that human life span is 120 years, the actual time you spend in any given incarnation is decided by your *karma*.

Karma is one of those doctrines that means different things to different people, but for most Hindus today it's a sort of moral balance sheet that determines both the circumstances and duration of your next life. Every deed is a seed, a quantifiable causal agent that adds to others of its kind to predestine your fate. The popular myth has it that a record-keeper called Chitragupta reads out your file in the Hall of Yama following your death. If you have managed to avoid even a single evil thought or act, you are dispatched at once to everlasting beatitude. The rest of us endure a period of reward or punishment, depending on our overall spiritual state, before being sent back to take on another body. That body may not be human: the morally bankrupt often have to face incarnation as an animal or insect.

There are, of course, many educated Hindus who accept the myth as the figurative description of a spiritual process. But the end result remains the same. We are all subject to *samsara*, a great wheel of birth, death, and rebirth that grinds relentlessly millennia upon millennia. This is the nearest thing a Hindu gets to the Christian ideal of "life everlasting"—and he hates the very thought of it. The whole thrust of Hindu spirituality is to achieve *moksa*, the final liberation from the wheel.

Although it would seem reasonable to suppose the only real road to *moksa* is a saintly life, many Hindu hopefuls rely on the proper observance of certain rituals. When the devout sense the approach of the Grim Reaper, they begin—if they are able—to chant the mantra *Om*, a sound associated with Brahman and believed to be the bedrock vibration of the universe. Those lucky enough to die while the mantra is sounding are guaranteed instant *moksa*.

Among other things supposed to help is dying on the floor, preferably on a space sanctified by Ganges water and cow dung. (Dying in the space between ground and ceiling—i.e., raised from the floor in a bed—risks reincarnation as an evil spirit.) To help the process, relatives place a *tulsi* leaf in your mouth, then pour in some water taken from the confluence of the Ganges and Yamuna rivers at Allahabad. White clay is smeared on your forehead. When you breathe your last, your body is wrapped in a clean cloth, the color of which announces your age. Your relatives walk clockwise around the corpse.

Cremation is more or less universal among Hindus. Bodies are looked on as offerings to Agni, the Fire God. This is something else that's changed over the ages. According to the ancient texts, Indo-Aryans once buried their dead. But later, fire was taken in a black earthen pot from the home and carried before the corpse all the way to the funeral pyre, which was then lit by the eldest son or grandson—a practice retained more or less unchanged to the present day. As the flames rise, the soul seeks refuge in the head from whence it is liberated when the skull explodes. If the skull fails to explode, it is shattered by blows from a cudgel.

The business of soul liberation is another of those areas where Hindus disagree. Some believe a shattered skull is entirely unnecessary—the soul can escape through the nose, eyes, or mouth. Others think the best route is through the anterior fontanel, that terrifying soft spot on the head of very young babies which mercifully closes over as they grow up. Yoga practice, or even intense meditation, is believed to reopen the aperture, allowing the soul free passage out after death. If you have been particularly wicked during life, you risk a soul exit by way of your rectum, a filthy way to go that will require considerable purification.

When your soul has escaped, from whatever orifice, it resides in the *linga sarira*, a nodule of vapor about the size of your thumb. As it emerges, it is seized by two lurking servants of Yama, the God of Death. They rush it off to their master, who checks your identity, then sends you off to the Abode of the Dead, where you hover on the threshold waiting patiently for those you left behind to create you a new body. (The desperate need of a soul for a body is one reason why cremations are carried out so promptly in India—it ensures the soul doesn't return to the original corpse.)

Ten days after your departure, the officiating priest and chief mourner have purified themselves sufficiently from the defilement of your death to start the construction of a new, albeit temporary, body for your soul. They do this by digging a small trench in consecrated land by a river and invoking the god Vishnu. A mixture of barley flour, sugar, curds, milk, honey, sesame seeds, and a clarified butter known as *ghee* is formed into ten balls that are placed, one by one, in the trench.

A prayer accompanies each ball. The first calls for the creation of a head, the next for neck and shoulders, and so on until the new body—just eighteen inches long—is complete. Vishnu is then asked to deliver it to Yama and the balls are thrown into the river. Later, further prescribed ceremonies take place, including one designed to turn your soul into an ancestral spirit. Once the formalities have been completed, you leave the earth in your new little body, clinging to the tail of a cow that leads you over a river of blood marking the outer boundary of Yama's kingdom.

It takes a full, somewhat perilous, year to cross the kingdom and reach the judgment seat where Chitragupta reads out your file and Yama dispatches your soul temporarily to heaven or hell. There, in bliss or agony, you will await your next incarnation.

Although some authorities speculate that Neanderthal humanity may have believed in reincarnation, our only really firm evidence points to the concept having first arisen in India. But more than five hundred years before the birth of Christ, something happened on the country's Nepalese border that was to lead to the widespread export of this Vedic idea: a young prince had his first sight of a corpse.

Siddhattha, the prince in question, was born to King Suddhodana and Queen Mahamaya in the Kingdom of the Sakyas. According to legend, the birth was foretold in a dream of the queen's in which a white elephant entered her womb. Brahman priests interpreted this as predicting the birth of a universal monarch or buddha.[65] When the baby appeared, the king's spiritual adviser, a sage named Asita, gave his verdict on the basis of body signs: a buddha it would be. Several Brahman body-sign experts hedged their bets. If the child remained at home, he would be a universal monarch; if not, a buddha.

Queen Mahamaya never found out who was right. She died a week after the birth and the child was brought up by his aunt. Pali scriptures record that while still a little boy he went into trance during a state ploughing festival, exhibiting a knowledge of yoga far beyond his years. This incident, combined with the Brahman predictions, began to worry King Suddhodana. He had absolutely no intention that his son should become one of those wandering ascetics who have been India's trademark for millennia and sought to keep the boy at home by showering him with every luxury. His clothes were tailored from the finest cloth. Lotus ponds were made for his enjoyment. He was even given three palaces, one for winter, one for summer, and one for the rainy season. In later life, the boy was to recall how he passed the four months of the rains royally entertained by female musicians.

When he was sixteen, Siddhattha was married off to his cousin, another sixteen-year-old. Like many a father before and since, King Suddhodana must have thought marriage would settle the boy. As it happened, it did nothing of the sort.

The crunch came when Siddhattha was twenty-nine. His sheltered existence had protected him from a great many of life's little trials, but while driving in his chariot, he chanced to see a bent, decrepit man walking with huge difficulty, leaning on a staff. In his innocence, Siddhattha asked what was wrong with the unfortunate. His charioteer explained the man was suffering from old age, something that came to us all.

This was to be only the first of four signs that combined to bring Siddhattha to the most important turning point of his life. The second was sight of an individual far gone with illness— again the charioteer explained this was something everyone risked. The third was a corpse with the attendant explanation that death is the fate of every living being. Finally, critically, the young prince caught sight of a yellow-robed holy man. The monk seemed absolutely serene, totally at peace with himself and the world. Impressed, Siddhattha realized his father's worst nightmares: he decided to go out into the world to find out how the holy man could remain so serene in the midst of so much misery.

In an interesting example of the way Murphy's Law operates even in the lives of buddhas, Siddhattha was en route home when he heard his wife had given birth to a son. His reaction is best judged by the fact that he promptly named the boy Rahula, which means "fetter." But fettered or not, he stuck to his decision. After a period of soul-searching, he left the palace to become a wandering ascetic. His action has since become known as the Great Renunciation.

Siddhattha apprenticed himself to two gurus in the course of his wanderings. In each case he quickly mastered what they had to teach and achieved advanced mystical states. But his accomplishments still fell short of *nirvana*, the realization of absolute truth, and he continued on his travels. Eventually he reached a village called Senanigama, near what is now Gaya, where he established himself with a small group of disciples on a beautiful stretch of land between a woodland grove and a river. Here he undertook a rigorous regime of austerity and self-mortification.

It didn't do with him at all. His hair started to fall out, his body withered so that his spine took on the appearance of a knotted string, his eyes grew sunken, his skin shriveled. He was so weak that he frequently fell on his face when he left his meditation posture to answer calls of nature. On one occasion he swooned so deeply that his followers thought he was dead.

This sort of thing is by no means unusual among Indian holy men and it took Siddhattha fully six years to realize it was getting him nowhere. When he started to eat again, his disciples were so disgusted that they left him. Siddhattha decided to trust his own judgment. He stayed put, slowly regained his strength, and continued to seek his salvation with diligence.

One morning he sat down cross-legged beneath a fine example of a fig tree, the *ficus religiosa* now universally known as the *bodhi* or *bo*. He determined not to get up again until he had achieved enlightenment and escaped the eternal wheel of birth, death, and rebirth.

Here, as so often happens in the lives of religious leaders, the scriptures take on a mythic flavor. According to the ancient texts, the Evil One, Mara, moved to foil the emergence of a new buddha and attacked Siddhattha with a legion of his most hideous demons. But Mara had misjudged his enemy. Over a series of previous lives, Siddhattha had perfected his virtues and these stood him in such good stead that he was able to meditate calmly throughout the attack. Mara knew when he was beaten and withdrew his demons.

(Once again this story may be taken figuratively. It's a matter of experience that demons of the mind—lust, inattention, greed, fugue, doubt, and all the rest—often arise to plague those trying to lose themselves in meditation.)

Over the course of the night that followed, Siddhattha first accessed the memories of his past lives, then developed the power to see the reincarnations of others. When finally he came to realize the "four noble truths," his mind became free and he achieved ultimate enlightenment.

The Four Noble Truths were—and are in Buddhism today—the

interlinked realizations that all lives, from beggars to kings, are defined by misery; that misery arises solely and directly out of craving; that craving can be eliminated; and that to do so, you need to follow a methodical path. Literally millions of words of commentary have been written about these insights as Buddhism became a religion in its own right, but in themselves they remain an elaboration of the fundamental Hindu worldview. For the Buddha, as for his fellow countrymen, humanity was caught up in *samsara*, the everlasting wheel of birth, death, and rebirth. The only worthwhile spiritual course was to stop the wheel and climb off. Where the enlightened Siddhattha differed from prior Indian tradition was his insight into the nature of what it was that kept you chained to the wheel and the methods by which you could break free.

His developed philosophy differed in another important respect as well. The enlightened Siddhattha concluded the Upanishads were wrong to assume the reality of a soul that somehow survived death. Indeed, he wasn't happy with the idea that there was any ultimate reality at all. To him, everything was impermanent, transitory, illusory. Life was no more than the sum of serial microseconds of experience by something that was itself impermanent, transitory, and illusory.

Although Buddhism recognizes the existence of a *self* in the practical sense of something that appears to be the focus of action and, indeed, morality, the Buddha was convinced the concept of ego was a delusion, albeit one most people shared. Even more deluded were the identifications people typically made, seeing themselves in terms of their bodies, their wealth, their families, their children. The unreality of such identifications would be readily accepted by Western psychology, but the Buddha went further when he concluded you should not even consider yourself a mind, since mind was no more permanent than anything else, consisting as it does of an ever-changing flow of thoughts and emotions.

Impermanence quickly assumed center stage in Buddhist philosophy and neither the Buddha nor his followers has shied away from the implications of the insight. If only the permanent and unchanging deserve to be called self, soul, or *atman*, then self, soul, or *atman* simply cannot exist, since nothing at all is permanent. What we think of as self, and postulate as soul, is no more than the sum of five aggregates—physical form, sensations and feelings, ideas, dispositions, and consciousness. Put these five things together and you have the illusion of a self or soul, but no more than an illusion. Nothing permanent survives death. The actuality is a process of continuous change with no fixed underlying entity.

The process continues across a daisy chain of physical bodies, leaving non-Buddhists bewildered about what it is exactly that reincarnates. Buddhists themselves remain comfortable with their *anatman* (no-soul, no-self) doctrine and see the reincarnatory relationship as analogous to fire, which is a different thing with every passing moment yet manages to retain its own distinctive appearance and characteristics—the curious continuity of an ever-changing entity.

The *nirvana* of Buddhism is not an afterlife in paradise: it is the state of having completely freed yourself from the delusion of ego and consequently also freed yourself from the need to reincarnate.[66] What is such a state like? Buddhists are absolutely certain that any attempt to describe it will distort it, and given the nature of the concept, you would be hard put to disagree. At the same time, the Buddha himself claimed, "There is an unborn, an unoriginated, an unmade, an uncompounded; were there not, there would be no escape from the world of the born, the originated, the made and the compounded." The world we know and experience may be illusory, but this is surely a broad hint that there is some sort of reality behind it.

Difficult though some of its concepts undoubtedly were,

Buddhism caught on. Siddhattha began by teaching his new insights to the five companions who had walked out on him when he abandoned self-mortification. After some initial reluctance, they listened and eventually agreed to become monks in the first Buddhist community. Others followed suit and before long the community had swollen to some sixty members. Fired with missionary zeal, they went out to spread the word. The Buddha himself continued to attract new disciples as he traveled, including King Bimbisara of Magadha.

As word of the movement spread, the new teacher began to receive invitations to visit various cities. One was Savatthi, today known as Shravasti, where a wealthy banker funded a monastery that became to all intents and purposes the headquarters of the new religion. More monasteries followed until there was one in almost every important city in the Ganges valley. Women as well as men began to flock to his standard. It was an embarrassing development: as a child of his time, the chauvinistic Siddhattha was not at all sure he should be teaching females. But his cousin Ananda struck an early blow for feminism when he finally persuaded him to establish an order of nuns.

Following the Buddha's death at the age of eighty in 483 BCE, Buddhism continued to grow. In a hundred years, monastic communities had spread throughout much of northern India while there were lay Buddhists in important areas of the nation's social and economic life. By the middle of the third century BCE, it was a major religion of the Mauryan Empire, which extended in a swathe from the Himalayas almost as far south as Sri Lanka. By the birth of Christ, Buddhism seemed firmly established in India and had begun its spread into central Asia and even China. But before long, there were signs of something amiss at home.

From about 300 CE, there was a strong revival of Hinduism in India, characterized by a devotional (*bhakti*) movement in which followers attempted to develop an intense love for a personal god. This movement actually led many Hindus to a devotion for the Buddha. But they did not become Buddhists. Instead they recognized Siddhattha as an incarnation of Vishnu and worshiped him accordingly. It was a tiny straw in the wind. For millennia, Hinduism had demonstrated a disturbing ability to swallow dissenting creeds whole.

Other factors came into play. As early as 399 CE, a Chinese traveler noted the destruction of numerous Buddhist monasteries in India by nomadic Central Asian Huns. At the same time, surviving Buddhists were turning by the thousands to Tantric practice, a fascinating set of psycho-spiritual and physical disciplines that promised power and enlightenment but nonetheless diverged from the original Buddhist message.

The Huns continued to rampage into the sixth century CE, weakening Buddhism further. By the eighth, there was a temporary revival under the Pala Kings, themselves Buddhists, but it was Tantric Buddhism that flowered. When the Pala dynasty collapsed in the twelfth century CE, Buddhism in India collapsed with it. The religion was heavily monastic, and when Muslim invaders razed the monasteries they destroyed its very foundation. A few pockets of influence remained, but in real terms Buddhism was dead in the land of its birth.

Not so elsewhere. Buddhism conquered Southeast Asia, profoundly influenced China, established itself in Japan (as Zen), and famously became the state religion of Tibet. It has even made something of a comeback in India since the early years of the twentieth century, when Indian intellectuals embraced it as an alternative to a Hinduism they could no longer accept. In the 1950s, Buddhist numbers were swelled by a mass conversion movement among the Untouchables, the lowest of all members of India's ancient caste system. Throughout this vast geographical area, Buddhists firmly believe that death is followed by reincarnated life.

The belief is shared by followers of another of India's great religions, Jainism. If the dating of Hinduism is uncertain, the beginnings of Jainism can be pinpointed much more precisely ... at least in a manner of speaking. Its historical founder was a man named Mahavira, the son of a clan chieftain, born in 599 BCE and a contemporary of Siddhattha. (His name comes up in Buddhist writings.) Much like Siddhattha, Mahavira felt called to an ascetic life when he was approaching thirty. After several years of meditation and considerable hardships, he achieved enlightenment, attracted followers, and soon had a whole new religion on his hands.

But that's just the historian's version. Jains themselves are convinced their faith is actually eternal. It was revealed through successive ages from the earliest of times by a succession of *Tirthankaras*, enlightened individuals who attained perfection, then preached Jainism to the world. The first Tirthankara—hence the real founder—was called Rsabha and lived in Vedic times. (His name appears in both the Vedas and Puranas but with no accompanying details of his life.) A succession of Tirthankaras stretches from Rsabha to Mahavira, but nothing is known about any of them with the sole exception of the 23rd, a sage named Parshva, who lived in the eighth century BCE—and little enough is known about him.

Whatever its foundations, the most far-reaching of Jain insights is an absolute conviction that life is sacred and should not be taken under any circumstances. That means *all* life. To this day, Jains typically wear face masks so they won't inadvertently inhale an insect and sweep the ground as they walk so they won't accidentally squash a bug.

Jains are also convinced the universe is divided into two broad categories, *jiva* and *ajiva*. The first of these (*jiva*) is an animating soul-substance that permeates all living creatures and certain categories of natural phenomena like wind and fire. Everything else (*ajiva*) is categorized as inanimate. *Karma*, that great law of cause and effect that so dominates Hindu and Buddhist thought, is seen by Jains as an actual fluidic substance, something real but intangible and unseen, like radio waves. This invisible fluid flows into the *jiva* and clogs it up, an unfortunate development that results directly in the process of reincarnation as humanity clings desperately onto life. The only way of stopping the influx of fluid karma is a series of lives marked by extreme discipline and penance. But once the karmic flow is stopped, liberation follows.

There is, of course, a great deal more to Jainism than this, but it is clear that where life after death is concerned, Jain belief is identical in principle to that of Hindus and Buddhists, although different in detail. For the Jain, as for his fellow countrymen, the bottom line is still reincarnation, and the fundamental desire is to break free of the eternal wheel.

Much the same thing can be said for another of India's major religions, Sikhism. Sikhs follow the precepts of Nanak, an early Indian guru, and nine of his successors, as contained in two holy books, the *Adi Granth* and *Dasam Granth*. But any speculation about cosmic origins is drawn largely from Hindu texts from which Sikhs accept completely the concept of *samsara*, the karma-driven wheel of birth, death and rebirth.

Indeed, the theory of reincarnation so pervades Asian thought that it is almost a surprise to find any major Eastern religions that do not embrace it. There are a few, of course. The Parsis of India, whose religion derives from ancient Persian Zoroastrianism, accept the postmortem survival of a soul that is fated for judgment rather than recurring incarnations. Chinese Confucianism, often seen more as a social philosophy than a religion, does not support the idea of a soul at all. Taoism, historically the great mystical religion of China, has led some of its followers to seek physical immortality through mundane or spiritual alchemy, but is not tied to any doctrine equivalent to *samsara*. But aside from these and a few more minor exceptions, Eastern belief systems generally hold that you have far more to fear from life than death, since your tomb is actually the entrance to another womb.

Even from our brief survey, it is clear that some form of life after death is an article of faith in almost all of the world's major religions, but the nature of postmortem existence is evaluated differently across an East-West divide. In the East, as we have just seen, the concept of reincarnation generally holds sway. In the West, there is a leaning toward the idea of survival in some immaterial realm with the possibility of physical resurrection at a later date. Despite their differences, both traditions agree that death is not the end.

You have to wonder if there might be any evidence to support this widely held notion.

13

The Nature of Mind

What is mind? Doesn't matter.
What is matter? Never mind.
Anon, but beloved by physicists and psychologists

YOU KNOW FROM personal experience there's something's going on inside your head. You're aware of a constant chatter, as if you were talking to yourself. With an act of will, you can probably "see" pictures in there too, some of them vivid, colorful and active. You're aware of awareness itself—a focus that places you at the center of the external world. You know you have a storehouse of memories that, if not present all the time, can usually be accessed without too much trouble. You experience something in there that figures things out, makes decisions, acts as the driver of your body every time you take a stroll. Most of all, you have the sense that this is somehow where you live—the essential *you*, the fundamental core of your being. If anything is to survive after death, it's surely this . . . whatever *this* may be.

Put the constituents together and you have what's commonly called your mind. You know it's there because you experience it, yet it can't be weighed or measured and there's not an instrument on earth that can detect it directly. It's as if this "mind" exists on some other level of reality beyond firsthand examination by anybody other than yourself.

To make matters worse, there seems to be a part of your mind that you know nothing about. Sigmund Freud, the father-figure of psychoanalysis, was among the first to suspect this[67] when he noticed behavior patterns in some of his patients that appeared to be driven by something outside of themselves—or at least outside their conscious awareness. Eventually he formulated his famous theory of the subconscious, defined as the collection of mental activities within an individual that go on without his or her awareness.

It sounds innocent enough when put that way, but Freud clearly thought of the subconscious as a dustbin, a layer of the mind littered with repressed material too frightening or unpleasant to be confronted consciously. The concept led him to postulate different levels of the mind. If what you're doing falls within your immediate field of awareness—like reading this book—Freud saw that as using the "uppermost" stratum of your mind. Beyond that, so to speak, is a preconscious level that contains a storehouse of data you're not immediately aware of but can tap into instantly the minute you need it. It's unlikely, for example, that you've been thinking of your father's first name while you've been reading, but there it is, in the full light of your consciousness, now I've brought it up. Your father's name, like your street address, the faces of friends and a host of other data, is stored in the readily accessible preconscious. At a deeper level still lies a wholly unconscious area that's far from easy to reach. Were you breast-fed as a baby? Without asking Mother, few of us have the least idea, yet the memory is in there. Experiments with depth hypnosis and electrical stimulation of the brain have convinced scientists we are walking recording machines who never entirely forget *anything*. But most of it is stashed away in that deep, dark cupboard with the difficult lock.

Except the deep, dark cupboard analogy isn't strictly accurate. Freud thought there was a constant seepage from the unconscious. Its images emerge in dreams. It generates irrational fears. It causes slips of the tongue—the notorious "Freudian slips"—in which you innocently reveal ideas, desires, or attitudes you never knew you had in the first place. Freud believed that when you absentmindedly left your umbrella behind, it meant that subconsciously you wanted to come back.

Freud's favorite disciple (until they quarreled) was Carl Gustav Jung, who enlarged this model of the mind by adding another layer that he called the "collective unconscious." This he presented as an inherited area common to humanity as a whole and reflecting the basic structure of the human brain. To Jung, the collective unconscious was something very different from the personal unconscious, which arose out of individual experience. The collective unconscious, by contrast, was a huge repository of primordial ideas and images.

There seems little doubt there really *are* unconscious aspects of your mind. You've probably even seen the evidence yourself. How often, for example, have you lit a cigarette, drummed your fingers nervously, tapped your foot in time to music, finished a third cup of coffee, or eaten the last chocolate in the box without the least awareness you were doing it? Something in you decided on those actions and enabled you to carry them out effectively, but that *something* was clearly unconscious.

Given there is more to mind than meets the eye, psychologists prefer to use the word *psyche* to describe the totality of your mental processes, conscious and unconscious. It's a useful distinction. The layperson tends to think of *mind* as consciousness in its variety of manifestations. Most laypeople instinctively think of the soul in much the same way.

That word "soul," which appeared so often in the last couple of chapters, is a lot more tricky than it sounds. The *Concise Oxford Dictionary* gives its premier meaning as "the spiritual or

immaterial part of a human being, often regarded as immortal"—
precisely the way, you would assume, it's been used in this book.
But for most of us, the word carries an unexamined assumption.
We assume that whatever survives is conscious.

Think about it. When you've considered, as you must have
done, the possibility of surviving death, did you imagine for a
moment the afterlife might be an unconscious state? The plain
fact is, an unconscious afterlife is no afterlife at all: you might as
well be dead. If anything worthwhile is to survive, it simply has
to be your conscious mind. The dispute has never really been
about whether or not you have an immortal soul. The question
that needs to be answered is, *Will your mind survive?* But before
you can hope to tackle that one, you have to answer another:
What is mind anyway?

To this day, many of our reflections on the second question
have been influenced by the ideas of the seventeenth-century
French philosopher René Descartes. It was Descartes who coined
the famous phrase *Cogito, ergo sum*[68] and in so doing sought to
establish the certainty of existence on the basis of thought—a
criterion that surely holds good for life after death. He began all
his speculations on the basis of doubt and accepted an idea only
when it was clear, distinct, and free from inherent contradiction—
an approach that helped lay the foundations of modern rationalism. What he had to say about the nature of mind remains
interesting to this day.

Descartes drew an absolute distinction between mind and
matter. He observed that the defining characteristic of matter
was to occupy space, which mind clearly did not. The defining
characteristic of mind, by contrast, was to think. (Or at least to
be conscious of something.) It was possible to view material
substance as a total continuum, although typically broken up
into packets that might, in themselves, endure only for a limited

time. He believed mind was something analogous—when taken as a whole, individual minds made up a continuum of mental substance. Mental and material worlds were each complete in themselves and wholly distinct from one another.

That said, Descartes admitted a special relationship between body and mind. He was not, he believed, an entity who existed inside his body as a captain might exist inside his ship. The relationship between the two was far more intimate than that, so that the mind could affect the body and the body could affect the mind. This was particularly true when it came to emotion, sensation, and imagination, which, while clearly mental attributes, only seem possible if you have a body. Sensation arises out of bodily experience, as do the forms of the mental pictures created by your imagination. Even your emotions, apparently so cerebral, are largely body-based. Next time you feel fear or joy, ask yourself how much of the emotion would be lost if the associated physical sensations disappeared.

Despite his hedging of the bet, Descartes soon found his ideas about separate mental and material worlds under strong attack. The English philosopher Thomas Hobbes left off his political theorizing for long enough to argue there was no such thing as mental substance. For Hobbes, the phenomenon of mind could be fully explained by the concept of matter in motion—the only thing that really existed in Hobbes's opinion. In this he was supported by the scientist Pierre Gassendi, who entered into correspondence with Descartes on the subject.

These early leanings toward materialism were a foretaste of much later developments. But before they arose, the Jewish philosopher Baruch Spinoza, perhaps the foremost exponent of seventeenth-century rationalism, rejigged the Cartesian concepts in a surprisingly mystical way. In place of Descartes' separate worlds of mind and matter, Spinoza proposed an ultimate Unity of Substance—call it God, call it Nature—which had an infinity of attributes, only two of which, mind and matter, were known to humanity.

As Spinoza saw it, the ways in which the Unity manifested itself were determined by its essential nature, not by any act of will. (You had to remember that will, a mental function, was by definition just a manifestation of the Unity, not the *cause* of its manifestations.) Because of this, what manifested under one aspect had to have its counterpart in all the others—everything that arose was a presentation, in different forms, of the nature of the single Unity.

This is not an easy concept to follow and I'm far from sure my précis has done Spinoza's speculations justice, but the bottom line of his thinking was clear enough: for every mental event there had to be a corresponding physical event, for every physical event there had to be a corresponding mental event. What this had to say about the mind was quite intriguing. Whatever you believed about yourself, you were not a pairing of two separate elements, mind and body. Rather, you were part of a single Unity, a single universal "substance" that—like everything else—manifested itself in a variety of attributes. In your own case, the only attributes you were aware of happened to be the mental and the physical.

Spinoza seems to have been the first European philosopher to propose the idea that mind and body should not be considered separately, that, in fact, every human being is a mind-body complex of two absolutely interdependent aspects—a notion that still finds considerable support among modern scientists.

By the eighteenth century, philosophers like Scotland's David Hume had dismissed the Cartesian theory of mental substance as nonsense. (He referred to it as a "chimera.") Hume saw the mind as nothing more than a bundle of perceptions, another idea that was to gain some currency among modern psychologists. Less understandably, he thought of the body in exactly the same way and accepted the principle of interaction between the two. At least he said he did. In practice he seems to have been as convinced as Descartes that the body was one thing and the mind another. Certainly there are few hints in his work of any serious attempt to explore relationships between the two. When Hume adopted Newton's scientific method and used it to try to describe how the mind works in acquiring knowledge, he came to the conclusion that there could be no knowledge at all that wasn't based on experience. As a sidebar, he announced his belief that no theory of reality was even possible—the sort of statement that makes you wonder why we ever bother to take philosophers seriously.

The Prussian philosopher Immanuel Kant bought into Hume's ideas about reality only insofar as he agreed that it might be difficult to get a handle on things as they really were. But he argued it was perfectly possible to know things reliably from experience. He reached the conclusion by deciding that time, space, and causation were not aspects of the external world but rather categories the human mind imposed on the flow of events. This is a particularly interesting idea that seems to reflect to some degree the Buddhist concept of the world as *maya*, an illusion created by human perception. You would imagine the implication must posit mind as the ultimate reality, but so far as I can determine, Kant never went down that road.

When Kant died in 1804, Georg Wilhelm Friedrich Hegel was thirty-four years old and still thirteen years away from the publication of his *Encyclopaedia of the Philosophical Sciences in Outline*, an attempt to explain his outlook on life, the universe, and everything. The work was divided into three parts, concerned respectively with logic, Nature, and mind.

When it came to his examination of mind, Hegel decided thought proceeded in an endless sequence of thesis, antithesis and synthesis. He'd noticed that when two people argue a point from diametrically opposite views, they sometimes end up by dropping both their original viewpoints in favor of something new that's broad enough to encompass each. That's the way he believed thought worked all the time. You start by laying down a proposition that's instantly and automatically contradicted by its opposite until further thought brings the two viewpoints together in a wider amalgamation. But this amalgamation becomes an original proposition in its own right, which is instantly and automatically contradicted by its opposite until . . . but you get the idea. You've also probably worked out—as Hegel did—that a process like this is likely to be circular, so that thinking must ultimately return to where it started, except that everything inherent in the original thought is now out in the open.

Hegel himself certainly followed this pattern in his exposition of the nature of mind. He examined the development of the subconscious, the conscious, and the will, showing how human history and institutions could both be seen as manifestations of human will. From there he looked at religion and art, which he saw as expressions of the human realization that we are essentially spirit and one with God. All very interesting, but not hugely helpful in deciding whether consciousness might survive physical death.

By the Victorian era, certainties had begun to creep in as scientists took over from the philosophers. The nature of mind was no longer an intellectual speculation but rather a matter to be decided by observation and experiment within the scientific paradigm. The scientific paradigm of the day was one of unrelenting materialism. The universe consisted of energy and matter, with matter more or less defined as something you could drop on your foot. The purpose of science was to weigh and measure and categorize. No wonder a respected practitioner forecasted it was only a matter of time before scientists would know everything and thus be out of their jobs.

In a universe like this, mind had very little place. You couldn't weigh it and you couldn't measure it. But you could ignore it; or in this instance, leave it to that woolly new breed of scientists, the psychologists. On the back of it all, there arose a fresh viewpoint on the nature of mind that dominated psychological thinking on the question for much of the twentieth century. It was formulated by an American psychologist named John B. Watson and labeled, in its developed form, behaviorism.

Behaviorism wholly bought into the Victorian proposition that if something couldn't be observed, measured, and recorded it wasn't worth bothering about. Psychological phenomena were studied only in their measurable manifestation—the behavior of the individual. Introspection was abandoned. Only third-person observation counted. Everything was seen as stimulus and response. The organism responded to stimuli presented by the external environment or its own biological processes. When you reach the stage of thinking of mind only in stimulus/response terms, it's a short step to denying that the mind exists at all. Behaviorists didn't hesitate to take it. Dr. Watson went on record with the fascinating statement that "*consciousness* is neither a definable nor a usable concept . . . merely another word for the 'soul' of ancient times."

It's something of a relief to report that Behaviorism is no longer as fashionable as it once was, but like so many other academic propositions about the nature of mind, its influence lingers. Today there are three main schools of thought about the nature of mind:

The first concludes, like Descartes did, that mind and body

are two separate things—the *you* who thinks is quite distinct from the *you* who tips the scales at two hundred pounds and needs coffee to get going in the morning.

The second is convinced the mind is simply an expression of the body, your personal experience of body function. In its most fundamental expression, this theory takes us back to Dr. Watson's idea that the mind is essentially behavior. In a rather more sophisticated form, mind results from the electrical activity of the brain, presenting the illusion that there's something separate inside your head when all that's really happening is the flow of electrons through neural pathways.

The third school of thought is almost a synthesis of the first two, although it leans much further toward the second than the first. Here the theory is that we're wrong to think in terms of mind *or* body but should rather see the *person* as the fundamental unit—a mind/body interlock, the elements of which are completely inseparable. Proponents of this school tend to think of the mind as the subjective experience of the brain; or if not, then something "given off" by the brain as a kettle gives off steam.

On the basis of these propositions, you might be tempted to conclude the chances of your mind surviving death are 2:1 against. But like virtually all major scientific theories nowadays, the three fail to take into consideration that disreputable area of human experience colorfully known as "wild talents."

The phrase "wild talents" is associated not only with so-called psychical abilities but also with what is commonly called the supernatural. Many, perhaps most, people have had experiences that fall within this area. They range from the sensation of being watched when someone is staring at the back of your neck to apparent postmortem communication with a loved one.

Typically such experiences are dismissed as imagination, quickly forgotten, or explained away in terms of known and understood causes. Yet they have also been the subject of scientific investigation, which, as we shall see, has presented substantial evidence for their validity. Interestingly, both the evidence and the investigation itself have been the butt of considerable ridicule within the intellectual community as a whole. But if American parapsychologist George P. Hansen is correct, the ridicule arises out of social rather than scientific foundations.

Hansen argues convincingly (in *The Trickster and the Paranormal*) that the reality of the paranormal undermines the belief structures supporting modern Western society. Consequently, even scientists ostensibly dedicated to the pursuit of truth are sometimes forced by the pressure of social psychology to deny paranormal phenomena and its supporting evidence. The result is an essentially religious attack—designed to preserve the status quo—masquerading as scientific rationalism.

Yet while the antisocial nature of the paranormal has led to an underfunding of paranormal research and widespread ignorance of its findings, the research itself has been and continues to be carried out by scientists of the highest caliber under laboratory conditions as strict, if not stricter, than those found in any of the hard sciences.

The most commonplace of the wild talents is telepathy. The word comes from the Greek, in which it means "distant feeling." In the modern era it was coined by the great British psychical researcher Frederic W. H. Myers in 1882. Myers defined telepathy as "the communication of impressions of any kind from one mind to another independent of the recognised channels of sense."

The experience seems to be as old as humanity. Australian Aborigines and many other ancient cultures consider it a normal faculty. Devout Jews will recall that the prophet Elisha always knew what moves the King of Syria was planning during his war with the Israelites. Devout Christians may remember that Jesus realized—

without being told—the woman of Samaria had had five husbands: she was so surprised she decided he must be a prophet. From the eighteenth century, practitioners of mesmerism and its derivative hypnosis regularly reported that entranced subjects seemed able to receive impressions from other minds.

Although comparatively rare enough in modern urban environments, telepathy is reported as a commonplace in tribal communities throughout the world. Brian Inglis quotes[69] the author Joseph Sinel whose son lived for some time among the tribespeople of southern Sudan and found telepathy "a constant." His Sudanese friends seemed to know where he was and exactly what he was doing, however far he wandered. On one occasion he found an arrowhead and was met on his return by two tribesmen who asked if they could examine it. On another, he managed to get himself lost . . . but was collected and brought home by cheerful tribespeople who had somehow sensed he was in difficulties.

American Professor Michael Harner reported similar talents among the tribespeople of South America's Amazon Basin. The psychologist Ronald Rose spent years living with Australian Aborigines and found many of them capable of determining when a friend had died a great distance away. "It comes awful heavy, that feeling," one of them told him. "When I had it last week I knew one of my people was gone. It was a feeling full of death."

Britain's Society for Psychical Research and its U.S. counterpart, the American Society for Psychical Research, have collected a mountain of anecdotal evidence for the existence of telepathy in the industrialized world. Unlike more agrarian societies, it tends to manifest spontaneously, perhaps only once in a person's lifetime, often in reaction to emergency, injury, or death. One typical case study describes how a woman dreamed she had been struck in the mouth and was bleeding from her upper lip. She awoke at 7 A.M. still feeling the sensation of the blow. It later transpired that at the time she had the dream, her husband, who was out sailing, had been struck on the mouth by the tiller of his yacht and bled profusely from his upper lip.

Systematic investigation into telepathy began in France and Britain during the 1870s and was carried forward with the foundation of the Society for Psychical Research in 1882. Society members, many of them physicists in those early days, structured experiments in which "receivers" were required to duplicate pictures drawn by "senders." Similar experiments have been repeated frequently since the turn of the twentieth century with tighter and tighter controls. While results can sometimes be impressive, the approach has always been dogged by the difficulty of deciding when a "received" picture really matches. If the target drawing is the sun, for example, do you score a sunflower a hit or a miss?

An American Doctor of Philosophy, Joseph Banks Rhine, sorted out that particular problem in the late 1920s when he adopted a completely new approach to psychical research. Although he started his academic career as a researcher in plant physiology (and before that was a U.S. Marine) Rhine's real interest was the possibility of life after death. Like many another in the field, he began by investigating the work of mediums, including the impressive Eileen Garrett, but quickly came up against an interesting problem. Some mediumistic communications certainly contained information the medium might not be expected to know. But how could you be certain it originated in the spirit world and not from a telepathic link with one of the sitters at the séance? Rhine and his wife, Louisa, who was just as interested in this area, turned their attention to telepathy.

At this stage they were both working in the department of psychology at Duke University in North Carolina under the distinguished psychologist William McDougall. But before long, the Rhines were heading up their own department of parapsychology at the same university. An important factor in the transition—and in their whole subsequent career—was Rhine's development of a statistical approach to psychical research. Broadly speaking, it all came down to this:

If somebody picks a playing card at random from the deck and asks you to guess what suit they're looking at, there's a one in four possibility you'll get the answer right purely by chance. (Because there are only four suits—spades, hearts, diamonds, and clubs—in the deck.) Should you repeat the experiment 100 times, you can confidently expect to make about 25 correct guesses by chance alone. But things get interesting if you start to get more than 25 guesses right in every 100 runs. Clearly, if every time the cards are run, your score has risen to, say, 30, then it's likely there's some factor at work other than pure chance. In other words, some form of extra-sensory perception (ESP) is at work.

Rhine took this sort of thinking into the laboratory. He didn't use playing cards, since there's a psychological bias against certain cards that might influence results. (People tend to avoid guessing the Ace of Spades, for example, since it's thought of as the "death card.") Instead he used a special deck designed by his colleague Karl Zener and called, appropriately enough, a Zener pack. This deck featured emotionally neutral symbols like a square, a cross, a circle, or wavy lines.

Working with his students, Rhine set up telepathy experiments in which a hidden "sender" would look at each card of a shuffled Zener deck in turn, while a "receiver" tried to determine what card was being viewed. It quickly became very obvious that in a number of cases, certain subjects were performing better than chance expectation—in some instances *far* better than chance expectation. On one almost unbelievable occasion, Rhine offered a subject the encouragement of a hundred-dollar bet against his calling the card correctly. By the time the student got twenty-five straight hits, Rhine owed him twenty-five hundred dollars, at the time roughly equivalent to the good doctor's annual salary.

Although Rhine's early methodology was severely criticized by his scientific colleagues—some experiments left the possibility of the "receiver" picking up sensory clues—controls were later tightened, similar experiments performed elsewhere, and rigorous mathematical analysis applied to the results. Subjects continued to score significantly above chance. In some instances the odds against chance ran into the millions.

Rhine's statistical approach yielded some wholly unexpected results. One researcher attempted to duplicate the telepathy experiments without significant results . . . until he noticed two of his subjects were guessing not the card the "sender" was looking at but the next card in the pack—that's to say the card the "sender" was *about to* look at. It seemed as if the "receiver" had gone beyond simple telepathy and was somehow predicting the future a second or two ahead. Later still, a modified form of the experiments indicated that some subjects seemed capable of directly sensing the sequence of Zener cards in circumstances that ruled out both telepathy and precognition. They were demonstrating something akin to clairvoyance.

As if this weren't spooky enough, Rhine became intrigued by gamblers' claims that they could sometimes get "hot" and influence the fall of the dice just by willing it. He and his colleague Carroll B. Nash set themselves to test the idea experimentally. They asked subjects to will the dice to fall a certain way, then analyzed the results. Similar trials were conducted in Britain by George W. Fisk. Once again results exceeded chance. Since these early experiments, investigation of psychokinesis has continued with ever-increasing sophistication and evidence of its reality continues to mount. At times that evidence has been spectacular. In the old Soviet Union, the Russian Academy of Sciences released movie footage of controlled experiments carried out with a subject named Nina Kulagina[70] who could move small objects like cigarettes and coins (and on one memorable occasion a journalist's sandwich) to order just by thinking at them.

As things stand today, there is a substantial body of accumulated scientific evidence to support the proposition that extreme abilities like telepathy, precognition, clairvoyance, and psychokinesis actually exist. It has also been shown quite conclusively that the exercise of such talents is in no way affected by distance. That's why I used the quotation marks around terms like "sender" and "receiver." In the early days, telepathy was seen as something analogous to mental radio. The theory was that some form of hitherto unknown telepathic "waves" were broadcast by a "sender" and picked up by a "receiver." Later, however, it became evident that this could not be the case. Physicists and engineers have long known that broadcast energy weakens with distance in accordance to a well-tested mathematical formula. Experiments have shown telepathy does not exhibit the decline effect. Whatever else may be going on here, it is not any form of biological radio transmission.

This is a discovery with implications. If one consciousness can interface with another without reference to the physical laws of distance, it suggests consciousness itself is independent of space, as does the exercise of clairvoyance. If it is possible for consciousness to obtain information about an event that has not yet happened—even an event just a few seconds in the future—then it suggests consciousness is independent of time. Both discoveries support Descartes's contention that the mind is essentially separate from the body. Indeed they point to the possibility that mind is somehow outside the physical universe as we know it.

The existence of psychokinesis—mind exercising a direct influence on physical events—may take us even further. It opens up the possibility that mind really does function like the captain of a ship, no matter what Descartes may have believed. But we have to be careful here. Just before the Second World War, a Russian engineer named Semyon Kirlian developed technology that produced photographs of a biological energy field surrounding the human body. Kirlian photographs of Nina Kulagina suggest she pulsed this field in order to move inanimate objects. If this is so, then at least some psychokinetic effects are *not* the result of direct action by mind on matter.[71] All the same, there is convincing experimental evidence from a wholly different source that mind is separate from the brain and can influence matter directly.

In 1969, the Eddington Memorial Lecture, a premier event in the scientific calendar for many years, was delivered by the distinguished British neurophysiologist, Dr. W. Grey Walter. He devoted his talk to a detailed description of a series of experiments he had recently carried out that, he believed, showed two things conclusively. The first was that the mind exists separately from any brain function. The second was that mind can influence matter without any possibility of an intermediary.

Grey Walter's procedures were based on the fact that the human brain generates small but measurable electrical signals. He attached electrodes to volunteer subjects' scalps over the area of the frontal cortex. These picked up any brain electrical activity that might arise and transmitted it via an amplifier to a specially constructed machine. Thus wired, his subjects were set before a button that, when pressed, caused what Grey Walter described as an "interesting scene" to appear on a TV screen.

Neurologists have discovered that when you decide to take any physical action (such as pressing a button) a twenty micro-volt electrical surge occurs across a large area of your brain cortex. This is technically known as a readiness wave. The machine Grey Walter designed amplified this readiness wave to such a degree that it directly triggered the TV picture a fraction of a second before the button was actually pressed. He called the process "auto-start."

Once subjects had a few runs with the button, they usually figured out the machine was anticipating their actions. Most were intrigued and delighted. Before long they managed to train themselves to "will" the pictures onto the screen without touching the button at all.

Grey Walter questioned his volunteers about exactly how they did this. He discovered that their mental state was all important. For the trick to work, the subject had to duplicate his/her mind-set in pressing the button. If attention wandered or the mind locked itself in on focusing on the necessity of con-centration, the brain-wave potential failed to rise and no picture was delivered. But once they got the knack, subjects could even combine auto-start with auto-stop—they could actually will pictures onto the screen, then dismiss them with the relevant thought when finished.

It's important to recognize clearly what was going on here. The triggering of screen pictures did not, of course, involve mind acting directly on matter. The switch was thrown by a per-fectly ordinary electrical surge originating in the subject's brain. But once subjects learned they could produce the pictures without pressing the button and began to do so by an act of will, their minds *were* directly influencing matter—the physical matter of their own brains.

This is a subtle point. What it comes down to is that a deci-sion of the mind, applied in a particular way, is all it takes to change the electrical potential of your frontal cortex. As Grey Walter discovered, there is no physical aspect to the cause: as the subjects got into their stride, the button was neither pressed nor attempted to be pressed. The totality of cause lay in the mind.

Although a twenty micro-volt surge is a small thing, its implications are enormous. It is enough to settle the controversy about the independent reality of the mind. Grey Walter's experiment shows it's the mind that controls the brain and not the other way around. Which means, in turn, that consciousness is a separate entity—and *that* means it's capable of surviving death.

Whether it actually does is another question.

14

Ghosts

*You may meet the spectre of an Edwardian lady
along the lanes of Braishfield.
Haunted Britain, 1973*

THE MORNING OF my thirty-second birthday was dry, warm, and sunny—unusual enough circumstances for an Irish summer. At the time, I was renting the gate lodge of a country estate in County Meath. One perk of the tenancy was the use of a delightful seventeenth-century walled garden that formed part of the main estate. I decided to take the day off work and enjoy a little sun bathing.

Equipped with a blanket, a novel, and a Thermos flask of fruit juice, I ambled into the garden at about 11.30 A.M., took off my shirt, spread the towel, and lay down to enjoy my book. The garden itself was large and rambling. Although originally planted in the seventeenth century, it had been reworked extensively during the early Victorian era. I was stretched out on an area of lawn with a shrub bed at my back, facing a formal layout of low-cut box hedge surrounding a rose bower.

As I recall, I'd reached a particularly exciting part of my book when the young woman appeared. She took my mind off the story at once. She was about twenty-eight years old, dark-haired and extraordinarily pretty. She was also wearing period costume, an ankle-length beige crinoline, full at the bottom and cut to leave her shoulders bare: the sort of thing you would associate with evening wear rather than a morning stroll. I assumed she was a guest at the main house and it occurred to me the owners of the estate must be planning a fancy dress party—the young woman was clearly trying out her costume.

She had appeared from behind some trees and now walked across the lawn so that she passed no more than a few feet in front of me. I called out a cheerful "Good morning" but to my surprise (and disappointment) she ignored me completely and continued on as if I didn't exist. I watched her cross the lawn toward the rose bower, frankly thinking she was extremely rude. When she reached the low box hedge she disappeared.

Even though I watched it I could hardly believe it. If you've ever seen the series *Star Trek*, her disappearance was almost exactly like the special effect that takes place when a crew member is beamed off somewhere by transporter. She shimmered, faded, then finally dissolved into briefly sparkling fragments. I jumped up and ran across to the hedge: only a matter of yards. There was no sign of my young woman, no sign of anyone or anything. The hedge was at most three feet high, too low to give more than minimal cover. Besides, I'd been watching when she vanished. Hairs raised on the back of my neck in an atavistic reaction. I'd seen a ghost.

I wasn't the first. An Egyptian text dated circa 1200 BCE describes how a high priest of the god Amun was haunted by the chief treasurer of Pharaoh Rehotep, who had lived and died some five hundred years earlier. According to the text, the cause of the haunting was the state of the treasurer's tomb. For an ancient Egyptian of high rank or noble birth, the tomb was seen as the individual's dwelling place throughout eternity, so the concern was understandable. The tomb of the treasurer had been lost for generations, but it was, according to the ghost, in a delapidated state. The phantom nagged the High Priest so effectively that he mounted a successful search for the tomb and had it renovated . . . whereupon the haunting stopped.

The idea that hauntings often follow improper burial is both cross-cultural and widespread. The Assyrians even coined a word for the type of ghost that resulted—an *ekimmu*—and special rites to send *ekimmus* on their way are preserved in a clay tablet that survives to this day. Suetonius, the Roman biographer and antiquarian born in 69 CE, mentions that the whole of Rome knew the mad Emperor Caligula haunted the Lamian Gardens after his assassination until his sisters eventually gave him a decent burial.

An even more detailed account of a similar case appears in the works of Pliny the Younger, whose commonsense mind-set makes the case study particularly convincing. Pliny described the haunting of a large, spacious house in Athens, manifesting first as the clanking of iron shackles, which drew nearer until the ghost itself appeared—a thin, bedraggled old man. The haunting proved so frightening that it became almost impossible to find a tenant for the house until a philosopher named Athenodorus arrived on the scene.

Athenodorus was immediately suspicious of the low rent asked and eventually found out about the haunting. But he decided to take the house anyway. He moved in, equipped himself with a lamp, pen, and notepad, sent his companions to bed and waited for the ghost.

At first nothing happened. Then came the distant clanking of fetters. When the sound appeared to manifest in the room, Athenodorus turned to find the old man's ghost beckoning him. After ignoring it at first, the philosopher eventually got up and followed the specter into a courtyard, where it promptly vanished. Athenodorus marked the spot and the following day asked the city authorities if they would dig it up. When they did, a fettered skeleton was discovered. The bones were collected and reburied at public expense. The haunting stopped.

(The circumstances of this ancient case-study were duplicated during the nineteenth century in a house in Tokyo, Japan. These premises too gained a reputation for ghosts and fell empty until a fencing master named Miura Takéshi moved in because he was too poor to go anywhere else. He returned home late one night to find his wife cowering beneath the bedclothes. She told him she had heard the ghost by a pond in the garden. The following night, Miura made a point of returning home early and a little before midnight heard the noise for himself. He opened the shutters and saw the ghost of a bald-headed man surrounded by a black cloud. Later, when he made inquiries in the neighborhood, Miura heard a story that a decade earlier a tenant of the house had decapitated a blind man and thrown the head into the pond. With the help of his fencing pupils, Miura drained the pond and discovered a skull at the bottom. When it was buried by a priest in a nearby temple, the haunting stopped.)

Another example of ghostly manifestations in Ancient Greece was recorded by the historian and geographer Pausanias, who claimed that the site of the bloody Battle of Marathon, fought in 490 BCE, remained haunted by the sounds of warfare for centuries. Interestingly, there have been ancient British battle sites where similar phenomena have been reported up to modern times, as we shall see shortly.

Although the reality of ghosts remains a popular after-dinner conversation topic, reports of hauntings worldwide run, conservatively, into hundreds of thousands. Ghosts, it seems, can appear anywhere at any time. Near Hays, Kansas, for example, a twenty-year-old Texan named Mark Gilbert was working a combine harvester late one summer evening when a woman in a long blue dress stepped in front of the machine. Gilbert braked sharply . . . and the woman vanished. Later, when climbing down from the combine, he was struck by the feeling that someone was watching him. When he turned, he saw the woman at the bottom of his ladder, surrounded by a haze of blue-white light. Again she disappeared after a brief moment.

Gilbert was only one of a number of people, including a police patrolman, to see the ghost in the blue dress. The earliest sighting seems to date back to 1917, when she was spotted by a farmer on horseback. Interestingly, the horse refused to take him close to her.

America also has its share of haunted houses, like the mansion on lower Summit Avenue in St. Paul, Minnesota, that was the site of various phenomena over a period of years. The house was originally built in the nineteenth century by Chauncy W. Griggs, a grocery and railroad magnate. It totaled more than thirty-thousand square feet of living space on three floors—not counting attic and basement—and was set in one of the most elite neighborhoods of the city, overlooking downtown St. Paul and the Mississippi River. It passed through various hands until, in the 1940s, its current owners, a prominent local financial family, turned it over to the St. Paul School of Art and Gallery. Although there were stories of earlier hauntings, this seems to have been the time the trouble really started.

Essentially there were three sets of phenomena:

The first involved the specter of a "tall thin man in evening clothes." An Art School employee was reading one evening in a basement apartment created from the original billiard room when the lights went out and he felt cold, clammy fingers at his throat. He struggled to his feet and managed to get the lights back on. As he did so, he saw the tall figure retreat through the door and disappear. This was the only reported instance of malevolent phenomena. After it occurred, several people, mostly evening students, saw the figure at a distance and asked about him. Sightings became so frequent that the phantom was eventually given a name—George.

The second phenomenon occurred at the south end of the basement, again in an apartment used by a school employee. The tenant claimed he was awakened with feelings of terror and saw a small glowing visage floating in space before him, something like a shrunken head.

The third phenomenon involved no ghostly sightings at all. Kitchen appliances were mysteriously turned on and off to such an extent that the presence of another ghost was suspected. This one was eventually named "Martha" and generally referred to as "George's" wife.[72]

In the early 1960s, the property was purchased by a young publisher named Carl Weschcke. As a former art student, he was aware of the building's reputation and was given more of the details at the time he negotiated the purchase. But he was a man with considerable interest in the paranormal, so the stories did nothing to dissuade him from his planned purchase.[73]

Weschcke became aware of ghostly phenomena even before he moved in. He had asked a contractor for estimates on replacing the outside storm windows. The man called him to report that one of the attic floor windows on the west side was open. Weschcke checked the next morning, found the contractor was right, and sent one of the workmen up to close the window. The following day it was open again, even though access—via a ladder and trapdoor—was extremely difficult. This time the workman nailed it shut.

After he moved in, Weschcke lived in only one room while major restoration work was carried out. He became aware of phenomena almost at once—the sound of footsteps, the slamming of doors. When he came home in the evening, he got into the habit of calling out, "It's just me, George—I'm back!" Window problems started up again. Third floor windows, still on the west side, would be mysteriously opened—always at night. After a while this stopped, but then a landing window on a circular staircase (still facing west) began to open of its own accord. Weschcke found himself awakened on winter nights with a cold wind racing down the stairs into his bedroom.

Later the phenomenon repeated on the second floor, then stopped for a long time until one evening when he was telling a visiting author about the problem and they heard the sound of a window thrown violently open. They both ran to the sound and discovered a first floor window (again facing west) had been opened.

When most of the restoration work was completed, Weschcke moved his office in as well. The old kitchen housed an accounting and billing staff of about six people. As the business grew, he later converted the third floor art studio into a production facility with editors, desktop operators, and art and advertising departments.

Several years later, "George" appeared again. Weschcke still had his office and library at home. It was a Saturday afternoon, with sunlight streaming in from the western windows. He got up from his desk to get a book and found himself looking at a tall thin man with bushy white hair standing with his back against the sunlight. As he watched, the apparition slowly faded away. It was not the last of the phenomena. During his bachelor days, Weschcke kept cats, who would often sleep on his bed. The animals developed the disconcerting habit of starting up and staring at the bedroom door facing the west circular staircase. Several times he was wakened to see a figure of grayish-white swirling mist.

As Weschcke learned more about the history of his home, he discovered that in the early part of the twentieth century, the third floor had several rooms used by maids. There was also a huge ballroom—the basis for what later became a studio. Out in the carriage house were rooms for the male servants, including a chauffeur. One of the maids, an immigrant girl still learning English, had an affair with the chauffer and became pregnant. When he declined to marry her, she was found hanging on the third floor landing of the circular staircase near the west-facing window. On one occasion, Weschcke was walking down this staircase when he suddenly found himself in space before crashing down. The sensation was as if he had been swinging like the maid who hanged herself.

When the story of the hauntings got around, a local newspaper reporter called to ask Weschcke if he could do a story. Weschcke agreed to have a medium investigate and to permit two reporters and a photographer to spend a night on the third floor. The medium claimed the place was full of spirits, but there were two stronger than the others. One was a military man[74] while the other was a sad young woman who had enjoyed watching the restoration of the house. Neither fitted the George and Martha stories.

After the medium left, both reporters and the photographer retired to the third floor, while Weschcke went to his own bedroom to sleep. The newspapermen spent their time in the ballroom-studio until the early-morning hours, when they heard footsteps in the hall that led to the circular staircase. Later they told Weschcke they thought he was coming up to check on them, but when no one appeared each in turn went to look. All returned with the same story of feeling an overwhelming sense of fear and depression. The photographer took pictures. When developed they showed some curious wavy lines that appeared like cigarette smoke over that stair.

Not all hauntings are associated with old houses or historic sites. In Wilmington, North Carolina, a department store erected in the 1950s was converted into a library[75] in 1981, after which ghostly manifestations began on the second floor—appropriately enough the historical wing. Over a period of about three years, various library patrons saw the apparition of a human figure. Most thought it was a woman, although the figure was indistinct. One witness described how the figure was already fading as it emerged around a corner of the stacks in the summer of 1985. When she moved closer and tried to touch it, it disappeared altogether.

The state librarian, Beverly Tetterton, reported other phenomena in the historical wing. On a number of occasions after the library closed for the night, sounds were heard as if it were still in use—footsteps, the rustle of pages, books being replaced on the shelves and so forth. Pamphlet file cases locked up for the night were often unlocked in the morning. Occasionally drawers would be pulled open as well.

Reports of ghostly manifestations are equally widespread in the Old World. In his comprehensive *Haunted Britain*, Antony Hippisley Coxe lists case after case. In Ipsden, Oxfordshire, there is a monument to John Thurlow Reade, whose ghost appeared to his mother there although he actually died in India. At Stonor Park, also in Oxfordshire, Coxe was told by Lord Camoys of voices in empty rooms and phantom footsteps on the stairs. A cowled figure was seen in the bedroom of an inn at Henley-on-Thames.

Culloden House in Nairnshire, Scotland, is reputed to be haunted by Bonnie Prince Charlie and sometimes manifests a phantom army in the sky. There is a phantom limo at Hook

Green in Sussex that disappears when other cars get closer than a hundred yards. Two Mile Down, in Wiltshire, is haunted by a coach and four gray horses. There are several ghosts at the stately home of Longleat, including one that knocks on bedroom doors. Forde Abbey in Somerset is haunted by a shade that hovers near a table in the Great Hall. Longnor in Shropshire has a White Lady. Capestone Hall is home to a disembodied spectral arm, a line of specters which descend into a vault beneath the chapel, and a Grey Lady who haunts a garden walk. One is irresistibly reminded of the lines of doggerel quoted by Brian Inglis in his introduction to Andrew Mackenzie's *Hauntings and Apparitions*:

> *The Stately Homes of England*
> *Though rather in the lurch*
> *Provide a lot of chances*
> *For psychical research*

Although most of the cases quoted above are anecdotal, many stately (and other) homes have benefited from the activities of psychical research from time to time. More than thirty years ago, psychical researcher Shiela St. Clair played me a fascinating tape of sounds she had managed to record in the empty rooms of Gillhall, a location she described bluntly as "the most haunted house in Ireland."

Until it was razed by fire in the 1970s, Gillhall stood in its own grounds near the little market town of Dromore in County Down. The house was associated with paranormal activity as early as 1693 when the pregnant Lady Beresford was awakened there by the ghost of her friend James de la Poer, the Third Earl of Tyrone. The apparition told her he had died the previous Tuesday and made various predictions about the child she was carrying. As proof of his reality, he wrote in her pocketbook and knotted the curtains of the four-poster bed, then gripped her wrist when she protested she might have done these things herself in her sleep. The wrist was discolored the following morning, and it's said that she wore a black ribbon around it for the rest of her life.

In the nineteenth century, visitors accommodated in a bedroom off a gallery on Gillhall's first landing reported the sounds of a phantom coach drawing up at the front door in the early hours of the morning. On looking out, they saw a young woman in a traveling cloak climb from the carriage.

Sheila St. Clair was asked to mount an investigation of the house in the summer of 1961. She put together an extensive team of technical experts who arrived on site on a warm June afternoon. Gillhall was a conventional enough example of period architecture: a three-story mansion with a basement. A wide, elegant staircase led up to the first floor gallery. There was a supposedly haunted bedroom on the second floor toward the front.

Technicians installed microphones in each of the main rooms, the hallway, and the cellar, connecting them up to a central tape bank that was continuously monitored throughout the night. Observers with walkie-talkie sets patrolled the grounds. The plan was to listen via the microphones for any paranormal activity with investigators walking round the house at intervals to report on any visible phenomena.

Shortly after monitoring began at 11:28 P.M., the door of the control room swung fully open of its own accord, although earlier investigation had shown the stiffened hinges would allow it to move only a few inches before it stopped and had to be forcibly pushed. The researchers jammed it shut and returned to their vigil. Ten minutes before midnight, the first of a series of loud crashes was recorded in the empty cellar. Microphones throughout the house were by now all picking up a curious, constant background growl, which at first the investigators thought might be an artifact of their equipment. But they quickly discovered this background noise swelled to a roar immediately before individual sounds manifested.[76]

Over a period of an hour and a half, the research team managed to tape sounds variously described as thuds, "the movement of heavy furniture," and "fingernails dragged across the face of a microphone." There was also the sound of whispered voices. Most of the manifestations were in the cellar and none of them were subtle. Volume levels were so high the equipment actually vibrated.

When the first patrol was mounted at 1:45 A.M., the house became silent the moment the control room door was opened. In the cellar, lengths of lead piping and some planks had been moved toward the center of the room. When the investigators returned to their control room, noises broke out in the cellar again, but this time the familiar thuds and crashes were joined by the sound of a cough, followed by someone humming a tune. Although the mansion itself had lain empty for some time, there were kennels at the back that housed the estate's gundogs. The investigators noted that the dogs showed a distinct tendency to howl about twenty seconds before each paranormal manifestation.

Although almost all the Gillhall phenomena were audible, there were two visible manifestations. When Ms. St. Clair went upstairs to check the rooms there, she saw a lighted chandelier reflected in the landing window, although no such chandelier existed in the house itself. (There was no electricity in Gillhall at the time—the investigators had to bring a portable generator to power their equipment.) Observers patrolling the grounds noted that at one point during the night there was a soft, bluish glow behind one of the first floor windows.

American ghosts have proven no more reticent at becoming manifest for psychical researchers. The files of the American Society for Psychical Research contain many convincing case studies, including one involving a haunted house in a Pennsylvania mill town.[77] The house itself is located on what was originally a farm, broken up in the middle 1920s for urban development.

In 1956, new owners moved in—a family of nine—and two years later a wide range of paranormal phenomena began. Family members experienced cold spots, footsteps, raps and bangs, the mysterious opening and closing of doors, sounds like the movement of furniture, objects moving of their own accord, and apparitions of human figures. Four family members reported being grabbed by phantom hands.

The family proved extraordinarily resilient under the circumstances and it was more than twenty years before they contacted the American Society for Psychical Research. In 1979, investigators Karlis Osis and Donna McCormick detected both audible and visual phenomena.

The various case studies presented in this chapter represent no more than the most minuscule review of the available evidence. But they are enough to indicate that extraordinary events occur. These events present themselves as supernatural—or at least paranormal—and while largely ignored by mainstream scientists, the sheer volume of material is indicative of something that must be taken seriously. Professor H. H. Price, a former president of the (British) Society for Psychical Research put the matter succinctly:

The tea-party question, "Do you believe in ghosts?" is one of the most ambiguous which can be asked. But if we take it to mean,

"Do you believe that people sometimes experience apparitions?"
the answer is that they certainly do. No one who examines the
evidence can come to any other conclusion. Instead of disputing the
facts, we must try to explain them.

For many people the explanation is self-evident. From the deepest reaches of human history, the common assumption has been that apparitions and other paranormal phenomena are caused by spirits of the dead. When Sir Shane Leslie, an author noted for his collections of ghost stories, saw an apparition in his bedroom, he had not the slightest doubt it was the shade of his uncle Moreton, who had died in 1925. The ghost even berated him for something he'd written.[78] But how safe is it to assume spirits are really involved?

The first thing that emerges from any careful study of hauntings is that there are ghosts and then there are ghosts. The Assyrians may have been the first to recognize different classifications of phantoms, and their example is followed by psychical researchers in the present day. Quite clearly, not all ghosts manifest in the same way. Equally clearly, not all manifestations are actually ghosts.

During my twenties, I lived for a time in an isolated apartment that formed part of a large country estate. One winter evening I was alone in the house when the noise of heavy breathing abruptly filled the room. It was the most terrifying sound I've ever heard—especially when I looked around and found the room empty. The breathing continued loudly, exactly as if an invisible someone, or some *thing*, was standing no more than a few feet away from me. But it wasn't a ghost. When I found the courage to investigate, I discovered the sound originated from my fireplace. An unusual change in wind direction had caused it to emit a noise exactly like heavy breathing.

Many ghosts are like that: essentially, cases of mistaken identity. Air trapped in central heating pipes or plumbing can cause unexpectedly loud metallic raps, knocks, and thuds that are often taken as ghostly manifestations. One case of an apparition seen through the window of an old house turned out to be a fascinating, but unghostly, freak of nature. A nearby lightning flash during a violent electrical storm had somehow burned the image of a woman into the glass of the window, creating an unusual natural "photograph."

Mundane circumstances that give rise to ghostly reports can sometimes be even more unpredictable than lightning photography. A research colleague of mine specializing in poltergeists was contacted by a young married couple whose lives were being ruined by a ghost. The entity first manifested when they moved into a rented house on a council estate in the north of England. Neither husband nor wife saw or heard anything, but day after day they would get up in the morning to signs of a midnight intruder. Furniture would be moved around, books and magazines opened. The entity would even clean work surfaces and wash dishes. Nothing was ever taken and there was no sign of forced entry, so it seemed burglars could be ruled out.

Although the manifestation had all the hallmarks of a friendly ghost, its presence terrified the young couple to such a degree that they twice moved house. In each case, the phantom followed. Eventually, in desperation, they decided to leave the country. They embarked for Ireland and took a house in the suburbs of Dublin. To their horror, the ghost came too. It was at this point that they sought help from the poltergeist specialist. He listened to their story, decided their concern was genuine, and agreed to an investigation.

With their permission he moved recording gear and infrared cameras into their new home, setting up in the living room and kitchen areas, where the manifestations typically took place. Then, when the young couple went off to bed, he switched off the lights and settled himself down in a comfortable chair to wait. Sometime around three o'clock in the morning, he was awakened from a shallow doze by a sudden sound. Now fully awake, he waited in the half-light filtering through the window from the street lamps as the door of the living room slowly opened. Then he watched with openmouthed astonishment as the young wife came in to tidy the room and do the washing up. She was sleepwalking.

Another cause of so-called phantoms may be hallucination on the part of the observer. It was once suggested that the most likely explanation of my attractive young woman in crinoline was that I dozed off while reading and dreamed the whole incident. Although it sounds plausible, this is actually unlikely. Research has shown that dream periods do not typically occur until about an hour and a half after an individual falls asleep—far too long to account for my experience. But there's no doubt at all I may have had a waking hallucination.

Carl Jung, one of the founding fathers of psychoanalysis and a career psychiatrist with a lifetime's experience, is on record as saying that hallucinations are far more common than most laypeople realize. The problem seems to be that we tend only to take note of dramatic hallucinations. If, for example, you enter a friend's home and notice an empty cup on the table, it would never occur to you to wonder if the cup was really there. Even if it disappeared next time you looked, you are likely to assume somebody tidying up took it away. Yet according to Jung, unnoticed hallucinations of this type occur quite often. They are part of the normal functioning of the human mind and do not, in themselves, indicate mental illness or any other pathology. From time to time, more spectacular hallucinations arise and my experience in the walled garden may fall into this category. I was alone when the young woman appeared and subsequent investigation failed to unearth any other reports of the figure— the walled garden had no history of a haunting.

But this interpretation will not do for all phantoms. When Carl Weschske was confronted with his tall, thin figure, he was experiencing something that had been previously reported by others. Clearly, if different people see the same ghost in the same place, the hallucination theory becomes less tenable—at least if we accept the definition of hallucination put forward by modern psychology. Although Weschske was aware of the earlier reports, there are numerous cases of multiple sightings where witnesses had no idea a particular site was supposed to be haunted, or by what. In such circumstances, it's difficult to see how hallucination provides a satisfactory explanation. A variation of the hallucination theory suggests a particular witness might be "psychic"—might, that is, have an unusual ability to see things others do not. There have certainly been many reported cases in which a ghost appears to one witness while those around him see nothing. But if the phenomenon recurs with different witnesses, then evoking psychism (second sight) is hardly a valid objection to the reality of the ghost. Something had to be there to stimulate the psychism in the first place.

That said, it is unwise to assume you are necessarily dealing with spirits of the dead, even where hauntings are clearly paranormal. Poltergeists form a commonly reported category of haunting. Although the term means "noisy ghost" and the phenomena include mysterious noises and the movement of objects like the occurrences in the cellar at Gillhall, poltergeists often seem to have more to do with the living than the dead.

In November 1967 a German lawyer named Sigmund Adam began to experience problems with his office lighting. The strip lights kept failing so often that he had a special meter installed that showed sudden, inexplicable surges of current. Adam's office was in Rosenheim, a small town southwest of Munich. Adam eventually complained to the *Stadtwerke*, the local electricity company, whose representatives concluded there was something wrong with the power lines. They tried installing a direct cable, but the lights still malfunctioned. Adam installed his own generator and replaced his strip lights with ordinary bulbs, but it made no difference.

He was still in the throes of his problem when his phone bill arrived. It catalogued a frightening increase in his calls. Phone company technicians installed a monitor that showed someone was dialing the time for hours on end, four, five and even six times a minute. When a local reporter published a report on the "Rosenheim ghost," the story was taken up by the national press and attracted the attention of one of Europe's leading parapsychologists, Professor Hans Bender of the Institute of Paranormal Research at Freiburg in Germany.

Bender mounted a full-scale investigation and quickly confirmed the phenomena. Lights swung for no apparent reason, pictures turned on the wall, a heavy filing cabinet was moved by unseen hands. But this was no ghost. Bender discovered everything was associated with a teenage girl named Anne-Marie Schaberl, who had joined the company two years previously. When she walked along the corridor, the overhead lights would begin to swing back and forth and the mysterious surges of current occurred only when she was in the building. When Adam fired the girl, she took a job in another office and similar phenomena occurred. When she went ten-pin bowling with her fiancé the electronic equipment malfunctioned. She took a mill job, but left when machinery ran amok and killed a fellow worker.

When initially tested by Bender, the girl gave no indication of paranormal abilities, but once her emotions were aroused she showed extraordinary ESP, including a high degree of telepathy. Bender concluded Anne-Marie was a powerful, if unconscious PK medium. Psychical researchers have come to similar conclusions in a wide variety of poltergeist cases. Typically the phenomena follow young people, often those passing through puberty, with strong but repressed emotions. It is as if their inner turmoil is somehow projected out into the environment, where it manifests as poltergeist activity.

And projected "poltergeists" are not the only question marks to be thrown over the theory that ghosts are simply spirits of the dead.

15

Recordings and Time Slips

The difference between a ghost and an apparition is that a ghost is usually less purposeful and more somnambulistic.
Encyclopedia of Parapsychology and Psychical Research

IN 1709, THE Rev. Thomas Josiah Penston saw not one ghost but more than a hundred. He was walking near Wroxham, in England's Norfolk Broads, when he was approached by an entire Roman legion. They marched past in good order, ignoring the astonished cleric completely.

It is a fact of history that the Roman armies left Britain in 406 CE, so these were ancient ghosts even in Penston's time. But Romans have continued to haunt Britain long after Penston himself died. There was a reported sighting in Bath—the former *Aqua Sulis* named for its healing waters—as recently as 1988. A workman saw a Roman walk across an underground chamber in that city, then disappear through a wall.

But are such sightings really spirits of the dead? Can we be confident that when Roman soldiers died, they rejoined their old legion and marched eternally across the Norfolk Broads? It would certainly seem an odd thing to do in light of the fact that the legions were called home to defend Rome against Alaric's Goths. You would imagine their spirits would be more inclined to guard the Eternal City in case the Goths came back. Another strange thing about hauntings of this type is that Roman ghosts are as old as you get in Britain. There are no reported hauntings by cavemen or Bronze Age hunters. If such ghosts are spirits of the dead, it is reasonable to ask what happened to the millions of spirits who were around before the Roman invasion?

The mystery deepens when you investigate other hauntings of this type. At first glance, there doesn't seem to be much in common between the Roman ghosts and the Grey Lady of Levens Hall, a stately home south of Kendal in Westmoreland, England. Yet there does seem to be a connection. Levens Hall is an Elizabethan mansion, built about 1586, and the Grey Lady—one of several ghosts—has been there for a long time. In the days when a coach-and-four was the aristocratic way to travel, she used to cause near accidents by appearing suddenly and star-tling the horses. Nowadays, the coaches have gone, but the Grey Lady has not. There have been several reports of her causing motorists to slam on their brakes as they negotiate the driveway to the hall. When they stop, she promptly fades away.

Grey Ladies are a fairly common type of ghost in Britain. In the Church of St. Michael and All Angels, a Department of the Envi-ronment property at Rycote in Oxfordshire, several people have seen one that glides from a pew to disappear into a stone wall. More startling still is the Grey Lady who occasionally visits the Lion and Lamb in Farnham, Surrey, a café run in converted inn stables that are more than five hundred years old. She waits patiently until a member of staff walks up with a menu, then vanishes. A common denominator of hauntings of this type is that the ghost always ignores the people who see it. A Grey Lady never speaks, never stops what it is doing, never deviates from a set routine. It will typically do the same thing over and over for years. The Grey Lady at Levens always appears in the driveway to the Hall. Every witness to the haunting of St. Michael and All Angels has seen that Grey Lady glide from the same pew and disappear at the same spot in the wall.

Even when they appear as warlike Roman legions, Grey Ladies will do you no harm. Should you find the courage to stand in front of them, they will walk right through you with not so much as an eye-blink. A member of the Bagot family, who own Levens Hall, once cycled through the Grey Lady there without disturbing her in the least. All this suggests Grey Lady ghosts may not be spirits of the dead at all. Certainly they do not exhibit the behavior patterns of sentient beings. Even sleep-walkers deviate to some degree from their established routines.

But if Grey Lady ghosts aren't spirits, what then are they?

Sheila St. Clair, the psychical researcher who conducted the Gillhall investigation, awoke in the night while a guest in an old manor house to find she had been visited by a Grey Lady–type haunting. The ghost was actually male, but in all other respects behaved as a Grey Lady. Ignoring his witness, he strolled in his nightgown from one side of the room to the other and made his exit by walking through a wall.

When Ms. St. Clair filed her report on this manifestation, it contained some very interesting details. One was that the ghost was walking some two and a half feet *above* the floor of the room. Another was that there had once been a door at the exact spot where it disappeared . . . but this door had been bricked up for more than fifty years. Yet another was that, according to the owners of the manor, the original floor of the bedroom was two and a half feet higher than the present floor. It had been low-ered in Victorian times during structural alterations to get rid of dry rot. Clearly, this specter was not haunting the bedroom as it exists today. Rather, it seems to have been walking across the bedroom as it was in Victorian times, its feet firmly planted on the *original* floor. The door through which it left is now bricked up but could have opened easily in another era.

Reports of this type—and there are literally thousands of

them—have led to the theory, widely accepted by modern psychical researchers, that these manifestations are not ghosts at all (at least not in the sense of spirits) but some sort of action replay, like a home run reviewed on television. It is as if something *recorded* a Victorian gentleman walking across his bedroom, then *played it back* to Sheila St. Clair more than a century later. This theory explains why the Rev. Penston could not distract his Roman legion, why heavy traffic at Levens does not disturb the manor's ghost.

The notion that some ghosts might be natural "recordings" is not new. In India, there is a widespread belief that stone can store impressions, a little like magnetic tape. The British archaeologist Tom Lethbridge noted that many hauntings are reported near lakes and marshes. Because of this, he put forward a theory that ghosts were somehow recorded on an electrical field set up by dampness. It seems possible both these ideas are true—that ghosts can be recorded on almost anything. But how does the recording take place? And, perhaps even more important, what causes the playback? According to some psychical researchers, the recording effect is caused by *high emotion*.

The actual emotion does not seem to be all that important. It could be anger, such as one might find in the midst of battle. It could be terror, of the sort you might experience while being murdered. Or it could be the sort of empty, grinding misery that leads to suicide. The important thing is that the emotion must be intense. According to the theory, emotions imprint on their surroundings—the reason why some houses feel happy when you walk into them, while others seem sad and unwelcoming.

In a house where a murder or suicide has taken place, there is often a particular spot that visitors find cold, upsetting, sometimes even terrifying. This, researchers hold, is where the emotions were recorded. Sometimes such spots can be dangerous. When Carl Weschcke walked past the spot where the maid hanged herself, he felt disorientated, as if he were falling—and might well have fallen since he was on a staircase at the time. The former Maynooth Seminary in Ireland had a haunted room where, many years ago, an unhappy student committed suicide by throwing himself out of a window. Although no visible sightings of the student's ghost were ever reported, visitors often found the room uncomfortable and several claimed they were seized by an almost overwhelming urge to throw themselves out of the window as well. What seems to be happening is that sensitive individuals pick up the original emotions and react as if they were their own. How imprinted emotions turn into visible specters is not entirely clear, but anniversaries may have something to do with it. It is noticeable that many Grey Lady ghosts recur at the same time in the same place, year after year.

There is some interesting evidence to suggest the theory of natural recordings is well founded. The Battle of Edgehill, between the Cavaliers and Roundheads, took place on October 24, 1642, the first real clash in England's Civil War. It involved a total of 27,000 men and, you may be sure, generated intense emotion while it was being fought. Two months later, a group of travelers, guided by some shepherds and countrymen familiar with the district, happened to be passing Edgehill shortly after midnight when they were startled by the sound of drums. This noise was followed by loud groaning, so that the party understandably decided to get out of the area as quickly as possible. But before they could do so, phantom armies appeared, carrying the standards of Royalists and Parliamentarians, and proceeded to fight the Battle of Edgehill all over again.

The illusion was complete. The terrified spectators could hear the neighing of the horses, the roar of cannon and muskets, the screams of the dying, the beating of the drums. They could see the two sides join. They watched the changing fortunes of the battle until, after a period of hours, the king's men with-drew. When the phantom battle was over, its quaking witnesses hastened to Keinton, where they awakened a justice of the peace named William Wood. Wood in turn woke up his neighbor, the Rev. Samuel Marshal. Both men listened while the party told their story under oath.

Wood and Marshal decided to investigate it for themselves. The next night, a Sunday, they went with the original wit-nesses and a substantial crowd from Keinton and neighboring parishes to the battle site. About half an hour after midnight, the phantom armies appeared and the battle was fought out exactly as before. Word went round the district like wildfire, but though hordes of curious spectators turned up the next night, nothing happened. The following Saturday, however, the ghostly armies were fighting again, with a rematch lasting four hours on the Sunday. The phenomenon recurred for several weeks. Regularly, on Saturday and Sunday nights, phantom armies refought the Battle of Edgehill exactly as it had been fought on October 24.

Word of the phantom battle eventually reached the king at Oxford and he was curious enough to dispatch six trustworthy investigators under the leadership of Colonel Lewis Kirke. The king's men interviewed witnesses, then set out to see the haunting for themselves. They reported back that the rumors were true. They even recognized the ghostly faces of several of those, like Sir Edmund Varney, who had been killed in the original battle.

This is one of the best-attested and most spectacular histor-ical examples of a haunting in the annals of psychical research. But clearly it was not caused by spirits of the dead, for while many men were killed at Edgehill, many more survived *and were alive and well elsewhere in England while their phantoms were fighting on those Saturday and Sunday nights*. It seems almost certain that what happened here was a replay, before scores of witnesses, of some sort of natural recording, an explanation underscored by the fact that after a time, the phantom armies stopped coming to Edgehill, as if the recording was wearing out.

There is a strong suggestion that such "recorded" ghosts *do* wear out eventually—something that would explain the puzzle mentioned earlier about why we never see ghosts of cave people: any that were recorded would simply have played out by now. Eric Maple and Lynn Myring, two veteran British researchers, reported a case[79] in which a ghost was seen to fade away as it got older, an even clearer indication that it was some sort of natural recording. The first sighting, in the eighteenth century, was of a ghostly woman wearing a red dress, red shoes, and a black head-dress. About seventy years later, another witness saw her, this time dressed in pink. By the nineteenth century, she had become a typical Grey Lady, now dressed in a white gown. In 1939, there were reports of phantom footsteps and the swish of her dress at the site of the haunting. The house in question was demolished in 1971 when all that was left was the faint sense of her presence.

An alternative theory to the idea of natural recordings suggests that some ghosts have been conjured through a hole in time—a hypothesis that seems even harder to swallow than the concept of spirits, yet one for which, again, there is substantial evidence, at least some of it from a highly respected academic source.

In the second week of January 1912, Arnold Toynbee was sitting at Pharsalus in Greece, staring down the slopes and thinking about a battle that had taken place there in 197 BCE. All of a sudden his surroundings changed. The bright Mediterranean sunlight disappeared and was replaced by a heavy mist. Somehow he knew there were two armies groping their way toward one another in that fog. One was the Roman legions, the other the men of Philip of Macedon.

The mist cleared and Toynbee saw the right wing of the

Macedonian army charging downhill and pushing the Romans before them. But the charge left a dangerous gap in their ranks. The Roman general seized his advantage, swung his men around to attack the exposed flank from the rear. The battle turned into a massacre. Even as the Greeks dropped their arms in surrender, the Roman soldiers hacked them to pieces. Sickened, Toynbee turned his eyes away. At once the battle scene vanished and he was again sitting in bright sunlight. This experience—and several others like it—led Toynbee to write his multivolume *A Study of History*, a work that established his reputation as one of the finest historians of the century.

Toynbee did not believe he was seeing ghosts (in the sense of spirits) reenacting that ancient battle. Nor did he imagine he was watching some sort of natural recording, like those we have been discussing. He thought he had slipped into a "time pocket." It's a theory that would sound extremely far-fetched were it not for the fact that something very similar has happened to other people. In the early 1970s, for example, a British visitor to Ireland was driving in the Wicklow Hills, an area riddled with roads so narrow that cars can only pass one another by pulling in tight to the verge; and sometimes not even then.

The visitor[80] passed a public house set just off the road, with sounds of people inside and a bicycle propped against the door. A few hundred yards further along, she realized she must have mistaken a turning some miles back and was on the wrong road. She did not have enough room to turn the car around and so drove on for perhaps another mile to where the road widened enough for her to turn and drive back the way she came. The road was twisting, but there were no forks or junctions so that she had little difficulty finding her way back to the point where she had turned off. It was only then she realized she had not passed the pub on the way back.

For a moment she thought she must have been concentrating so hard on her driving that she'd simply failed to notice it. But she didn't really believe this and eventually turned back up the same narrow road. Driving slowly and carefully she came to the place where the public house had stood. There was an open space to the side of the road, but no pub. She drove on, all the way back to where she had turned. There was no public house anywhere on the route. On the way back down, she stopped her car beside the open space and got out to investigate. There, in the undergrowth, she discovered the foundations of a ruined building.

The woman herself has no doubt at all she saw a ghost pub. And given all the circumstances, it's difficult to imagine another explanation. But what does "ghost" mean in this case? Certainly not a soul of the dead, since we're talking about a building. And not a natural recording either, since there was no drama, no emotion associated with the sighting. The ruins, invisible from the road, showed there had once been a building on the spot. Did the tourist drive through a pocket in time, slipping briefly back thirty or forty years to the days when the pub still stood, then drive out again into the present?

Hallucination is an outside possibility in cases of this sort. Toynbee knew a great deal about Greek and Roman history and freely admits he was thinking about the battle before his time-slip took place. Yet there were details of the battle he had never read about before—a group of horsemen fleeing the scene, for example. Hallucination does even less to explain the experience of the English tourist. She was not familiar with the district, had never visited it before, and reached the spot where she saw the pub by taking a wrong turn. As she drove past, there was nothing to indicate a building had ever been there, since the remains of the foundations were hidden by undergrowth. It was an isolated spot, not the sort of place you would expect to find a pub.

Hallucination is an even less likely explanation for the ghosts seen by the mountaineer Frank L. Smythe in 1940. He had entered a grassy defile near Glen Glomach in the Scottish Hills between Morvich and Lock Duich when he was seized by a feeling of dread. He decided to stop for lunch and try to figure out what was making him feel so miserable. Suddenly he saw twenty or more men, women, and children, ragged, pitiful, and weary, struggle through the defile as if they had walked a long way and were close to exhaustion. Then, as Smythe watched, an ambush was sprung. Hidden men, armed with spears, axes, and clubs, rose up on either side, raced down the hillsides, and butchered the exhausted people. Smythe staggered from the place with screams ringing in his ears. Only later did he discover the site was known for massacres. There had been one in 1715, when a group of Highlanders were murdered by General Wade and his men, and another in 1745, following the Battle of Culloden.

Smythe recorded his experience in a book called *The Mountain Vision*, which was published in 1941. It is difficult to be sure from his description of the events whether he was experiencing a time-slip or a natural recording, but there is no doubt at all about the most remarkable account of a time-slip ever—the "ghosts" of the Trianon Palace.

The story of these ghosts goes back to a hot August afternoon in 1901 when two respected Victorian ladies, on holiday in France, set out to explore the Palace of Marie Antoinette in Versailles. One of the ladies was Miss Charlotte Anne Elizabeth Moberly, Principal of St. Hugh's Hall at the University of Oxford in England. The other was Miss Eleanor Frances Jourdain, a teacher who had founded her own girl's school in Watford. These were the days when it was thought girls needed "finishing" and the only civilized place to finish them was Paris. In order to finish her young pupils, Miss Jourdain had rented a flat there.

In 1901, Miss Moberly and Miss Jourdain met for the first time. Miss Moberly was impressed and suggested Miss Jourdain might like to become Vice-Principal of St. Hugh's. Before making a decision on this offer, Miss Jourdain invited Miss Moberly to stay with her in her Paris flat to see how they got on together. Miss Moberly agreed. They traveled to France for a three-week holiday and decided to visit various historic sites in and around Paris. One place on their itinerary was the magnificent Palace of Versailles, only a short distance from the city. On August 10, the two companions boarded a train for Versailles.

There was a lot to see in the former seat of the French court. Misses Moberly and Jourdain spent much of the day touring the rooms and galleries of the palace itself, then rested in the Salle des Glaces. It was not until about four in the afternoon that Miss Moberly suggested they should visit the Petit Trianon, one of the minor palaces at Versailles, an imposing building set in extensive gardens and built during the reign of Louis XV. Its most famous resident was the ill-fated Marie Antoinette, who was given the house by her husband, Louis XVI, in 1774.

The Petit Trianon lies about a kilometer and a half northwest of the main palace. The two ladies consulted their guide map and set off to find it. They arrived eventually at the Grand Trianon, a companion building, and there lost their way. Instead of turning right as they should have, they went straight ahead and entered a narrow lane running roughly at right angles to the main drive. After walking north, then circling a number of buildings, they asked directions from two men they took to be gardeners. They were told to go straight on, but in their confusion managed to make a detour to the left. They passed a smallish building they described as a "kiosk" (but which they later decided must have been the Temple de l'Amour) and there, quite suddenly, began to feel distinctly strange.

"From the moment we left the lane, an extraordinary depression had come over me," Miss Moberly recorded later, "which, in spite of every effort to shake it off, steadily deepened. There seemed to be absolutely no cause for it. I was not at all tired and was becoming more interested in my surroundings."

Not wanting to spoil the outing, Miss Moberly said nothing about the way she was feeling. But as it happened, Miss Jourdain was just as uncomfortable. "There was a feeling of depression and loneliness about the place," she wrote in her account of the experience. "I began to feel as if I were walking in my sleep: the heavy dreaminess was oppressive."

With each determined to maintain a stiff upper lip, they continued on and in the gardens of the Petit Trianon met (and on two occasions spoke with) a number of people, all of whom seemed to be wearing very old-fashioned clothing. The brief conversations—mainly to ask directions—were conducted in French. Both noted odd pronunciations and Miss Jourdain concluded that at least one man used an old form of the language. They emerged eventually into the front drive and the odd feeling of oppression suddenly lifted. Without discussing their experience, they took a carriage to the Hotel des Réservoirs and had tea.

For a week, neither spoke about the Petit Trianon, but then Miss Moberly started to write a letter home and found creeping over her the same depressed mood she'd felt during the Versailles visit. On impulse she asked Miss Jourdain if she thought the Petit Trianon was haunted. Miss Jourdain at once said she did. At this stage, the two women began to compare notes and together started to wonder about the way the people they had met were dressed. But while their suspicions were aroused, it took three months for Miss Moberly to discover that one woman she had seen was not seen at all by Miss Jourdain. Yet "it was impossible that she should not have seen the individual: for we were walking side by side and walked straight up to her, passed her and looked down upon her from the terrace."

Since they now realized they'd not necessarily seen the same things, they each agreed to write down a full, detailed account of what they *had* seen and then investigate further. Their investigations continued over a long period. It was not until three years later that they returned to Versailles and again visited the Petit Trianon. They found it had been modernized. But by consulting guidebooks and officials, they soon discovered the modernization had not taken place in the last three years. There should have been no changes at all from their first visit. Now thoroughly intrigued, the two ladies began to study history books that showed the Trianon as it was in the time of Louis XVI. The features then were hauntingly familiar. Their first visit, in 1901, had taken them to the Petit Trianon as it had been toward the end of the eighteenth century. They concluded that one woman they had seen might have been Marie Antoinette herself.

This was not, of course, a haunting by spirits, since the entire place was changed when the two ladies first visited it. Nor was it any sort of natural recording. The denizens of the Trianon were aware of their modern-day visitors and quite capable of talking back. Taken as a whole, we seem to be looking at an experience that has more to do with the nature of Time than life after death.

Author Colin Wilson described a time-slip at Fotheringhay Church in Northamptonshire,[81] the place where Mary Queen of Scots was executed. For some time, the building had a reputation for being haunted, and a number of people reported hearing Elizabethan music coming from its interior when no one was inside. But this was unknown to Mrs. Jane O'Neill, a Cambridge schoolteacher, when she visited the church in the early winter of 1973. The visit seemed normal enough and she spent a good deal of time admiring a splendid picture of the

Crucifixion behind the altar on the left side of the church. It had, she said, an arched top and within the arch was a dove with its wings following the curve.

Some hours later she was in her hotel room with a friend named Shirley, who was reading aloud from an essay that mentioned a particular type of arch. "That sounds like the arch of the picture I saw in the church," Mrs. O'Neill remarked. But Shirley looked at her blankly. Although she had visited the church many times, she had never seen the picture. Shirley's reaction worried Mrs. O'Neill who'd had a bad shock two months previously that left her with a tendency to "see things." She rang the local postmistress, a woman who arranged flowers in the church every Sunday. The postmistress told her there was no picture of the Crucifixion, although there *was* a board behind the altar with a painting of a dove.

A year later, Jane O'Neill went back to Fotheringhay Church. The outside was exactly as she remembered it, but when she went inside she knew at once she was in a different building. It was much smaller than the Fotheringhay she had visited before. There was, as the postmistress had insisted, no painting of the Crucifixion. And even the dove behind the altar was totally different than the one she had seen. Thoroughly disturbed by now, Mrs. O'Neill got in touch with a Northamptonshire historian, who told her that the original Fotheringhay Church had been pulled down in 1553 and the present building erected on the site. Further research soon confirmed that the church Mrs. O'Neill had entered in 1973 was the one that had been demolished more than four hundred years previously.

Yet for all the ghosts that can be classified as mistakes or genuine paranormal phenomena that have nothing to do with life after death, there are a vast number of cases that seem to involve a level of spirit intervention. The phantom that beckoned

Athenodorus and showed him where its bones were buried is clearly something other than an imprint or hallucination and had none of the hallmarks of a time-slip. There are many cases of this type, some involving an exchange of information unknown to the living witness. Cases like this certainly suggest there is an element of us that survives, a phantom body that has much the same appearance we had while we were alive.

Curiously enough, there is considerable evidence that something of this sort exists. For phantoms, it seems, can sometimes be phantoms of the living.

16

Phantoms of the Living

*. . . whether in the body I cannot tell; or whether out of the body I
cannot tell: God knoweth . . .*
St Paul. *II Corinthians 12:2*

SHORTLY BEFORE HIS death in 1916, the Californian author John
Griffith Chaney published a novel called *The Star Rover* under
his familiar pseudonym, Jack London. Like so much of his previous work, the adventure dealt with one man's struggle for survival. It was a novel that appeared to contain a strong element
of fantasy, yet its fictional hero was based on an actual person,
an American convict named Ed Morrell.

Morrell held strong anticapitalist views, which endeared him
not one bit to the authorities. He was also a difficult prisoner,
which endeared him even less. At the time, the prison where he
was held—the Arizona State Penitentiary—had a barbarous
policy towards difficult inmates. They were strapped into a
double straightjacket and water was poured over it. As the material dried, it shrank. The first time this treatment was given to
Morell, he found himself unable to breathe and stars danced
before his eyes. Then something entirely unexpected happened.
Morell was suddenly outside the prison, walking free. At least
that's how it seemed to him. To his warders it looked as if he'd
simply fallen asleep.

Remarkably, this proved to be Morell's standard response to

the straightjacket torture. Every time the pain started—and he was subjected to the treatment fairly often—he found himself wandering the streets of San Francisco like a ghost, as if he had left his physical body behind.

This type of out-of-body experience (OOBE), mercifully without the help of a wet straightjacket, is far more common than you might imagine. In 1954, a student survey in Britain showed 27.1 percent of those polled reported having left their bodies and returned safely. Most of them claimed they'd managed it more than once. Over a decade later, the British director of the Institute of Psychophysical Research, Celia Green, carried out a study of Oxford undergraduates and found the incidence among them was even higher at 34 percent. Both surveys were conducted using a small base and were hardly representative of the population as a whole, but in 1975 a wider sample was taken. This showed 25 percent of students reported OOBEs, while the rate across the general population was 14 percent. A year later, a mass-circulation American magazine asked readers about their experiences in the area. Some 1,500 responded. Almost half— 46.6 percent—said they'd left their bodies.

Common or not, Morell's experience scarcely seems worth reporting, on the face of it. The warders noted that he fell asleep, so the most obvious explanation must be that he dreamed; and if the type of dream was unusually consistent, this was surely a response to his treatment and circumstances—his unconscious provided him with a temporary respite from the horrors of the penitentiary. But there seemed to be more to it than that. When Morell returned to his body and his cell, he was able to describe events outside the jail—like a shipwreck in San Francisco Bay—that he had no way of knowing about. This curious ability was confirmed by the governor of Arizona at the time, George W. P. Hunt.

It transpired that Morell was not the only one to manage this

trick. As psychical researchers became interested in the phenomenon, subjects who claimed to be able to leave their bodies were
subjected to controlled tests. The American businessman
Robert A. Monroe, who was convinced he was dying the first
time it happened to him, eventually learned how to generate
OOBEs at will and underwent scientific testing. On one occasion he was required to read a target number set up in a different
room than where his body lay. When he emerged from his
OOBE, he had been unable to read the number but reported
accurately that a laboratory assistant and her husband were in the
room where it was located. Charles T. Tart, an American psychologist with an interest in altered states of consciousness and a
distinguished record in the field of psychical research, reported at
least one subject, an unnamed "young lady," was able to read a
target number under strict test conditions. In Britain, Professor
Arthur Ellison, a vice president of the Society for Psychical
Research, structured similar number-reading experiments over
distances of several hundred miles and reported limited success.
(His star subject, I'm particularly pleased to report, was my wife,
the therapist and author Jacquelene Burgess.)

During the late 1960s and early '70s, I experimented in this
area myself using hypnosis to trigger OOBEs in subjects who
did not experience them spontaneously. Although not so tightly
controlled as the work of Tart or Ellison, some of the results
were intriguing. In one experiment a U.K. businessman named
Arthur Gibson "traveled" from Ireland to India. The experience
proved so vivid that on his "return" he could not believe he had
not made the journey physically. While out of the body, he was
able to provide a detailed description of parts of Bombay. This
did not, in itself, prove anything, since he had lived and worked
in the city for several years at an earlier stage of his career and
knew it well. But while "walking" through the old quarter of

the city, he discovered his favorite restaurant had been redecorated, while nearby a brand-new wall had been built.

My initial conclusion was that the experience had been a fantasy constructed by Gibson's unconscious mind using elements drawn from memory. (The vivid nature of the experience was not unexpected, since he was capable of reaching an exceptionally deep level of hypnotic trance.) I believed the details of the wall and restaurant redecoration, which were not part of his memories of Bombay, represented nothing more than the sort of embroidery you experience in dreams. Gibson was not so sure. He understood clearly enough that his mind might have fabricated the experience, drawing on his knowledge of Bombay, but he thought the changes odd. The problem nagged him so much that he wrote to a friend in the city . . . who confirmed that the wall had been built and the restaurant redecorated.

This information led directly to a second experiment in which the entranced Gibson "visited" a nearby house he had never entered physically. He was able to describe its layout, furnishings, and decor to a high degree of accuracy and claimed to have seen the owner and a houseguest. Curiously, there were details he got wrong. He "saw" a firescreen in a different room than where it actually was and the houseguest, when I checked afterward, proved not to exist.

Another long-distance experiment was conducted with the help of a teenage volunteer named Denise Alexander who was hypnotised and asked to read a target note set up about a hundred miles away. The contents were known only to two colleagues who were out of the country when the experiment took place. Ms. Alexander achieved the OOB state, reached the target site, but failed to read the note "because it was too dark." When I suggested that a light might be switched on in the room, she still could not read the note but said it was block printed on unlined blue paper and contained just five words. These details were later confirmed.

Even limited results require an explanation, and there seem to be only four possibilities—fraud, telepathy, clairvoyance, or the detachment of some sort of "second body" that carries consciousness to the target. Scientists like Tart and Ellison enjoy impeccable reputations, and in the case of my own experiments I had the luxury of knowing that no fraud occurred.

Telepathy may be a possibility in some of the experiments. Professor Ellison was aware of the target numbers his subjects were trying to read, so they might have fished them from his mind. But this seems somewhat unlikely, since Ellison never knew exactly when attempts to read the target number were being made—the numbers were left for several weeks and subjects made attempts to read them at random during this time. Thus the likelihood of his actually thinking of the number while a subject tried to read it was very low. If telepathy *was* at work here, it would have had to involve access to Ellison's preconscious or unconscious mind.

In the case of Arthur Gibson's Bombay trip, telepathy is even less likely, since no one involved—except for Gibson himself—had ever visited the city or was particularly interested in it. Certainly nobody knew about the restaurant redecoration or the wall. Nor did anyone, myself included, know where Gibson would end up when the experiment began: the suggestion was simply that he should leave his body and take a trip. Thus there was no opportunity of obtaining advance information. I deliberately tried to structure the experiment with Denise Alexander in a way that would rule out telepathy completely. While in retrospect I don't think I succeeded—the subject knew the couple who created the target note and might thus have "tuned in" to one of them even though no one knew their whereabouts at the time—I do believe I minimized the possibility.

Clairvoyance has always been a problematic aspect of OOBE experimentation. There is substantial evidence to suggest that clairvoyance—the direct extrasensory perception of distant events—really does exist, and while the mechanism of the talent remains uncertain, it is possible that it might be used to collect data on experimental targets. But if clairvoyance can't be entirely ruled out, there is a difficulty with it as a complete explanation. The *subjective* perception of clairvoyance is typically that of "knowing" something intuitively or, alternatively, "seeing" something in a more or less vivid mental vision. In both instances, the seat of consciousness remains static. In other words, your mind is where it should be—firmly seated behind your eyes in your physical body.

Any OOBE is characterized by an entirely different subjective sensation. When I had my first spontaneous OOBE—the impetus for my experimentation in this area—it took me quite a long time to realize that anything was amiss. I was aware of my body exactly as it had always been, complete with appropriate clothing. It seemed to be functioning normally in a normal world except for the curious fact that I could walk through doors without opening them. Even when I noticed my *actual* body stretched out on a bed, I did not recognize it. (The sensation was similar to hearing your voice recorded for the first time.) Certainly, seeing it did nothing to shake my conviction that I was real and solid, despite all evidence to the contrary.

This subjective perception appears to be typical of the OOBE generally. Arthur Gibson was so convinced he had physically visited India that when challenged, he said he assumed he must have caught a plane. So if clairvoyance was the mechanism by which Tart's young lady read the target number, it was clairvoyance accompanied by a vivid, detailed, and entirely consistent hallucination. Even this is not entirely impossible—we are in uncharted territory here and nobody really knows how any of it works—but there is a substantial body of evidence to suggest the "second body" everyone experiences during an OOBE is something more than a subjective reality.

In 1845, for example, a Livonian linguist named Emilie Sagee was sacked from her job as a teacher. It wasn't the first time this had happened, yet no one questioned her abilities, qualifications, or skills. The problem was she frightened her pupils. At no fewer than eighteen different schools, they kept seeing two of her. The second Mlle Sagee might be standing near the first beside a blackboard, or eating the same school dinner. Sometimes the second figure would sit quietly in a corner, watching the first at work. Sometimes it would leave her to get on with the lesson while it strolled through the school grounds.

I stumbled on an anecdotal account of something similar when asked to lecture on OOBEs in Britain during the spring of 1990. After the talk I was approached by a woman, also a schoolteacher, who detailed a very curious experience of her own. Staff and pupils of her school had planned a summer trip to the mountains the previous year, but since she was attending a course she decided not to go. On the day of the trip she deeply regretted her decision. The weather was oppressively hot, so that instead of paying attention to her course, she sat uncomfortably daydreaming about cool, fresh mountain air and imagining herself with her colleagues and students. When she returned to school the following Monday, she asked a fellow teacher how the trip had gone. He looked at her in bewilderment and said surely she knew how the trip had gone, since she was there—he'd spent most of the afternoon talking to her. It subsequently transpired that others had noted her presence, even though she had been nowhere near the mountains that day. But something that looked like her certainly had, apparently with sufficient autonomy to maintain a conversation.

One of my earliest published short stories was called "House Haunting" and described how a young couple discovered the home of their dreams only to find it was on the market at a suspiciously low price. When they quizzed the estate agent, he reluctantly admitted the house was haunted, but added, "Don't worry, Madam—you're the ghost." The story drew on a factual case involving an Irish family named Butler. The wife had pictured her dream house for years, imagining herself walking through its rooms. When the real estate agent showed her husband and herself the property, she recognized it at once from the mental picture she'd carried so long and was able to describe the interior in detail before they actually went in. She made only one major mistake, mentioning a green door that did not exist, but the bemused agent confirmed it had once existed and been bricked up several years earlier.

Another example of essentially the same thing occurred in 1863 when the steamship *City of Limerick* hit a mid-Atlantic storm. An American manufacturer named Wilmot was on board. During the night, he dreamed his wife visited him in her nightdress and kissed him. Although he said nothing of the dream, his cabin mate teased him the following morning about his "midnight visit from a lady." When he arrived home in Bridgeport, Connecticut, his wife at once asked him if he had received a visit from her in the night. She'd been worried by reports of shipwrecks and decided to try to find out if he was safe. Consequently she visualized herself flying over the ocean, finding the ship, and going to his cabin. A man in the upper berth looked straight at her, but she went ahead and kissed her husband anyway. When pressed, she was able accurately to describe the ship, the cabin, and the man who had shared it with Mr. Wilmot.

Like so much paranormal phenomena, cases of this type are

more common than you might imagine. As long ago as 1886, the Society for Psychical Research published *Phantasms of the Living*, which detailed 350 examples. In 1951, Sylvan Muldoon and Hereward Carrington added another 100 in their book, *Phenomena of Astral Projection*. Three years later, Hornell Hart was examining 288 cases in the *Journal of the American Society for Psychical Research*. Another psychical researcher, Robert Crockall published no fewer than nine books of case histories between 1961 and 1978. Author John Poynton added one with 122 more in 1978.

These collections are reinforced by various folk traditions. The Azande of Africa believe you have two souls. One of them, the *mbisimbo*, is capable of leaving the body while you're still alive and often does so during sleep. The Bacairis of South America, talk of a *shadow* that leaves the body when we fall asleep. Native traditions in Burma also list a second body that's often likened to a butterfly. According to one survey, some 57 contemporary cultures throughout the world have beliefs about a second body. Such beliefs appear to have been historically widespread as well. In Ancient Egypt, as we've already seen, religious faith held that people had three souls. One of them, the *ka*, was thought to be a double of the physical body, composed of finer matter. Such doubles, under various different names, appear in the yoga systems of India, Tibet, and China. Oriental yoga in general postulates a series of subtle bodies, one within the other, like Russian dolls. This idea was carried into Europe and America by Madame Blavatsky and her Theosophists, reinforcing the existing tradition of the doppelgänger, a German word for the double supposed sometimes to appear as a herald of death.

With so much smoke, you have to ask, where's the fire? Why should a woman's brooding cause her image to appear in a ship's cabin? How could my schoolteacher appear in two places at once and even carry on a conversation? What *is* the *mbisibmo* of the Azande, the *butterfly* of Burma, the *andadura* shadow of the South American Bacairi?

No matter about the cross-cultural beliefs just quoted, the consensus of Western scientific thought assumes you have only one body—the one holding this book. But a few individual scientists haven't been so sure. In the 1920s, for example, Dr. Duncan McDougall of Haverhill, Massachusetts, carried out a macabre series of experiments designed to show that something tangible left the body at the point of death. His idea, which had an elegant simplicity once you get beyond your natural revulsion, was to *weigh* several of his patients as they died from tuberculosis. To do this, he placed them, bed and all, on a precision scale. At the point of death, he discovered in four out of six cases a weight loss of between two and two and a half ounces.

I'm not aware of any attempt to confirm or refute McDougall's findings, but I have been able to discover reports of two Dutch physicists, Drs. Malta and Zaalberg Van Zelst, who came to similar conclusions by a different route. While Dr. McDougall was weighing his hapless patients, they were hard at work building something called a *dynamistograph*. The device seems to have shared certain characteristics with a ouija board, since it had a pointer and a lettered dial. But unlike a ouija, which requires people to operate it, the dynamistograph was capable of functioning in an empty room. The Van Zelsts watched spellbound through a tiny window while spirits used it to spell out lengthy messages.

How you use something of this type to examine a hypothetical second body, I have no idea,[82] but the Van Zelsts subsequently announced they had discovered a soul body composed of widely separated atoms, with a density 176.5 times lighter than air. It was capable of expanding by about 1/40,000,000 of its own volume and contracting by some 1/6,250,000.

Although there is nothing to suggest they were in contact with Dr. McDougall, or even knew of his experiments, they concluded this second body weighed just short of 70 grams, (two and a quarter ounces), which falls neatly within the range of the good doctor's findings.

While it's difficult to take seriously anything with a name like "dynamistograph," a noted scientist in a prestigious post has done work that commands respect, even though its impact on modern scientific thought has been far less than the findings deserve. While an anatomy professor at Yale in the 1930s, Dr. Harold Saxton Burr became interested in the electrical potential of living systems. He developed equipment capable of detecting electrical field phenomena associated with trees and plants, animals, and human beings. These fields, he discovered, fluctuated in response to external conditions like moisture, electrical storms, and even moon phase.

His work in this area convinced Burr he was dealing with life-fields that determined and maintained the physical structure of an organism. This is an interesting observation and one that goes a long way to solve one of the persistent mysteries of biology—how you manage to recognize a friend you haven't seen for over a year. It's well known that, at the cellular level, your body is in a constant process of change. The physical *you* who started reading this book is quite different than the *you* who's reached this point in the narrative. Unless you are an extraordinarily fast reader, your entire liver has been replaced, as have much of your other internal organs and most of your skin. There is scarcely a molecule of your face that has survived, yet your spouse had very little trouble recognizing you this morning. What is it that maintains the old familiar patterns?

This is no trivial question. The magnificently complex specimen reading these words was once a group of undifferentiated cells programmed by nature to split and grow. But the time very quickly came when they ceased to be undifferentiated. Some grew into stomach lining, some into eyes, some into a brain. Biologists unfamiliar with Burr's research are at a loss to explain how cells somehow "know" their individual identity. But know it they do. If you sieve a living sponge through silk to separate its constituent cells—as biologists with nothing better to do have already tried—the creature will nevertheless reform as it was before. Even more impressively, you can mix together the cells of two different sponges without disrupting the process. They'll reform as separate individuals.

Clearly there's some sort of organizing principle at work here. It doesn't seem to be chemical. Scientists have looked hard in that direction without so far finding an answer. Could it be electrical, as Dr. Burr suggested? In 1958, an orthopedic surgeon named Robert Becker showed that it could.

Becker was interested in the fact that certain reptiles are capable of regrowing amputated limbs, while mammals—and, indeed, other reptiles—are not. By taking careful electrical measurements on the extremities of salamanders (which can regrow limbs) and their near-relatives frogs (which can't) he found a tiny 0.000002 amp negative current in both. He then discovered experimentally that when either of the creatures lost a limb, there was still a small electrical flow in the stump, but now with a positive polarity. As the wounds healed, there was a divergence in the electrical activity of the two species. As scar tissue formed on the frog, the electrical flow gradually reverted to its original negative polarity. In the salamander, the electrical potential also turned negative but rose to three times its original level.[83] This high negative potential was maintained while the salamander went about regrowing the missing limb.

This proved to be a practical discovery. When Becker induced a salamander-style electrical potential into the amputated stump of a frog, the creature grew an entire new limb, something it was incapable of doing naturally. In 1972, the regeneration process was induced in a mammal. A laboratory rat implanted with a tiny electrical battery managed to regrow part of a missing limb. The idea that electricity may be able to play a direct part in therapy is gradually gaining ground with orthodox medical practitioners. Battery implants now speed the healing of broken bones, and TENS machines[84] are routinely used for pain control.

Research of this type suggests a "second body" might be taken seriously as an electrical field phenomon, although it doesn't solve the mystery of how an electrical field becomes visible to others and even talks to them. All the same, it's interesting to discover there are some people who seem able to detach the second body at will. One of the most carefully studied was an American named Sylvan Muldoon.

Although Muldoon was only twenty-five years old in 1927 when he contacted the well-known psychical researcher Hereward Carrington, he had been having OOBEs regularly for thirteen years—more than enough time to bring them under conscious control. Carrington visited Muldoon and carried out experiments to test his claims. He was so impressed by the results that they wrote a book together, *The Projection of the Astral Body*.

Muldoon was not the only one to claim a detailed knowledge of the second body and how to separate it safely from the physical;. Carrington discovered another source of information by the time he came to edit Muldoon's manuscript. This was the publication, in France, of a book called *Le Fantome des Vivants*— The Living Phantom—by someone named Hector Durville. Durville was interested in projections resulting from "magnetic" trances and described a fascinating series of experiments that included attempts to photograph the second body.

Charles Tart carried out sophisticated tests on the American OOBE expert Robert Monroe between September 1965 and August 1966, using the facilities of the Electroencephalographic Laboratory of the University of Virginia Medical School. During these experiments, Monroe's brain waves, heart rate, and eye movements were all monitored while he was out of his physical body. Brain-wave patterns were those associated with dreaming sleep and were usually accompanied by rapid eye movements. His heart rate remained normal, but blood pressure typically dropped suddenly as he moved out of his body and stayed low until he returned, when it made a sudden surge back to normal.

More than ten years later, Monroe was tested again, this time at the University of Kansas Medical Center. Dr. Stuart Twemlow and Dr. Fowler Jones took left and right occipital electroencephalograph readings and used a Beckman polygraph. The Beckman equipment is commonly called a "lie detector" but actually measures a variety of physical functions such as the electrical potential of the skin, temperature variations, and blood pressure fluctuations. The EEG tests tended to confirm that Monroe left his body in a state very similar to dream sleep but not, apparently, identical to it. There was also a dramatic reduction in alpha and theta brain waves. The polygraph showed an unusually high galvanic skin response of 150 microvolts when the sessions began but no response at all while he was out of the body.

But back in the 1920s, Hereward Carrington was far more interested in whether OOBEs were what they appeared to be than in the sort of physical reactions they induced. On one occasion he experimented by willing himself to project into the presence of "a certain young lady" reputed to be psychic. The experiment produced nothing in the way of a conscious OOBE, but the lady in question reported waking to find him standing in her room at the time he made the attempt. He remained for a few moments before fading away.

In January 1957, an American woman named Martha Johnson tried something similar. She generated an OOBE that allowed her to travel from Plains, Illinois, to visit her mother nearly a thousand miles away in northern Minnesota. She found her mother at work in the kitchen and leaned against the dish cupboard to watch. Eventually her mother grew disturbed and turned to look at her. Later her mother confirmed she had actually seen Martha Johnson briefly—and apparently physically present—before she disappeared. She added the interesting detail that her dogs became agitated, as if they too could see or sense the apparition.

The use of an animal as a sort of "second body detector" formed the basis of a series of experiments carried out at Duke University, the North Carolina home of modern psychical research. The subject was a young man named Stuart Blue Harary, who, like Muldoon and others, had developed the ability to generate OOBEs at will. Harary's pulse, blood pressure, galvanic skin response, breathing, eye movements, and brain waves were all monitored. A target room approximately half a mile away was packed with thermistors, photo multipliers, and various devices for measuring electrical conductivity and magnetic permeability.

When Harary projected, his heartbeat and respiration increased and, like Monroe, his blood pressure dropped. There was a similar decrease in galvanic skin response. Some rapid eye movements were noted, but he was not asleep, since the EEG showed a steady alpha rhythm associated with relaxed alertness. He was instructed to try to influence the various pieces of equipment in the target site but failed to do so. He did, however, manage some effect on a unique piece of biological equipment, a caged kitten named *Spirit*. Spirit disliked confinement and meowed thirty-seven times during a control period in which nothing happened. But throughout the entire time Harary reported stroking her while in his second body, she meowed not at all.

Although there seems to be little risk associated with the typical OOBE—Robert Monroe once remarked that he had regularly left his body for twenty-five years without suffering harm—the research that has been carried out into this intriguing phenomenon certainly seems to have a bearing on what may happen to you after death. There is every indication that, whether you realize it or not, you were born with an electrical image of your body that, when separated from the physical, manifests in much the same way ghosts of the dead have long been reported to manifest.

Could it be that upon death this second body separates permanently from the first and is capable of supporting your consciousness afterward? In other words, does the existence of a second body provide an additional basis for confidence in post-mortem survival? At the present stage of scientific research, the answers remain uncertain, although the evidence is suggestive. Fortunately, it is not the only evidence we have left to consider.

17

Mediums

*Since I come up here, I've learnt that a lot of influencing goes on from
above what we don't know nothing about.*
Cockney spirit guide named Alf, died on the Somme, 1915

IN 1913, HARRY Houdini received news of his mother's death.
Most biographers of the great escapologist record it was a profound shock. A movie of his life was later to suggest he turned
to Spiritualist mediums in the hope of making contact with her.
Whether this is true or not, he certainly launched a highly pub-
licized investigation of séance-room phenomena . . . and
denounced every medium he met, often exposing them for
what he believed were fraudulent practices.

The *Concise Oxford Dictionary* defines a medium as "a person
claiming to be in contact with the spirits of the dead and to
communicate between the dead and the living." By this definition, mediumship has a long history: shamans have claimed
contact with the dead all the way back to the dawn of time. But
the term as it's used today really only dates to 1847, when a
Methodist farmer named James D. Fox moved with his wife
Margaret and daughters Margaretta and Kate into a house in
Hydesville, in upstate New York.

The house had something of a reputation. Talk in the area
was that it might be haunted. The previous tenant, a man named
Michael Weekman, said he'd heard loud knockings while he

stayed there. But the Fox family enjoyed a period of peace until the end of March 1848, when they too were disturbed by banging noises. Even then, nobody took much notice. The weather was bad, with frequent storms. The assumption was that wind was causing noises in the timber framing.

Then, on the night of March 31, things changed. At the time, everyone slept in the same room in two separate beds. As the parents were coming to bed, raps started up again and somehow it didn't sound like the wind. Kate Fox, then age twelve, suddenly said, "Mr. Splitfoot, do as I do!" and snapped her fingers. At once, the banging sounds changed to something very like finger-snapping. The fifteen-year-old sister, Margaretta, also shouted, "Do as I do" and clapped her hands. The snapping noises changed to the sound of hands clapping.

The girls themselves quickly came to the conclusion somebody was playing a joke on them. (March 31 is followed by April Fool's Day.) Their mother wasn't so sure. She decided to test the ghost—or whatever it was—by asking it to rap out the ages of her children. If somebody was acting the fool, it was unlikely they would know. But the ghost complied, rapping out the ages of Kate and Margaretta correctly. Then, eerily, it rapped again, this time counting out the age of a third child who was dead.

Mrs. Fox asked if the noises were being made by a human being and suggested two raps if they were. There was no sound at all. A spirit then? At once there were two raps, so loud that the house shook. Over a lengthy questioning session, Mrs. Fox discovered that what claimed to be making the raps was the ghost of a man who had been murdered in the house at the age of thirty-one.

By now thoroughly excited, Mrs. Fox called in fourteen of her neighbors, among them a man named William Duesler, whose cynicism about ghosts evaporated abruptly when he went into the bedroom and was faced with raps so loud and definite he concluded a spirit had to be involved. Duesler then suggested working out a code so that the ghost—if it was a ghost—could communicate properly. By means of this code and careful questioning, he discovered the spirit claimed to be a peddler named Charles B. Rosma. The entity said he had been attacked and murdered in the house five years earlier and robbed of five hundred dollars he was carrying. After the murder, the body was buried in the cellar. A maid called Lucretia Pulver later confirmed that a peddler had stayed in the house briefly about five years before. She had once been sent home for some reason, and when she came in for work the next day the man was gone.

When news of the spirit messages began to spread, hundreds of people headed for the Fox home to see and hear the miracle for themselves. The raps and coded communications never faltered. There was some digging in the cellar at this time, but the place flooded and excavations had to stop. Although clearly impressed by the phenomena, the visitors were far from naive. They set up an investigatory committee that began its work by collecting statements from witnesses, then embarked on no less than three cautious experimental examinations. Despite various precautions—at one stage the girls were made to stand on pillows with their ankles tied—the raps continued.

It was eventually decided to separate the children. Kate went to her sister in Rochester, Margaretta to her brother in Auburn. The ghost followed them . . . or rather, several ghosts followed them, for the original peddler stayed in the house at Hydesville and produced gurgling noises so terrifying that Mrs. Fox's hair turned white. Young Kate started communicating with a dead relative named Jacob Smith. Raps continued to be heard around Margaretta. Their sister Leah, who lived in

Rochester all along, suddenly found she could talk to spirits too. Then suddenly the phenomena jumped out of the family altogether. In Auburn, a sixteen-year-old named Harriet Bebee, who was unrelated to the Foxes, came to hear the raps and was followed about by something invisible that produced more raps at her home twenty miles away.

Once the initial novelty wore off, the Fox family began to tire of the flood of visitors to their farm. Eventually they moved to Rochester in the hope of getting away from the noisy peddler. The raps continued. A turning point of sorts came with the visit of a man named Isaac Post. Using an alphabetical code, the spirits spelled out the following message:

Dear friends, you must proclaim this truth to the world. This is the dawning of a new era. You must not try to conceal it any longer. God will protect you and good spirits will watch over you.

It was no empty promise. From that time on, things got a lot more exciting. Tables turned and tapped messages with their legs. Objects moved around rooms. Invisible presences played musical instruments. The spirits insisted they could make contact better in darkness. On November 14, 1849, in the gloom of Rochester's Corinthian Hall, the first Spiritualist meeting took place. It was not the last. Public interest in talking with ghosts proved enormous. In a matter of months, Spiritualism had swept through America. Everybody, it seemed, was trying to communicate with dead relatives and provoke spirits into making raps and moving tables. Among them was a young Republican congressman from Illinois named Abraham Lincoln, who, when elected president in 1861, attended séances at the White House during which he was berated by a spirit about the necessity of freeing the slaves.

The interest jumped the Atlantic. Even Queen Victoria was caught up in the wave of Spiritualist practice. Buckingham Palace was the setting for a number of séances; and both the queen and her consort, Albert, engaged in table-turning and similar experiments. Psychics and mediums were presented to Victoria, who showed an enthusiastic interest in their talents. One was the clairvoyant Georgiana Eagle, who demonstrated her powers before the queen at Osborne House, on the Isle of Wight, in July of 1846. Victoria was so impressed that she had a watch inscribed to Miss Eagle for "meritorious and extraordinary clairvoyance." But the psychic died before the gift could be presented and the watch later went to Etta Wriedt, an American direct-voice medium.

Spiritualism also swept through Europe. Most crowned heads on the Continent followed Queen Victoria's example and held frequent séances. Thousands of their subjects followed suit. In November 1904, over fifty years after the events in the Fox household, a cellar wall in the house collapsed to reveal a second wall behind it. When workmen dug between the two walls, they uncovered a skeleton and a peddler's tin box.

Although the craze died down eventually, séances still take place in their thousands throughout the world each year. The question naturally arises whether Houdini was right in claiming they were all frauds.

From the earliest days of the Spiritualist movement, situations have arisen that suggest Houdini, for all his expertise and indignation at what he judged to be unfair advantage taken of grieving families, may have overstated his case. One concerned Queen Victoria herself. Shortly after Prince Albert's death on December 14, 1861, a thirteen-year-old medium, Robert James Lees, held a séance in Birmingham during which, it was claimed, the spirit of the prince consort came through with the message that he wished to speak with his wife, the queen. The development received a measure of publicity—one of the sitters happened to be a professional editor. His published account of the séance was subsequently brought to Victoria's attention.

Despite her earlier interest in Spiritualism, the queen was by no means credulous. She was aware how often spurious communications follow the death of a public figure. Besides, her position dictated a tactful, low-key approach. She instructed two courtiers to attend the next Lees séance but warned them they were not to use their own names or reveal their status as emissaries from the court. I've not been able to pinpoint the identities of the courtiers concerned, but if they were not themselves believers in life after death, the séance they attended must have come as something of a shock. The voice produced by Lees was instantly recognizable as that of the late consort. Worse still, the spirit addressed the courtiers by their real names. Eventually, reluctantly, they were forced to admit they had been sent by the queen.

It seems there followed a great deal of evidential material, including intimate details of life at the palace that only Albert could have known. The courtiers were impressed. So, when she received their report, was the queen. But before she could take action, she received a letter from the schoolboy Lees. This letter was an example of something called automatic writing. According to Spiritualist theory, the shade of the deceased takes over the body—or at least the hand—of the medium long enough to pen a message.

The message in this case was signed by a pet name used only between Albert and his wife and was packed with personal details. Victoria was utterly convinced that it represented a genuine spirit communication. She sent at once for Lees and a séance was held in the palace. The voice of Albert came through the medium and spoke to his delighted widow. Lees paid nine visits in all to Buckingham Palace, and his séances impressed the queen so much that she asked him to join the royal household as resident medium.

It's easy to be cynical when studying this case. Sorrowing widows are not particularly difficult people to impress and Victoria's emotional state was such that she would have been easy prey for an impostor. But if Lees was a fraud, it's difficult to imagine what his motives may have been, for he refused the offer of a court position, apparently on the advice of his spirit guides. But he did not leave the queen without solace. His final message to her (or Albert's final message through him, if you accept the Spiritualist viewpoint) assured her that another medium had been chosen to keep the line of communication open. This medium was "the boy who used to carry my gun at Balmoral." The boy who used to carry Albert's gun was a Scottish gillie named James Brown, who subsequently became so close to the queen that there were rumors they were lovers. But decades after Victoria's death, investigations by the British journalist Hannen Swaffer unearthed evidence to suggest Brown, like young Lees, was a medium and this, rather than any sexual attraction, formed the basis of his relationship with the queen.[85]

With so much going on, it was only a matter of time before the phenomenon of Spiritualism attracted scientific attention— some of it of an extraordinarily high caliber. Sir William Crookes, for example, was a research chemist and president of the Royal Society who had the discovery of no less than six new elements to his credit and was widely considered to be the greatest scientist of his age. In 1882, he became a founder member of the Society for Psychical Research and devoted much of his time thereafter to the investigation of séance-room phenomena, notably levitation.

Other enthusiastic investigators in the same field were Cromwell F. Varley, a pioneer of ionization research; J. J. Thompson, who discovered the electron; and Alfred Russell Wallace, the naturalist who theorized about evolution before Darwin published his ideas. In America, Thomas A. Edison became such a convinced Spiritualist that he experimented with electrical equipment designed to communicate with the dead. After Edison's death, the inventor of television, John Logie Baird, believed he made contact with him through a medium. Sigmund Freud, the founding father of psychiatry, went on record as saying that had he his life to live again, he would devote it to parapsychology. Carl Jung went even further. He personally investigated mediumship and claimed that certain "psychological" phenomena could be better explained by the spirit hypothesis than any other.

What exactly was it these scientists were investigating? A good many years ago, I set myself to find out and my first séance proved a good deal less than edifying. I climbed endless narrow wooden stairs before reaching the séance room, in Belfast, Northern Ireland, which was laid out with rows of wooden chairs and a lectern at the front so that the whole thing had the feel of a small-town gospel meeting. Of the twenty or thirty people present, only two others besides myself were male. There was only one really young person there, a girl I would judge to have been about eleven. The average age must have been approaching sixty. Proceedings began with hymn singing and the reading of a biblical passage about speaking in tongues, exactly like the start of a religious service. But then things changed.

The medium came in, a small, painfully thin man with long (and very dirty) fingernails. He switched out the lights except for one dim, dull red bulb of the type photographers use in darkrooms. Everyone sat nervously in the gloom and waited.

The medium slumped in his chair and began breathing deeply and heavily. He was, it appeared, going into trance. Eventually he stood up, picked out a woman from the audience and told her he'd made contact with her mother, who had died five years previously. The mother, he said, wished to send her "love and flowers." There were several more messages of this type before the medium invited anyone else who was receiving "impressions" to share them with the rest of the sitters. Several elderly women jumped up and delivered messages from the dead to anyone who cared to listen. I recall there was one for me, telling me not to worry about an examination.[86] The séance ended with more hymns and a brief communal prayer. I subsequently discovered the medium involved had been thrown out of the SNU (the Spiritualists National Union) for faking a trumpet séance. Trumpet séances are held in total darkness. An aluminium trumpet, with luminous rings painted around each end, is set in the middle of a circle of sitters. If all goes well, the spirits will use the trumpet to speak through. On the occasion in question, everything appeared to be going very well indeed. Startled sitters watched the trumpet shiver, then rise up into the air. But then some cynic switched the light on and the medium was discovered on hands and knees, waving the trumpet above his head.

Not all séances resemble my early experience. Where there are several sitters, the group will often form a circle, sometimes round a table. Lights are typically dimmed or, occasionally, extinguished altogether. Members of the group may or may not link hands. The medium will often, but not always, enter a trance state.

What happens next will vary with the talents and specialties of the medium involved. Some, known as impressionistic mediums, go no further than announcing an intuitive response to questions posed by sitters or the possibility of spirit visitations. Others are more spectacular. Among the phenomena that have arisen at séances are:

• *Automatic writing.* Here it is believed that a spirit takes control of the medium's body (or at least hand and arm) to write out messages.

• *Spirit visions.* The medium reports the presence of a spirit or spirits, describes their appearance, and reports any communications.

• *Overshadowing.* The medium's physical appearance seems to change as he or she takes on the features of the over-shadowing entity.

• *Direct voice.* A spirit takes control of the medium's vocal apparatus—tongue, larynx, etc.—in order to speak directly to the sitters. The term can sometimes refer to an even more spectacular phenomenon—voices sounding out of thin air from various parts of the room.

• *Audible effects.* Raps, knocks, sometimes whispers, snatches of music or other sounds that seem to emanate from the air.

• *Poltergeist effects.* Various objects may be moved or even levitated. Bells might be rung or musical instruments played by unseen hands.

• *Spirit touch.* Sitters report tactile experiences that resemble fleeting touches by spirit hands, or, occasionally, more intimate phenomena like light kisses.

• *Sudden cold.* A drop in temperature believed to be associated with the presence of spirits, often accompanied by unexplained air currents.

• *Ectoplasm.* A white, sometimes slightly luminous substance extruded from the medium's mouth or other bodily orifices.

• *Materialization.* The appearance, with a greater or lesser degree of solidity, of spirit faces, limbs or, occasionally, a fully manifested body.

• *Table turning.* Gross physical movements of a heavy table, usually but not always touched by the sitters, which can sometimes turn into coded communications.

• *Ouija.* An upturned glass or ouija board that moves under the fingers of sitters to spell out messages using the letters of the alphabet.

Author C. J. Ducasse reported that in 1961 there was a factory in Columbus, Ohio, devoted to the manufacture of talking trumpets, ectoplasm, and life-size spirit manifestations that could be ordered as séance kits to terrify your friends or extract money from the gullible. But while there is not the slightest doubt, as Houdini discovered, that all séance room phenomena may potentially be faked and some of it most certainly is, there remains a considerable body of evidence for the genuine article, much of it painstakingly built up by skeptical scientists over a period of years. A particularly convincing example was the lengthy investigation of the American trance medium Leonora E. Piper from Boston.

Mrs. Piper was born in 1857 into a working-class family, a factor that had considerable bearing on her career. At the time she began to practice as a medium, class-consciousness pervaded the Spiritualist movement, even in America. A lady or gentleman who professed psychic abilities was considered incapable of cheating, but someone from Mrs. Piper's background was instantly suspect. As a result, she remains to this day one of the most thoroughly investigated mediums of all time.

Among those who examined the Piper phenomenon firsthand was the arch skeptic of the (British) Society for Psychical

Research, Richard Hodgson. Like Houdini, if a little less publicly, Hodgson had established a fearsome reputation for unmasking cheats. He had branded Madame Blavatsky[87] a fraud and was one of the first to expose Eusapia Palladino, another famous medium of the day. When he turned his attention to Mrs. Piper, he was widely expected to unmask her as well.

They loathed one another on sight. Mrs. Piper found him arbitrary and cold and made no secret of the fact that she disliked working with him. But despite the personal antipathy, both persevered. Convinced that the information Mrs. Piper produced during her séances was procured not from spirits but confederates or secret inquiries, Hodgson hired private detectives to watch her day and night. They followed her when she went out, reported back on anyone she met, even intercepted her mail. When none of this gave any indication of fraud, he introduced sitters of his own choosing to her séances, individuals unknown to anyone except himself, well briefed not to let slip any information about themselves. It made not the slightest difference. Mrs. Piper continued to produce the goods.

Among the goods she produced were messages for the Rev. and Mrs. S. W. Sutton, a couple who attended her séances in 1893 in the hope of obtaining news of their recently deceased daughter. Hodgson, who was investigating Mrs. Piper at the time, described the Suttons as highly intelligent and arranged for a stenographer to takes notes at their sittings. The record of what happened is preserved in SPR archives and makes interesting reading. An entranced Mrs. Piper claimed to have made contact with the child and produced a great deal of evidence.

The Suttons had, for example, brought along some buttons belonging to their daughter and left them on the séance room table. The spirit recalled accurately that she used to bite them while alive. She went on to make reference to a (genuine) Uncle Frank and a friend who had died from a cancerous tumor. She named the girl's doll, Dinah, and talked about a toy horse she'd played with. She referred to the girl's brother by his pet name and accurately named her sister, Maggie. She peaked the performance by singing two songs the girl had been singing immediately before her death. The Suttons had no doubt at all they were listening to their deceased daughter.

Hodgson himself wasn't nearly so sure, at least at first. But the evidence continued to mount, some of it very weird indeed. On one occasion he watched while an entranced Mrs. Piper verbally delivered a spirit communication to a sitter while her hand wrote a wholly separate message, on a different subject, to Hodgson himself—an extraordinarily difficult thing to fake. Hodgson began to suspect she might have paranormal abilities, although he still stopped short of accepting that she was in contact with a spirit world.

Like a majority of mediums, Mrs. Piper worked through what's called a "control." In Spiritualist theory, a control is an entity more or less permanently attached to a medium, who acts as a guardian angel cum gatekeeper in selecting which spirits are permitted to contact her—a sort of celestial bouncer. Many mediums work with the same control throughout their entire lives. Mrs. Piper had several. One of the earliest was an entity called "Phinuit" who was associated with her from 1855 to 1892.

Phinuit was far from shy about his background. He claimed to be the spirit of Dr. Jean Phinuit Scliville, a Marseilles man who had studied medicine in Paris, France and in Metz, Germany. He was able to give the name of his medical school, Merciana College, and the woman he had married in later life, Marie Latimer. Regrettably, no amount of investigation confirmed these details, while it very quickly became clear that this French-born spirit spoke little or none of his native language. Hodgson began to suspect that Phinuit was no disembodied spirit but rather a split-off portion of Mrs. Piper's subconscious, an entity essentially similar to those that emerge in multiple-personality disorders. It was a theory with a reassuringly scientific ring about it, but one that failed to explain how a split personality could obtain detailed knowledge of the dead.

Then, toward the end of 1892, something occurred that was to challenge Hodgson's skepticism. A colleague of his named George Pellew died, shortly after which Mrs. Piper obtained a new "control" who introduced himself as "G.P." Although initially this was expanded into "George Pelham," it quickly became evident that Pelham was actually Pellew. This was a particularly interesting development for Hodgson, who was able to quiz the contact on things Hodgson actually knew. Although "G.P." made mistakes, he was certainly aware of an impressive amount of detail about Pellew. When, for example, he was challenged to identify those sitters he had known in life, he accurately named 30 out of 31 from a total sample of 150. His only mistake was failing to recognize someone he hadn't seen since she was a little girl.

Three years later, while "G.P." was still her main control, a communicator identifying himself as Stainton Moses came through. W. Stainton Moses was a well-known English medium and author who had died three years earlier. While alive, Moses had functioned with no fewer than forty-nine spirit controls—he called them his Imperator Band—and now brought four of them to help Mrs. Piper. These four, known as Imperator, Rector, Doctor,[88] and Prudens, gradually took over from G.P. as her principle controls, although G.P. himself never actually disappeared. It was at this stage that Mrs. Piper proved herself capable of delivering verbal messages from one control while simultaneously producing written messages from another.

While fulfilling their expected function as controls, the four Imperator Group members presented evidential material about their identities while living and also came to act in the manner of those "channeled" entities so popular with today's New Age movement. That's to say, they propounded teachings designed to help sitters lead worthwhile and moral lives. Hodgson was so impressed both by the evidence and the doctrines that he eventually capitulated his initial position. In an 1892 report published in the *Proceedings* of the Society for Psychical Research he concluded, "I cannot profess to have any doubt but that the chief communicators to whom I have referred in the foregoing pages, are veritably the personalities that they claim to be, that they have survived the change we call death, and that they have directly communicated with us whom we call living, through Mrs. Piper's entranced organism."

He was not the only skeptic to find himself impressed. The psychology pioneer and founder member of the SPR, Frederic W. H. Myers, went on record with the statement that "messages were given to me and certain circumstances indicated with which it was impossible that Mrs. Piper should be acquainted." The great American psychologist William James expressed "absolute certainty" that the entranced Mrs. Piper knew things impossible for her in the waking state. The eminent British scientist Sir Oliver Lodge claimed he had assured himself that much of the information supplied by Mrs. Piper could not have come through normal sensory channels.

As mediumship entered the twentieth century, Mrs. Piper laid the foundation for one of the most puzzling of all Spiritualist phenomena—something now known as cross-correspondences. Three of the original founders of the Society for Psychical

Research—Edmund Gurney, Henry Sidgwick, and Frederic Myers—were particularly interested in the question of life after death. Gurney, who died in 1888, was a skeptic. Sidgwick, who died in 1900, was more open-minded but essentially agnostic. Myers, by contrast, seemed to be convinced of the possibility of survival and expressed his intention of communicating when he passed on.

After Myers died in 1901, Mrs. Piper announced she had established contact with all three men through automatic writing. Both her claim and the quality of information contained in her texts attracted a great deal of publicity. As a result, about a dozen other mediums decided, quite independently, to try the same thing. A considerable body of writing was produced in this way and eventually examined by Society investigators. At this point, the cross-correspondences were noticed. Margaret Verrall, an English medium and classical scholar, received an incomplete message purporting to come from Myers. To their astonishment, the investigators found the conclusion of the message in an automatic text produced by Rudyard Kipling's sister, Alice Fleming. It was only one of many examples of a phenomenon that continued for several years and involved an ever-widening circle of independent mediums. Some of the references were unusually obscure—one set of correspondences combined Syracuse, the heel of Italy, and the so-called Ear of Dionysius—stone quarries with peculiar acoustic properties where Athenian slaves were once imprisoned. Even classicists had a difficult time with the separate elements, but taken together, the references made sense.

The scientific investigation of mediumistic phenomena continues to this day. In March 2001, the University of Arizona announced the results of a study that "produced findings so extraordinary they raise fundamental questions about the survival of consciousness after death."[89] The university project involved five mediums working with two sitters they had not met before. In the first run of experiments, all contact between medium and sitter took place under video surveillance, a screen between the two blocked off any possibility of visual clues and the sitter was confined to yes/no answers. Sessions ran for an hour, during which time each medium was independently required to describe the sitter's dead relative. Afterward the tapes were analyzed for accuracy. Results showed the average success rate of the mediums was 83 percent. One scored 93 percent. Around eighty pieces of information were produced at each session and the quality of information ranged from the relative's name to the circumstances of death. One medium claimed to have made contact with the sitter's dead mother three days before the experiment began and repeated a prayer she'd taught the sitter as a child. A second run of experiments with a new sitter who was not permitted to communicate with the mediums in any way produced similar results.

In a control experiment, the University of Arizona required a sample of more than sixty people to duplicate the results obtained by the mediums. The most successful showed a 54 percent accuracy by guesswork alone, but the average was a low 36 percent. The university team leader, Professor Gary Schwartz, was reported as saying that all data so far gathered was consistently in accord with survival of consciousness after death.

These results are just part of a vast body of evidence that suggests something very strange has been going on in the world of mediumship for a very long time. Reluctant to accept the strangeness as (necessarily) proof of postmortem survival, investigators have worked hard in structuring experiments designed to test alternative hypotheses. Some have produced intriguing results.

In one experiment, readings taken during a séance showed substantial and near-instantaneous temperature drops varying between 10 and 20 °F, coincident with psychical phenomena. In another, American professor Charles Hapgood, whose theories on polar shift were endorsed by Einstein, took EEG readings of the medium Elwood Babbitt while he was controlled by three separate "spirits." All three readings were different from one another and from Babbitt's own reading while in the waking state. Furthermore, the trance EEGs indicated the "spirits" were of different ages and could not, in the opinion of experts, have been produced by a single person.

Voice prints—visible representations of an individual's unique speech patterns—taken during sittings with Australian medium Shirley Bray indicated that three of the spirits that regularly manifested through her were different people. Variables of pace, rhythm, accent, and even breathing patterns mean that voice prints are as individual as fingerprints, and the technology used to test Ms. Bray was the same as that which led to the conviction of the British serial killer known as the Yorkshire Ripper.

Perhaps the most intriguing experiments involved the Irish-American author and trance medium Eileen Garrett, who in a lifetime of willing cooperation with scientists became one of the most thoroughly tested psychics of all time. Although Mrs. Garrett herself did not believe her trance controls were independent entities—she was convinced they were dramatized projections of her own unconscious—psychological tests indicated she might well have been wrong. Psychologists used a standard Jungian word-association test on Mrs. Garrett while in normal waking consciousness, then compared the result with similar tests carried out on her main spirit control Urvani and several "visiting" intelligences supplied by Urvani for the occasion. As with the EEG traces and voice prints, no fewer than eight entities, including Urvani himself, showed up as different intelligences from each other and from Mrs. Garrett herself. Most psychologists accept that the test, which measures response times down to a tenth of a second and involves long lists of associations, would be near impossible to fake. There is not the slightest doubt that voice prints and EEG traces are well beyond conscious fakery.

By the time of her death in 1970, Mrs. Garrett had been extensively tested by scientists throughout the world, including the pioneer of statistical research in America, Dr. J. B. Rhine. In experiment after experiment, Mrs. Garrett demonstrated telepathic and even precognitive abilities. Rhine referred to the experiments as a "turning point in parapsychology." But ironically, it was her well-attested psychism that threw doubt on the evidential nature of her spirit communications.

The problem has been a long-standing one. As the late astronomer Carl Sagan once remarked, extraordinary claims require extraordinary proofs. For scientists, the claim of post-mortem survival is the most extraordinary of all, so that evidence that appears to support it must have no other possible explanation. From the very foundation of the Society for Psychical Research, investigators have been aware that if telepathy is a fact of life—as it certainly seems to be—then it is almost impossible to decide whether the information provided by a medium at a séance derives from disembodied spirits or is extracted telepathically from the minds of the sitters.

The problem is obvious once you start to think about it. If a medium gives you details of your dead grandmother, you judge the accuracy of the information by comparing it with what you already know; that's to say, with information already in your mind while the medium was delivering her message. Even skeptical investigators like Hodgson and Frank Podmore, who were extremely reluctant to accept the evidence for telepathy in any other circumstances, insisted it provided a better explanation of séance phenomena than the spirit hypothesis.

While it's difficult to see how telepathy can explain phenomena like cross-correspondences or, as has happened, produce information known only to the deceased but verified after the séance has finished, the objection is now so deeply ingrained that some scientists have been moved to look beyond mediumistic communications for absolute proof of survival.

A number of them believe they may have found it.

18

Recording the Dead

Kostulit, ta tove mote. (Kostulit, this is your mother.)
Spirit communication recorded on tape by Latvian psychologist
Dr. Konstantin Raudive

IN 1959, AN amateur ornithologist named Friedrich Jürgenson went into the woods near his Swedish home to record birdsong. He had made similar recordings many times before, but on this occasion he found a faint, strange noise on the tape, like someone using his name. He ran the tape again and again, adjusting the volume, concentrating hard. The voice was definitely audible and after a while he decided it belonged to his mother. It sounded as if she had been somewhere deep in the woods calling to him. But Jürgenson's mother had been dead for years.

This was the beginning of a whole new chapter in the annals of psychical research. Jürgenson went on to produce many more mysterious recordings. In 1964, he went public. Toward the end of that year, a Stockholm publisher brought out his book *Rösterna från Rymden,* or *Voices from Space.* Among those who read it was a Latvian psychiatrist with a lifelong interest in the paranormal, Dr. Konstantin Raudive.

As Raudive began reading the book, he was not particularly impressed. He was familiar with most of the scientists engaged in psychical research at the time, and Jürgenson was definitely an outsider. Perhaps more important, he came across as a highly imaginative man—perhaps even overly imaginative—and Raudive suspected he might be capable of conjuring up visions in an empty room or voices out of the silence. But as he continued to read, Raudive found himself fascinated by the central theme of the book—that spirit voices, "voices from space," could actually be recorded.

Three years later, Jürgenson was to give technical details of his methods in a second book, *Sprechfunk mit Verstorbenen,* Radio-Link with the Dead. The original work contained no hint of how it might have been done. Jürgenson confined himself to claims that he had recorded not only the voices of dead relatives and friends but historical personages like Hitler and the recently executed Caryl Chessman, an American who became a best-selling author while on death row for attempted rape. It was all very frustrating for someone like Raudive whose whole instinct was to investigate such claims for himself. In April 1965, he contacted Jürgenson and asked to hear some of his tapes. Jürgenson agreed.

Raudive traveled to Sweden with a colleague, Dr. Zenta Maurina, and took a liking to Jürgenson at once. The Swede seemed sincere and deeply committed to his research. He allowed the visitors immediate access to his tapes. The voices were audible enough against a background hiss, but Raudive and his colleague found it impossible to make out what they were saying. They were faint and spoke very quickly with a peculiar rhythm. But as the tapes were repeated several times, their ears gradually attuned.

At this point, of course, they had only Jürgenson's word that the tapes were genuine. The man was a movie producer and could have hired actors to pretend to be spirits. His story about recording in the woods might have been pure fabrication. But Jürgenson agreed to make a new recording on the spot. When he played back the tape, there were voices on it that Raudive believed could not have come from anybody in the room. Nor did they seem to be glitches on the tape or sounds that Jürgenson had somehow prerecorded. The incident that ruled out both these possibilities arose when Dr. Maurina remarked she was under the impression that inhabitants of the Beyond led a happy, carefree existence. Her comment was duly recorded on the tape . . . as was the reply of "*Nonsense!*" from a wholly unknown voice. The spirits had become interactive.

All the same, Raudive was not entirely convinced. Although he was now certain Jürgenson was not faking the tapes, he thought there might be explanations for the phenomenon other than the spirit hypothesis. There was, for example, the obvious possibility of a freak pickup of radio transmissions. Clearly more research was needed. In June 1965, Raudive joined Jürgenson on his Swedish estate at Nysund to carry it out.

At first they managed to produce only faint, scarcely audible voices, but at 9:30 P.M. on June 10, they got a clear, good quality recording. Raudive later found anyone who listened to it could make out the voices easily. First there was one that called "Friedrich, Friedrich." Then a woman's voice said softly, "*Heute pa nakti. Kennt ihr Margaret, Konstantin?*" After a brief pause, the same voice sang, "*Vi tálu! Runá!*" Finally a different female voice said, "*Va a dormir, Margarete!*"

Almost all these phrases are a mixture of languages. Raudive, himself a formidable linguist, identified German, Latvian, English, and French. Putting these together, the translation would be: "Frederick, Frederick! Tonight. Do you know Margaret, Konstantin? We are far away! Speak! Go to sleep, Margaret."

The name "Margaret" struck Raudive forcefully. He had been deeply affected by the recent death of a friend named Margaret Petrautzki and the coincidence of the name gave him much food for thought. He decided to continue serious research on his own. It was a decision that was to influence the course of his entire career, for the voice phenomenon came to fill almost his whole life.

There are three ways of producing electronic voice recordings, two of them very simple. All that's needed is patience and some basic equipment.

The method that gives the clearest voices requires a radio, a short antenna (somewhere between 6 and 10 cm), a tape recorder, and something called a diode, which is readily available in any specialist radio or electronics outlet. The antenna is attached to the diode and the diode to the radio. You then turn on the AM waveband and tune the set to what's technically known as an inter-frequency—anywhere on the waveband where no station is broadcasting. This tuning produces "white noise," a constant hiss of static. The tape machine is set to record from the radio, either via a microphone or, better, a plug-in jack. If an open microphone is used, it will obviously pick up sounds made naturally within range, and these have to be carefully differentiated from any paranormal voices that might arise. Open microphone recording, conversely, allows the possibility of recorded interactions between the voices and the experimenter. The diode method is likely to give best results unless the equipment is set up too close to a strong radio transmitter, which can cause interference.

A second method is almost identical to the first except that no diode is used. The radio is joined to the tape recorder exactly as for recording a program and once again tuned to an interfrequency.

The third and simplest method of all involves setting up a recorder and microphone in an empty, quiet room and recording the silence for half an hour or so. It was this method Raudive used initially in his solo experiments and it took him three months of patient work before a taped voice answered one of his own spoken observations with the words "Pareizi tá büs!"— Latvian for "That's right!"[90]

Interestingly, while this was the first voice he heard, it was not the first he actually recorded. When he replayed earlier tapes he discovered many other voices he had not noticed before. This is a commonplace in the electronic voice phenomenon. Most people are able to distinguish only seven levels of volume and seven levels of pitch in the ordinary course of events. Because of this, most of the voices remain inaudible until the ear is attuned through practice. It is only when the individual is experienced enough to distinguish single phonemes—the smallest individual units of sound—that it becomes possible to hear all the voices properly. Individuals with musical training typically experience far fewer problems in this type of research than others, and it was Professor Atis Teichmanis of the College of Music in Freiburg, Germany, who was first able to confirm accurately that the electronic voices specifically differed in both pitch and volume from those of the average human voice.

But if the voices were so difficult to distinguish, how could anyone be certain they were more than psychological projections of the listener? The human nervous system is so well designed to distinguish patterns that it frequently discerns them even when they aren't there. Hence we see faces in the clouds and pictures in the fire. More to the point, it's perfectly possible—especially when we are tired—to "hear" whispers in white noise that are nothing more than the listener's expectations.

In 1968, the Otto Reichl Verlag (publishing house) of Remagen published Raudive's account of his experiments in German under the title *Unhörbares Wird Hörbar* ("The Inaudible Becomes Audible"). On October 13 the following year, the British publisher Colin Smythe was handed a copy while at the Frankfurt

Book Fair. In 1971, he brought out an expanded version of the book under the rather more commercial title, *Breakthrough*.

Breakthrough was not a particularly readable book. Most of its 391 pages were devoted to an increasingly tedious transcript of Raudive's polyglot tapes. But it did contain an indication that scientists other than himself were working on the voice phenomenon and some were prepared to take a strictly nuts-and-bolts approach. The work was sufficiently successful to persuade one of Colin Smythe's executives, Peter Bander, to write a book of his own on the subject. This offering, which was published by Colin Smythe in 1972, was much more superficial than the Raudive original but also far more readable. It dealt in part with the promotional activity that surrounded *Breakthrough* and the way in which the media dealt with the idea that ghosts might be recorded on tape. But more important, it detailed some of the work that had been done to establish the objective reality of the voices. Much of it has been impressive indeed.

First, tests were carried out to ensure that the voices were actually present as magnetic traces on the tape and not simply psychological projections into the white noise. Jochem Sotscheck, director of the Acoustics Research Group at the Central Office for Telegraphic Technology in Berlin, made use of a voice printer to show not only that the voices really existed but occurred in the same frequency range as human speech.

Once it was realized that *something* was impressing onto the tape, the next stage was to rule out any question of freak electronic intrusions—radio broadcasts, high-frequency transmissions, or even, as one authority suggested, low frequency communications used by the CIA. This was done by attempting a voice recording from inside a Faraday Cage.

A Faraday Cage is a device named for the nineteenth-century British pioneer of electromagnetism Michael Faraday. A wire mesh screens out all known forms of electromagnetic radiation and consequently creates a quarantine area into which no broadcast energy can penetrate. The recording device was set up inside the cage. Although a rational electronic explanation was now ruled out, the voices still appeared on the tape.

As the media became increasingly interested, more and more tightly controlled experiments took place. Typical of them was that set up by the British *Sunday Mirror* newspaper at the Pye Laboratories. Under the watchful eyes of twelve observers, Raudive was challenged to produce a voice while completely isolated from the machines and control devices set up by electronics engineers. In eighteen minutes there were two hundred voices on the tape, twenty-seven of them clear enough to be played back through a loudspeaker. Pye's chief engineer of the day, Ken Atwood, tried everything he knew to stop the voices or at least explain them within known electronics theory. He failed to do so and afterward commented philosophically, "I suppose we must learn to accept them."

Other experts came reluctantly to the same conclusion. The eminent parapsychologist, Professor Hans Bender of the University of Freiburg[91] went on record with the statement that examination with high-quality technical equipment in May 1970 "made the paranormal hypothesis of the origin of the voice phenomena highly probable." The physicist and electronics engineer A. P. Hale examined tests carried out in a screened laboratory and could only say, "I can not explain what happened in normal physical terms."

With the reality of the voice recordings and their paranormal origin established beyond all reasonable doubt, it becomes possible to embark on a logical analysis of their content. The picture that emerges is extremely interesting.

First, the voices are fragmentary. There are no lengthy messages on the tapes and little direct continuity. An entity will typically record a few words—a sentence or two at most—then disappear. Sometimes the same entity will return later but will seldom attempt to pick up where he left off. Where there are multiple voices on a tape, the impression one gets is of people jostling for attention while using a difficult and often faulty telephone connection.

Even when a voice gets through in solitary splendor, the messages are frequently clipped ("Here is Ivarits") and sometimes nonsensical, as in the bewildering "Statowitz one man eight nought one inch rub off." It is also clear that the individual entities attempting to communicate all have their own agendas. One complains of being a slave. Another insists it is surrounded by scoundrels. A third cuts through the words of a fourth with the testy exclamation, "Oh you chatterbox!"

Despite this, certain of the entities appear willing, even anxious, to enter into a dialogue with the experimenter. Many are interested in the process of communication and will sometimes put forward their own theories as to how it works. (Raudive was once told he functioned like radar.) Others attempt to describe their current state, but such descriptions tend to be vague, confused, and often contradictory. You are left with the impression of an unreliable connection to . . . somewhere, filtering through fragmentary scraps of conversation on a severely overloaded line. Thus the importance of the electronic voices is not what they say, but the fact that they exist.

Raudive alone recorded more than thirty thousand of them. At first they claimed to be dead relatives and friends. Later he discovered he had recorded what purported to be the voices of Tolstoy, Jung, Stalin, Hitler, Mussolini, and Churchill. Although Tolstoy and Stalin both spoke Russian, almost all the rest showed the now familiar mixture of languages. As other researchers began to work independently with the phenomenon, it became obvious that multilingual messages were very much a Raudive trademark—others got them only rarely, if at all.

This discovery led to the suspicion that Raudive somehow influenced the type of voices that came through. Although he remained cautious in his public pronouncements, Raudive himself came to believe there could be a mediumistic aspect to the whole phenomenon.[92] That is to say, he thought the investigator was himself a channel that allowed the voices to manifest. Several others have speculated along the same lines.

Although there was a flurry of publicity following the publication of Raudive's book, the idea of electronic contact with the dead was far from new. I mentioned briefly in the last chapter that Thomas Edison tried to build communication apparatus. So did Guglielmo Marconi, inventor of the telegraph and radio, and Nikola Tesla, who developed alternating current. There is no suggestion any of them was successful, but at the turn of the twentieth century, an American anthropologist, Waldemar Bogoras, claimed to have made phonograph recordings of spirit voices evoked in the air by a Tchoutchi shaman in Siberia. During the 1920s, the Anglo-American author and psychical researcher Hereward Carrington reported that he—and others—heard an unexplained voice emerge from equipment in a sealed room of a recording studio. (It asked, "Can you hear me?") In the same decade, an Italian medium claimed he had successfully made gramophone recordings of direct voice phenomena.

From 1934 to 1936, a great many people in Sweden and Norway picked up unexplained radio signals, but whether these originated in a spirit world remains questionable—there were reports of UFOs over Scandinavia at the time. But in 1936, a London ham radio operator named Gordon Cosgrave claimed to have intercepted Morse code messages from the *Titanic*, which sank on its maiden voyage in 1912. In 1950, there was a curious preview of the Raudive experience when a group of radio hams in Chicago reported unexplained signals carrying rapid bursts of speech in a mixture of languages. In 1956, three years before Jurgenson made his first recording, the American Society for Psychical Research received a report of faint whispered voices recorded on tape, wire, and phonograph discs by the medium Atilla Von Szalay.

Raudive's own work proved eminently repeatable. Several hundred thousand "spirit messages" have been recorded using his techniques by experimenters worldwide, including many who were initially skeptical. But Raudive's achievements may have been no more than a modest beginning.

In August 1981, the American author John G. Fuller received a letter from North Carolina signed by someone called George W. Meek. The letterhead was that of the Metascience Foundation, which Fuller was vaguely aware of as an organization involved in paranormal research. Meek said he had been working on a project that might make a new book for Fuller and suggested they meet. In November they did. Fuller's reputation was based largely on his nonfiction books about psychical phenomena. One of them—*The Ghost of Flight 401*—became a best-seller. But the story he heard from Meek went far beyond anything he had come across before.

Meek proved to be a retired engineer with a lifelong interest in the paranormal. While engaged in mediumistic experiments with a group in Philadelphia, the spirit of a deceased scientist came through to suggest a cooperative project with any engineers interested in developing an apparatus that would establish two-way electronic communication with the dead. The idea appealed to Meek hugely and he volunteered his services.

With the aid of a $70,000 grant from an interested aircraft

manufacturer, he started to put the equipment together. He was later joined by a Philadelphia medium and electronics engineer named Bill O'Neil, who brought discarnate entities other than the original deceased scientist into the project. One, known as "Doc Nick," suggested certain audio frequencies might provide an energy source. Meek claimed that by making the suggested modifications, O'Neil was able to establish two-way communication with the deceased doctor using ham radio equipment. A second spirit, named Dr. George Mueller, took over when Doc Nick eventually ceased to communicate. By September 1980, the equipment was capable of providing clear, audible conversations. Meek named it "Spiricom" and the two partners began work on an even more advanced project—"Vidicom"—designed to build equipment that would produce visible images of spirits.

Meek presented Fuller with more than five hundred documents on his researches, plus many hours of taped recordings purporting to be conversations between O'Neil and the spirit doctors. Fuller had a hard time deciding whether they were genuine. Even when he came to write his book about the developments,[93] he was still sitting on the fence. (An author's note began, "This is a strange story. It is either true or it is not. This determination has to be left up to the reader.") On the one hand, the supposed results obtained by Spiricom were not repeatable. As Raudive suspected about his own work, there was a mediumistic element to the Meek/O'Neil experiments. Spiricom equipment only seemed to work for O'Neil; and even then, both Doc Nick and Dr. Mueller had ceased to communicate by the time Meek was ready to go public. It all seemed very suspicious.

On the other hand, it was difficult to see what either Meek or O'Neil hoped to get out of an elaborate fraud if that was what they were engaged in. Meek declined to patent his apparatus and was quite prepared to hand out schematics to anybody who wanted them. No commercial corporations were established, no investments sought. Clearly nobody was in this for the money. They didn't seem to be in it for the fame either. Apart from a single press conference in April 1982, they made little effort to promote their discoveries. O'Neil in particular was a retiring individual who shunned personal publicity.

Independent examination of the tapes established conclusively that they contained two different voices—O'Neil certainly wasn't talking to himself. Nor, it seemed, was he talking to Meek, but nobody could rule out the possibility of an unknown confederate and one scientist suggested the possibility that the "spirit" voice was computer generated. Meek himself freely accepted that the tapes in themselves did not constitute scientific proof and said so at the press conference.[94] All the same, a great many scientists and engineers took them seriously and worked to duplicate the results.

In Germany, Professor Ernst Senkowski, a physics lecturer, came close. Although he failed to get the fluent two-way conversation of the Spiricom tapes, he was able to demonstrate an interactive contact to Fuller. Using a Raudive-like setup, he first recorded a question on tape, then allowed the tape to continue for a time. Although nothing audible occurred during this process, when the tape was rewound both Senkowski's original question and an answer could be heard. Since the answer contained the code word "aurora," specifically requested by Senkowski, there was no doubt that the electronic voice really *was* giving an answer.

In Scotland, an electronics engineer named Alex MacRea used a device originally designed for stroke victims to pick up paranormal voices. He discovered many of the voices had the same distinctive vocal quality as those on the Spiricom tapes.

Some of them called him by name, and, like Senkowski he was able to get answers to recorded questions at playback stage.

At about the time MacRea was conducting his experiments, another electronics engineer, Germany's Hans Otto König, defeated the problem of audible and immediate interaction using an ultrasound technique that he demonstrated on Radio Luxembourg. König's equipment generated a complex mixture of harmonics in the 30,000 Hz range—well beyond the capabilities of the human ear—and, like Spiricom, was designed to permit audible two-way conversations with the mystery voices. Early in 1983, König accepted an invitation (or perhaps "challenge" would be a better word) to demonstrate the apparatus on air.

The "König generator" he brought to the studio was carefully checked for fraud by Radio Luxembourg technicians and an agreement was reached that staffers of the station, rather than König himself, should carry out the experiment. Despite these precautions, the "König generator" achieved results comparable to Spiricom. The experiment began live on air with one of the station staff asking aloud for a voice to come through. A few seconds later, a voice did. "Otto König makes wireless with the dead," it said. A brief conversation ensued, interrupted at one stage by an excited assurance from program presenter Rainer Holbe that "on the life of my children" nothing had been manipulated and no one was playing any tricks. Afterward, an official station statement reiterated that the experiment had been closely supervised and added that staff and engineers were convinced the voices were genuine.

Later, König demonstrated his generator at a meeting of the German EVP Association.[95] Not only was he able to establish two-way communication, but when a woman asked to speak to Dr. Raudive, who died in 1974, a voice answered her that appeared almost identical to recordings made by Raudive while he was alive. Since then, an American researcher and author, Mark Macy, has claimed to have received a fifteen-minute *telephone call* from Dr. Raudive in the spring of 1996 and published a sound file of the communication on the World Wide Web.[96]

Macy's experience was just one example of what is now being called "instrumental transcommunication" or ITC, an umbrella term that covers apparent spirit contacts using phones, fax, television, and computers. Some of the claimed contacts have been, to put it mildly, quite extraordinary. In 1985, an engineer named Klaus Schreiber hit on the technique of aiming a video camera at a television set displaying static and instantaneously feeding the output of the camera back into the TV. This produced a swirling fog of static out of which images would gradually emerge. From time to time the images would be identified as specific people or things by electronic voices. Schreiber believes he has communicated with both his deceased wives in this way. Around the same time, Britain's Kenneth Webster was claiming a total of 250 computer-based communications from a sixteenth-century spirit, many of them accompanied by poltergeist phenomena. The text-based communications were consistent with the speech patterns of the time and contained historical details that were later verified.

Two years later, the husband and wife research team of Jules and Maggie Harsh-Fisch-bach from Luxembourg managed sustained computer contacts and high-quality television pictures of the type produced by Klaus Schreiber. On one occasion, according to Maggie Harsh-Fisch-bach, she received a three-page *fax* from the French science fiction author Jules Verne (who died in 1905) giving details of the afterlife. By 1995, the first electronic cross-correspondence was in place. Maggie Harsh-Fisch-bach received a television picture of the spirit of a French child named Anne Guigne at about the same time as a second picture of the girl was received by the German researcher Adolf Homes.

Reports of similar phenomena continue to pour in without, however, attracting much attention from the mainstream scientific community. The result, so far as I can ascertain, is that the entirety of the EVP and ITC phenomenon has yet to be subjected to the sort of rigorous laboratory scrutiny that would establish conclusively whether or not we are now bombarded consistently with electronic communications from the dead. But clearly something very odd is going on, and unless you subscribe to the idea of an international conspiracy to defraud, it seems to have a paranormal element.

Taken in tandem with certain ghostly sightings and a wealth of mediumistic communications, the tens of thousands of electronic voices now on tape provide a wealth of circumstantial evidence for the survival of your consciousness after death. There is also a considerable body of evidence indicating where your consciousness may ultimately end up after it has survived.

19

Coming Back

It is conceivable I might be reborn as a Chinese coolie.
If so, I shall lodge a diplomatic protest.
Sir Winston Churchill, when asked his views on reincarnation

IMAD ELAWAR LIVED in Lebanon, in a very remote and somewhat primitive village—one of those areas where time stands
still and most people don't travel very far from the place of their
birth. Though he had never traveled very far, Imad one day began
to claim he'd lived before as someone called Ibrahim Bouhamzy
in the village of Khriby, about thirty kilometers from what was
then his present home.

One day Imad bumped into somebody he recognized from
his past life, a man who actually came from Khriby. When questioned, it transpired this man was a neighbor of . . . Ibrahim
Bouhamzy. With an incentive to investigate, it was quickly discovered that of forty-seven items of detailed information made
by Imad about the Bouhamzy family—including names and the
fact that he'd had an affair with a woman called Jamile—forty-four
were accurate. When Imad Elawar first mentioned the
Bouhamzys, he was only two years old.

This is not the only well-investigated case of its type. In 1929,
three-year-old Shanti Devi began to tell her parents about her
"husband" and "children." Although the Devi family lived in
Delhi, India, where belief in reincarnation is a religious tenet, the

middle-class couple decided their daughter had dreamed up some imaginary companions, as children often do. They hoped she would soon grow out of it. In fact she didn't. By the age of seven, Shanti was still talking about her husband and was now able to name him. He was called Kedarnath and they had lived together in the town of Muttra, where she had borne him three children. She recalled she had died in 1925 giving birth to a fourth baby.

All this was too much for Shanti's parents, who decided she might have a mental illness and hurried her to a doctor. The physician listened to her story, concluded there was no indication of mental illness, and told the parents these were medical details of childbirth and death a seven-year-old could not possibly know.

Not long afterward, a business acquaintance of Shanti's father called at the door. The child happened to open it and recognized him at once as a cousin of her supposed husband. At this point, things took a distinctly weird turn. Shanti's parents both knew the town of Muttra actually existed—it's located a short distance from Delhi. Now the businessman confirmed he did have a cousin called Kedarnath who lived there. The man had married a woman named Ludgi (the name Shanti claimed was hers in the previous life) who had indeed died in childbirth. The amount of detail weakened the possibility of coincidence, but Shanti's parents were still a long way from accepting that their daughter was Ludgi reincarnated. Unknown to Shanti, they arranged for Kedarnath himself to come calling. Shanti recognized him at once.

Gossip began to spread and soon interest in the case was running so high that the Indian government set up a special committee to investigate. Members of this committee took Shanti to Muttra for the first time in her young life. The place proved so familiar she was able to lead them through it blindfolded. She successfully found her former home and correctly named several of the family. When Ludgi's children were brought out, she recognized three of them. The fourth was the baby Ludgi had been carrying when she died in childbirth.

Shanti took the investigating scientists to the home of Ludgi's mother where she pointed out changes that had occurred since Ludgi's death. The climax of the investigation came when the child insisted Ludgi had buried some rings in the garden just before her death. Shanti led the way to the spot and a small bag of rings was subsequently dug up. Ludgi's mother confirmed they had belonged to her daughter. The cautious committee later reported they could find no evidence of trickery or fraud.

Sometimes cases of this type can take a macabre turn. In 1968, two-year-old Reena Gupta began to claim she had been murdered in a past life by her husband. The child's behavior became increasingly bizarre. She took to criticizing her mother for the way she ran the house and spent much of her time in crowded streets searching for her past life husband and four children. A colleague of Reena's mother, Vijendra Kaur, discovered a Sikh couple named Sardar Kishan Singh whose daughter, Gurdeep Kaur, seemed to fit the stories Reena had been telling. Gurdeep had been murdered by her husband on June 2, 1961. Reena later identified Mr. and Mrs. Singh as her "father and mother," then went on to identify Gurdeep in a photograph. She also identified Gurdeep's sister both by name and nickname. When Surjeet Singh, the murderer of Gurdeep, was released from jail in 1975 after serving ten years of a life sentence, he took it on himself to visit Reena, by now nine years old. The child warily posed for a photograph of the two of them together.

Belief in reincarnation is, of course, widespread throughout India, as it is among the Druze community of Lebanon, and some investigators have theorized that cases like these are somehow no more than artifacts of the prevailing belief system. It's an idea that seems to be contradicted by the facts. Childhood memories of past lives have arisen in countries with no tradition of reincarnation belief. One example was Joey Verwey of Pretoria, South Africa, whose past life recollections were carefully recorded by her mother over a ten-year period beginning when the child was six. (The memories themselves had begun to emerge three years earlier but weren't taken seriously at first.) The records were subsequently investigated by Dr. Arthur Bleksley, who decided the sheer volume of detail pointed to genuine past life recall.

Closer to home, three-year-old Romy Crees of Des Moines, Iowa, began to recall a past life in 1981. She had detailed memories of living as a man named Joe Williams, who went to school in Charles City, married a woman named Sheila, and fathered three children. His mother's name was Louise, who had an injury to her right leg. He had died as the result of a motorcycle accident.

Romy's parents didn't believe in reincarnation (they were both Roman Catholics) but they didn't think their daughter was fantasizing either. After some soul-searching, they called in a professional researcher, Hemendra Banerjee. Banerjee discovered a place called Charles City—actually quite a small town—some 140 miles away from Romy's home and decided to take her there. He put together a party consisting of his wife and himself; a research colleague, a Des Moines specialist, Dr. Greg States; Romy's father, Barry and Romy herself.

Nobody told the child where they were going, but as they approached the outskirts of Charles City, it became clear she recognized the environment. She insisted on buying her (past life) mother blue flowers and mentioned that when they visited, they wouldn't be able to use the front door, but would have to go around to the side. The party eventually found the home of a Mrs. Williams who lived in Charles City but were unable to call at the front door due to a large notice directing them around to the side. The seventy-six-year-old woman met them on crutches due to an old injury on her right leg. She confirmed she'd had a son named Joe, who was married to a woman named Sheila. He had been the father of three children before he died in a motorcycle accident near Chicago two years before Romy was born.

Past life recall by a child is particularly impressive, since very young children, by and large, do not have easy access to the sort of data that might allow them to construct a detailed fiction. But adolescents and adults can have spontaneous recall as well. Dr. Arthur Guirdham, formerly chief psychiatrist for the city of Bath, England, was treating a thirteen-year-old schoolgirl toward the end of World War Two when she began to recall—through dreams and visions—a past life as a Cathar in France. The information she provided built up a vivid and highly detailed picture of life in thirteenth-century Languedoc. The girl was able at times to transcribe her visions into medieval French and even the distinctive tongue of the area where she said she had lived.

At the time the information emerged, very little was known about Catharism and some details given by the girl were held by historians to be inaccurate. A critical example was the color of Cathar priest robes, universally believed to have been black, but stubbornly held by the girl to have been dark blue. It was not until 1965, more than ten years after the girl's memories emerged, that the French historian Jean Duvernoy published evidence showing the consensus wrong and the girl correct. Guirdham himself was moved to investigate the historical realities behind her story and, starting only with her Christian name, eventually discovered the names of her family and friends, then went on to pinpoint the day, more than seven hundred years previously, when she faced the Inquisition.

Guirdham's schoolgirl was in therapy, a situation that encourages introspection, but there are indications that specific circumstances can trigger past life recall in much the same way that something reminds you of the milk you promised to pick up for your spouse on the way home. The trigger may be trauma, as was the case with a German coppersmith named Georg Neidhart who began to see images, then complete scenes of a past era following the unexpected death of his wife and child. It may also be exhaustion, as happened to the American aviator Charles Lindbergh, who reported falling asleep with his eyes open during a long-distance flight. When he did so, he had the curious sensation of simultaneously experiencing past, present, and future, and recalled voices, friendships, and individuals from a series of past lives. Injury triggered past life recall in the German racing motorist Hermann Medingen. After a serious crash in 1924, he found himself outside his body viewing several past lives of both sexes. One European investigator has suggested past life memory almost invariably results from leaving the body, but while this is not supported by the evidence, some connection between OOBE and past life recall has been well established over a number of cases.

Something as simple as a meeting can act as the stimulus. In Italy, a policeman named Lanfranco Davito was approached by a stranger while on patrol duty and was immediately struck by a highly emotive memory of life in a primitive tribe when the man clubbed him to death in the course of a quarrel. A rather more pleasant example arose in the life of the German parapsychologist Gerda Walter, who was out for a walk with a friend in 1930 when they met up with a retired army captain. The friend made the introductions and Ms. Walter was struck by the feeling she had met the man before. Almost at once she had a clear mental vision of the captain riding through a gloomy forest to escape from a besieged castle. She said nothing, but a little later the captain hesitantly told her he had been seized at the moment of their meeting by an overwhelming feeling he had known her in a past life.

The Dutch researcher Hans TenDam conducted a poll in the hope of discovering how common spontaneous recall of this type might be and discovered only 44 percent of respondents had no past life recollection at all.

I had personal experience of a case involving spontaneous recall by an adult following some newspaper publicity about my work on reincarnation research. A middle-aged woman approached me in the hope of an explanation for a recurring dream she'd been having since her teens. In the dream, she was crossing an ancient amphitheater, something like a Roman arena but smaller and with rather more sympathetic spectators. She was younger than her current age, dressed in a Grecian-style tunic. The totality of the dream was that she was walking across the arena sand, driven by an urgent need to reach the other side before some unknown disaster occurred.

Subsequent investigation stimulated more detailed memories and a comprehensive past life story began to emerge. In this life, the woman was named Andreas, a Mede princess who lived in a city called Xanthus. The name of her father, the king, was Adah. His country seemed to be one of those ancient maritime civilizations bordering the Mediterranean and now long disappeared. The woman recalled that King Adah was overthrown by his brother Pericles who was leading a rebellion of provincial governors. Andreas herself was imprisoned in a subterranean cell, but later released to appear in the public arena as proof she was still alive. She determined to accuse Pericles of her father's murder, since under Median law such an accusation would have to be investigated, even if it involved the new king. But by the time she entered the arena, Andreas was ill and she died before she could cross the sand to the king's box and make her accusation.

The story failed to check out historically—at least at first. The ancient kingdom of Media occupied what is now north western Iran, but, with only a small area of coastline, it was far from being a maritime civilization. It did have a sophisticated legal system, but the capital was Ecbatana, not Xanthus. Indeed there was no city of Xanthus anywhere in Media. Although the kingdom endured for a millennium, neither Adah nor Pericles appear in its lists of rulers. I could find no reference to a provincial rebellion either.

But it later transpired that the problem was the starting point of the research, all of which was based on the assumption that since Andreas was a Mede, the country she lived in had to be Media. A different assumption—that Mede or not, she was living elsewhere—produced a whole different picture. Part of the Median Empire was a maritime country called Lycia, which once occupied what is now the Anatolia area of Turkey; and Lycia fit the Andreas story perfectly: it was governed by a Median ruling class, the capital city was Xanthus, and a rebellion of provincial governors placed a King Pericles on the throne.

The technique that produced such a wealth of detail in this case was hypnotic regression, something that permits what appears to be past life recall in 93 percent of subjects, according to a study carried out by Dr. Jim Parejeko of Chicago State University in 1980. The use of regression dates back to Sigmund Freud and followed on his discovery that many emotional problems were rooted in forgotten experiences often dating back to childhood. His psychoanalytical method, known in its day as the "talking cure," was designed to help patients recall them. His followers tried different approaches, including hypnosis and drugs, but all had the same broad aim: to help patients remember by regressing them to an earlier stage of their lives.

The technique produces valid results. Subjects regressed through hypnosis will typically exhibit personality changes and behavioral patterns appropriate to the target age. Their voices will often alter and their vocabulary reduce. Handwriting becomes childlike. Involuntary reflexes revert to those of childhood. Examination of eye movements has indicated that when subjects are regressed to an early age, their ocular coordination degenerates. In two specific cases, ophthalmic examination produced even more impressive results. With one subject, who had worn glasses since the age of twelve, regression to the age of seven produced a measurable improvement in vision—a development most opticians would insist was impossible. The second subject had actually suffered blindness in the left half of the right eye, due to the presence of a colloidal cyst in the third ventricle. When the cyst was surgically removed, his sight returned to normal. But when regressed to a time before the operation, the visual defect reappeared. All this suggests a literal regression, not simply role-play.

Early therapeutic use of regression stopped at the appropriate childhood level, but in 1898, a Parisian colonel named Albert de Rochas succeeded in regressing a subject beyond the point of birth so that she reported inter-uterine experiences. When he discovered it was possible to create regressions of this type in others, de Rochas decided to see what would happen if he suggested they should go beyond the womb. Almost without exception, they presented what purported to be memories of past lives. In the twentieth century, British psychiatrist Alexander Cannon regressed more than fourteen hundred subjects, all of whom presented past life memories and there have been reports of work in Australia designed to validate the existence of a "cellular memory" believed to record past lives.

Cannon gradually came to believe the memories were genuine,

but whether or not he was right, there is something of a mystery here. If the material is fantasy, the question arises as to why the fantasy takes this particular form. We are not dealing with subjects whose religious convictions predispose them to a belief in reincarnation. Much of the work has been carried out with westerners, heirs to a Judeo–Christian culture that, as we have seen, looks forward to resurrection rather than literal rebirth. Even those with no belief in survival after death seem to remember past lives.

There is, of course, the possibility that the "memories" do not represent past lives at all. Daniel Dunglas Home, the famous medium, once remarked, "I have had the pleasure of meeting at least twelve Marie Antoinettes, six or seven Marys of Scotland, a whole host of Louis and other kings, about twenty Great Alexanders, but never a plain John Smith." Anyone with the slightest interest in reincarnation research soon attracts a stream of people claiming they were once the bard of Avon or the queen of Egypt. They are seldom convincing. Their "proof" is often confined to personal intuitions or the proclamations of some psychic. And their status in this life seems to be in inverse proportion to the status of the claimed incarnation—the lower their social station in this life, the higher it appears in former existences.

Even where there is no question of self-aggrandizement, research has shown that people sometimes resurrect material they have read and present it as past life recall. As long ago as 1906, what appeared to be a highly persuasive study collapsed for just this reason. A hypnotized subject, identified only as "Miss C," described her fourteenth-century life as Blanche Poynings, a close friend of the countess of Salisbury during the reign of Richard II. The account was detailed and seemed historically accurate, but investigation eventually proved the information was drawn in its entirety from a nineteenth-century novel entitled *Countess Maud or the Changes of the World, a Tale of the Fourteenth Century.* Miss C had read the work shortly after its publication in 1892 and forgotten all about it in the intervening years until she unconsciously used it as the basis of her ostensible past life "memory."

In another well-documented case, a woman produced vivid recall of a life in Ancient Rome with an impressive wealth of detail and substantial accuracy in portraying the period. Years later, investigators discovered the novel (long out of print) from which she had unconsciously drawn the story, complete with the names of her Roman husband, sisters, and lover.

But if some of this material may be fiction, it would be wrong to assume all of it is. The same woman who "remembered" life in Ancient Rome produced equally detailed memories of a life as a Jewess in medieval York. This material included reference to a church crypt in which she had hidden to escape pogroms. When the material was first published, no such crypt was known to exist. Only afterward was it discovered by workmen engaged in renovations. Prior to this point, it had been sealed, lost, and forgotten for centuries. It's difficult to see how this sort of data can be dismissed as fantasy or the unconscious dramatization of a forgotten book.

It's also clear that circumstances can arise where genuinely paranormal "memories" may not relate to a past life, whatever the superficial appearances. During World War Two, for example, Berliner Hermann Grundei was checking some financial records during an Allied bombing raid when he was struck by the feeling he had lived like this before. He kept the books in an old safe in a dark corridor and checked them routinely every Sunday. Now he recalled the ending of a past life in which he went to inspect his books, which were also kept in a safe in a dark corner. The inspection of long ago showed he was bankrupt, the result of embezzlement by his bookkeeper. Unable to face the future, he committed suicide.

These memories first arose in 1943, but more detailed recall emerged subsequently. Grundei gradually became convinced he had lived in a small seaport town in the nineteenth century and died sometime between 1870 and 1885. His bankrupt business had been concerned with ships and timber. By 1952, he was sufficiently sure of his information to begin writing to the authorities in various German seaports in the hope of confirmation. Eventually he received it. Not only did he discover there had indeed been a man whose background and history matched the memories, but the man's son was still alive. In 1956, Grundei went to visit. He and his "past life son" looked and spoke so alike that people mistook them for brothers.

On the face of it, the case appears to present evidence for reincarnation. But careful comparison of dates indicated that Grundei was born more than a month before his "earlier incarnation" shot himself. This would seem to rule out reincarnation as it is generally understood, although it does leave room for another altogether more sinister form of postmortem survival—possession. As it happens, the Grundei case is not the only pointer in this direction. A well-attested study involved a thirteen-year-old American girl named Lurancy Vennum.

In July 1877, Lurancy had a fit at her home in Watseka, Illinois. Soon after, she began to fall into frequent spontaneous trances during which secondary personalities emerged, several of them quite unpleasant. Her worried parents called in a doctor named W. W. Stevens who was able to see the problem for himself, since Lurancy went into trance while he was present and he was able to have a conversation with two of the personalities. They identified themselves as Katrina Hogan and Willie Canning. Dr. Stevens decided to try hypnosis. Lurancy proved a good subject and told him her symptoms had been due to possession by evil spirits. She then announced there was a spirit named Mary Roff in the room and she would permit Mary to possess her for a time. The following morning, Lurancy woke claiming to be Mary Roff.

It seemed the claim was valid. Mary Roff was a local girl who died in 1865, about a year after Lurancy was born. When Lurancy was taken to Mary's home, she was able to greet her "relatives" by name and recognized an old schoolteacher. She then went on to detail scores of incidents from Mary Roff's childhood. The Roff family was so convinced they were talking to their dead daughter that they agreed to let Lurancy/Mary live with them. The Mary persona explained that the angels would only let her stay for three months. For that period of time, she stayed with the Roffs as their daughter, never once saying or doing anything to convince them she was anyone other than Mary. At the end of the time, Mary's "spirit" withdrew; Lurancy returned and walked back to the Vennum household. The case was thoroughly investigated for the Society for Psychical Research by Richard Hodgson, who reported his conviction that the phenomenon was genuine and felt the only possible alternative to spirit possession was the unlikely appearance of a secondary personality with paranormal powers.

Despite the problems, scientific investigation has produced a large—and growing—body of evidence to suggest reincarnation is a fact of life. The earliest systematic study was carried out by Colonel de Rochas, the French investigator who first discovered it was possible for regression to reach beyond the womb. In 1904, he worked with nineteen subjects, all of whom produced past life memories under hypnosis, but was unable to unearth historical confirmation, largely due to lack of records but in some instances because what records were there contradicted his subjects' memories.

Interest in the subject received an unexpected fillip when a book by American businessman Morey Bernstein, *The Search for Bridey Murphy*, became a runaway international best-seller. In 1952, Bernstein conducted a series of hypnotic experiments with a twenty-nine-year-old housewife from Pueblo, Colorado, named Virginia Tighe. His original objective was to investigate regression in the purely clinical sense—that is, within the subject's known lifetime—but before long Mrs. Tighe began to present memories of a life lived as Bridey Murphy, an Irishwoman born in County Cork in 1798.

The amount of detail that emerged about Victorian Ireland was impressive. It included information on coinage, furniture, food, farming methods, books, popular songs, and a great deal more. Bernstein thought he had some serious evidence for reincarnation on his hands and wrote it up. The enormous success of his book attracted both scientific and media attention and inevitably there were those who set out to debunk his findings. A newspaper reporter eventually discovered Virginia Tighe had had an Irish nurse during childhood and printed an "exposé" claiming this must have been where she obtained the information.

It was the sort of glib explanation that satisfies skeptics, and interest in Bernstein's book declined steadily thereafter. But it scarcely stands up to close scrutiny. Mrs. Tighe was born in 1913, which means a childhood nurse would have had to have been more than a century old to claim personal experience of Bridey Murphy's early life and times. Secondhand knowledge, drawn from conversations with parents or grandparents, seems an unlikely source, given the extraordinary nature of the detail presented. In one instance, for example, "Bridey" claimed to have slept in an iron bedstead as a child. In 1952, specialist historians were claiming iron bedsteads only came into use in

Ireland after 1850. Later, however, it was discovered they were being advertised in the country as early as 1802.

The case attracted the attention of a young, Montreal-born investigator, Dr. Ian Stevenson. Thirty-four years old at the time, Stevenson had begun a distinguished academic career culminating in his appointment as chairman of the department of neurology and psychiatry at the University of Virginia School of Medicine. He was already showing an interest in the paranormal and later became president of the (British) Society for Psychical Research. But the Bridey Murphy story may have proven something of a turning point, since he not only decided the evidence Mrs. Tighe presented supported the reincarnation thesis but went on to become one of the most conscientious and respected investigators in the field.

Today, Dr. Stevenson has substantially more than two thousand verified[97] case studies on his files, and his investigations have carried him into the curious area of xenoglossy—the ability to speak a foreign language you have never learned. One study involved a thirty-seven-year-old Philadelphia housewife, identified as "T. E.," who, when hypnotised by her husband (a qualified physician), produced memories of a life as a Swedish peasant named Jensen and demonstrated an astounding ability to converse in colloquial seventeenth-century Swedish. Another involved a Hindu girl named Swarnlata Mishra, who began to sing in Bengali at the age of four, although she had never been exposed to the language. The child claimed to have been a Bengali in a past life and that she learned the songs from a friend.

Some two hundred of the cases investigated by Stevenson apparently indicate that birthmarks and some wounds can be "carried over" from one life to the next. A typical case he investigated involved a Tlingit fisherman in Alaska named William George. Although George's tribe subscribed to a belief in reincarnation, George himself began to doubt it in later years and eventually promised his son Reginald he would come back as Reginald's child "if there was anything in it." He told Reginald he would recognize the reincarnation by the recurrence of two birthmarks, one on his left shoulder, the other on his left forearm. For good measure, George handed his gold watch to Reginald and swore to reclaim it if he did manage to come back.

In 1949, William George was drowned at sea. During May the following year, Reginald George's wife, Susan, gave birth to a baby boy who exhibited birthmarks identical to those of his grandfather. The couple named him William George Jr. and the baby quickly grew into his name. He looked like his grandfather, walked like his grandfather, and displayed a precocious knowledge of boats and fishing, although he turned out to have a fear of water. His family relationships were bizarre—his eight elder brothers and sisters called him grandfather, he referred to his uncles and aunts as sons and daughters, and he insisted his great-aunt was actually his sister. At the age of four, he walked into his parents' bedroom and claimed the gold watch.

Stevenson's discovery of wounds carried over from one life to the next would suggest the possibility that certain illnesses might have past life roots. The Canadian psychotherapist Dr. Roger J. Woolger, an Oxford graduate who began working life as a skeptic about reincarnation, now devotes almost his entire career to a form of past life therapy that, he claims, has produced results in cases of insecurity, depression, unexplained phobias, and sexual difficulties. Typically, Woolger uses regression techniques that permit his patients to access past life memories that are then explored in a therapeutic context in order to discover what circumstances led to the current emotional problems.

But it seems this type of therapy is capable of alleviating

physical as well as psychological conditions. A case in point is that of the Toronto fashion model Bonnie Brown, who had a history of bronchitis from childhood until regressed by hypnotherapist Beverly Janus in 1972. Ms. Brown had recall of five different lives, including one as an eastern European woman transported to a Nazi concentration camp during World War II. Her lung problems began on the chill train journey and by the time she reached the concentration camp, she was coughing blood. When Janus suggested Brown need no longer be influenced by this past life trauma, Brown's bronchitis cleared up completely for the first time in twenty-nine years.

The American psychologist Dr. Helen Wambach used a similar technique to treat twenty-seven-year-old Shirley Kleppe-Moran, who had been suffering from unexplained seizures since the age of seven. Under hypnosis, Ms. Kleppe-Moran recalled a life as a sixteenth-century French girl accused of witchcraft by villagers who subsequently chased her over a cliff, where she fell to her death. Once the memory of this experience was brought into the light of consciousness, the seizures ceased.

Evidence of this type suggests specific individuals may have lived before, but a comprehensive ten-year statistical survey carried out by Dr. Wambach has gone a long way to establishing the possibility that reincarnation may be universal. Using a sample of more than one thousand regressed subjects, she collated data on sex, race, social status, clothing, and utensils reported across the broad base of past life memories. Her findings were fascinating. The ratio of reported female-to-male lives exactly reflected the population balance of the time. Less than 10 percent were of high social status, again reflecting actual population statistics. The number of lives reported from each time period between 2000 BCE and the twentieth century was consistent with historical population growth. Racial distribution also conformed with historical statistics. With only eleven exceptions, all descriptions of past life clothing, utensils, and footwear were historically accurate.

Dr. Wambach's dry statistics are eerily convincing. Where individual case studies might prove (at best) that a chosen few have been reincarnated, these figures seem to suggest it happens to us all. When you factor in the evidence of ghosts, of mediums, of out-of-body experience, electronic voice phenomena, and the rest, it begins to look as if consciousness does indeed survive the demise of the physical body.

In face of this, the time has come to find out what you might expect to happen to you when you die.

20

The Death Experience

IN 1962, I had the unexpected pleasure of meeting a woman who died and lived to tell the tale. Maureen Cowan went into a Northern Irish hospital for a routine operation and died on the table. Her heart stopped for four minutes, close to the maximum time the brain can survive without damage. Then the frantic efforts of the medical team got it started again, the operation was concluded without further mishap, and Mrs. Cowan was wheeled into the recovery room.

When her husband introduced us, I asked her if she could remember anything about being dead. "Quite clearly," she said matter-of-factly and proceeded to tell me all about it.

The first indication that anything was amiss came when she found herself drifting out of the anesthetic. She felt no pain, but became dreamily aware of the lights and the masked surgical team around her. Her perspective was wrong. Instead of looking up at the surgeons working on her innards, she found herself looking down on them. Then it seemed she was sucked into a long tunnel and moved toward a bright light before finding herself in a sunlit parkland.

"Did you realize you were dead?" I asked.

"I thought something might be wrong," she said without a hit of irony, "because I was met by Jesus Christ."

Maureen Cowan described Jesus Christ as a tall, handsome, full-bearded man in a long, luminous white robe. They chatted for a while—she could no longer remember the details—before he told her she would have to be getting back. Although she was happy and peaceful in the parkland and didn't want to go anywhere, she felt an irresistible pull before the vision faded and she eventually woke up in the recovery room.

Mrs. Cowan's operation and experience occurred in 1960 about eighteen months before she described what it was like to me. This was more than fifteen years before Dr. Raymond Moody Jr. published his book *Life After Life*, which introduced the term "near death experience" (NDE) to a fascinated public. Yet her description of dying tallied in all important particulars with those of others who went over the edge but somehow survived.

Dr. Moody interviewed more than a hundred patients in his attempt to construct a picture of the afterlife. His findings were anticipated by Dr. Elizabeth Kubler-Ross and confirmed by a host of other investigators who rushed into the field following the publication of the Moody best-seller. Broadly speaking, this is what you can expect when the Grim Reaper eventually comes calling:

As you've already learned from this book, there are three main highways out of this life—illness, accident, or old age. None of them is very much fun, so the chances are you will approach your death in some degree of discomfort or even pain. The good news is it isn't going to last; and whatever you might think, it isn't going to become unbearable either. If you're receiving medical attention, you'll know the worst is over when you hear the doctor pronounce you dead. (It may, of course, be a friend who performs this service for you. Listen out for a tearful "I think s/he's gone!")

At this point—perhaps even a little before—you can confidently expect the pain to stop, but not necessarily all the discomfort. You are likely to hear a loud, unpleasant buzzing in your ears, maybe even ringing sounds. But none of it will last long. By the time you leave your body, things will have quieted down considerably.

Leaving your body at death is a lot like the out-of-body-experience you may, statistically, have had while you were still very much alive. One minute you're lying on the bed. The next you're out there floating somewhere near the ceiling. Perhaps the most interesting thing at this stage is that you don't feel any different (except maybe a lot less sick.) You've got two arms, two legs, a body, and a head, all of which feel real and solid, and everything functions as it's always done. In fact, it functions better. If you lost a limb during your life, you'll find it's back now and working well. Same goes for any physical impairment.

In this curious but essentially benign state you can look down on your own corpse, watch the doctors try any last-ditch revival, and listen to your loved ones bewail their failure or discuss whether you've remembered them in your will. What you won't be able to do is communicate. You can talk all right, even yell at the top of your voice, but while you can hear them, they clearly can't hear you. If you try to grab their arms and shake them, you'll discover that even though everything looks solid, it actually isn't. Any attempt to touch will just lead to your hand passing through like a special effect in a movie. Either they've stopped being solid or you have; and the smart money is on you.

When I investigated the out-of-body experiences of various people over a period of years, most of my subjects wandered about their physical environments like ghosts, but one reported an awareness of a new "direction." It's a matter of common experience that you can move up, down, left, right, forward, back, and points in between, but this was somewhere else—a direction that doesn't exist in the familiar world. Having discovered it, my out-of-body subject traveled in this new direction and found herself in a whole different reality. Many other OOB practitioners—most recently Robert A. Monroe, whom we met in chapter 16—have reported experience of different realities, although no one else, so far as I'm aware, has mentioned the "direction" that gets you there.

Once you die, I suspect, you not only become aware of the nonphysical direction but are actively drawn to it. The experience is one of a tunnel, leading toward a distant light. Typically you'll pass through it very quickly—one of Dr. Moody's patients used the phrase "super speed"—and emerge at the far side into a reality very different from the gloomy old deathbed you've just left behind. Maureen Cowan said she was in a parkland, a description echoed by a great many other subjects. When I read the accounts, I was struck by the similarity with the Spiritualist "summerland"[98] where the sun shines all day on a neat, well-watered garden.

At this point, you'll discover you're not alone. There are people about and some of them you'll almost certainly recognize as relatives or friends who predeceased you. You may or may not stop to talk to them, but unlike the mourners at your deathbed, you *will* be able to communicate. Anyone you meet now will be on the same plane of existence as yourself.

Very soon you will meet somebody you haven't met before, unless, I suspect, you were a mystic or a saint during your life— a luminous being of light who seems capable of communicating with you telepathically. Mrs. Cowan decided this being was Jesus.[99] Others have differed in their identifications—Buddha, Krishna, Moses, and various saints have all been mentioned in different accounts—so that it seems your "being of light" will simply fit your personal expectations. Whatever about this, the being will usually present you with a sort of "playback" of your life—the main events at least—and require you to evaluate how you did from a moral standpoint.

At some point after this, a majority of those interviewed by Dr. Moody and the others reached a barrier, often invisible, beyond which they could not pass. When it happened, the being would typically tell them they had to return to their former life on Earth. Very few of them wanted to. By this stage they had left any initial confusion behind and their experience was one of peace, often joy, sometimes ecstasy. The last thing they wanted was to go back to the mortgage and the heart condition. But it turned out they had no choice. Before they knew it, they were in the deathbed again, now no longer a deathbed but the first stage on their road to recovery. The implication, of course, is that the "barrier" represented the ultimate moment of transition between life and afterlife. Only when you cross it have you absolutely, irrevocably, permanently left your old body and passed on to something new.

It all sounds too good to be true, the sort of naive wish-fulfillment that's constructed by those who prefer to take no responsibility for their actions and hope some supernatural father-figure will eventually lead them to a world of sweetness and light. Yet near-death reports of this sort have been presented again and again by individuals from various backgrounds, including atheists with no expectation of an afterlife at all. The order of events may vary and you won't necessarily experience everything I've mentioned, but you'll go through most of it, whoever you are, wherever you live, whatever your beliefs.

The near-death phenonemon has been taken very seriously by some scientists. In December 2001, the prestigious journal of the British Medical Association, *The Lancet*, reported on a study carried out in the Netherlands in which researchers questioned hundreds of patients resuscitated after suffering clinical death. About 18 percent reported some memories of the time during which they were dead, while 8 to 12 percent reported typical NDEs. The study answers objections that NDEs reported long after the event are the result of distorted memories and led researchers to suggest that science needs to take a second look at the nature of human consciousness and the possibility of postmortem survival.

Even psychologists determined not to take anything literally have been forced to abandon explanations like religious beliefs or cultural conditioning and fall back on the curious idea that these vivid experiences are somehow driven by body processes at the point of dying.

Whether physically driven or not, the evidence is that this— or something very like it—is what you're fated to experience at the point of your death. It seems quite a pleasant prospect, characterized by calm, freedom from pain, the possibility of continuity, and even some hint at a sense of purpose. But it has one irritating limitation. It doesn't tell you what will happen when you cross that final barrier.

Mediumistic communications, electronic voice phenomena, and the rest are surprisingly little help. It is a hard, brutal fact that most descriptions of the afterlife from these sources are banal, contradictory, or both and few go any distance toward explaining the gaps in the hard evidence for survival. Fortunately there is one source of experiential information that may be worthy of note, even though, for most of us, it is drawn from a distant, unfamiliar culture.

In 1956, Chinese authorities in occupied Tibet set up a twelve-man committee to tackle what was for them the nightmare of the local language. It had no words for the important things in their lives like guided missiles, trucks, airplanes, machine parts, or atom bombs. To make matters worse, it was jam-packed with different terms for a vast range of incomprehensible mental states.

The situation that so bewildered the Chinese arose out of Tibet's national preoccupation with meditation and self-examination. Although fueled by a religious impetus—the arrival of Buddhism in the seventh century CE—the effect was to develop a system of psychology that, in its scrutiny of subtle states and unconscious depths, is literally unrivaled anywhere in the world today. Although the terminology is unfamiliar to Western ears, this experiential study of the human mind is as scientific as anything the West has to offer, since it is firmly based on the principles of experiment and observation.

What has been observed is fascinating. One of the earliest conclusions of Tibetan meditators was that the mind itself is not at all what we experience it to be. They agree with Western psychology that there are whole areas of which we are normally unaware, but postulate mind/energy interactions unsuspected in the West. Eastern medical theory accepts there is an energy system operative within the human body.[100] Tibetans believe your mind is closely associated with it.

In 1992, the Dalai Lama spoke about mind-energy interdependence at the Fourth Biennial Mind and Life Conference in Dharamsala, India. He maintained that neither mind nor consciousness could be seen as separate things unto themselves, since each exhibited many subtle levels. It is the Tibetan belief that the consciousness we experience in everyday life depends on the brain for its existence. Once brain death occurs, the familiar experience of consciousness can no longer arise. But it was also the observation of Tibetan meditators that a subtle "essence of mind" existed independently of the brain and pervaded the body's energy system. This meant that from the Tibetan perspective, mind could survive brain death, at least for as long as the body's energy system remained functional.

Mainstream Western psychology has nothing much to say about this idea, but it does link rather neatly with the findings of psychical research and the work of Dr. Burr as they pertain to a human energy field and out-of-body experience. If, for example, out-of-body experience really is a field phenomenon that involves the detachment of a second "energy body," then Tibetan theory would explain why consciousness travels with it. The same theory would go some way toward explaining entities like Athenodorus's ghost, which showed the philosopher where its body was buried and clearly wasn't any type of natural tape recording, since it exhibited the ability to communicate. From this perspective, it is clear that certain phenomena usually described as "supernatural" simply represent the manifestation of systems and effects not yet examined by Western science.

Tibetan psychologists accept that an essence of mind survives even when the entire physical basis of the energy system has ceased to exist. They have developed a view of the death process more detailed and subtle than our own, but one that does not necessarily contradict the NDE findings of Kubler-Ross, Moody, and others. According to this picture, the first symptom of death is weakness, followed by sinking and melting sensations as if your body had begun to shrivel. Your vision blurs. It feels as if you're looking at an underwater world.

You begin to lose sensation. Your body numbs; sights and sounds fade away. You are aware of growing cold and your consciousness begins to fade. Nothing seems to matter very much anymore. The upside of the experience is that any pain or illness you've been suffering will fade away as well, just as Western near-death patients have reported. A curious sense of calm descends. Smell, touch, and taste diminish, then disappear. Your breathing weakens and eventually stops.

At this point, you are clinically dead. Heartbeat, blood circulation, and electrical brain activity have all ceased. But you retain consciousness and there is still activity, unsuspected by Western science, in the energy channels. Although your thoughts have dimmed and you have lost touch with the familiar physical world, there is a dreamlike perception of luminous darkness before you undergo an experience very similar to falling asleep. Your awareness passes into what the Tibetans refer to as the "clear light" (a mystical form of all-embracing consciousness few of us are likely to have encountered before) and finally departs from your body. This, the Tibetans believe, is the real moment of death. Your mind has become so tenuous it is scarcely detectable, even to yourself.

What happens next depends on your level of spiritual evolution. Saints tend to stay in the "clear light." The rest of us never even recognize it. You pass through it in total ignorance of its importance and experience a temporary loss of consciousness. Afterward, you awaken to darkness, but your essential self has begun to rebuild the structures you require to take your place in the phenomenal world again. Any memory of the clear light quickly disappears.

So, after a moment of darkness, you again become aware of what's going on around you. Your innermost self has built you a new body, but it is a tenuous, immaterial body like that of a spirit or a dream. Your senses return so you can see and hear those gathered around your deathbed, but—just as the NDE reports confirm—you can't communicate with them. By now, you've completely forgotten the sensations of your dissolution.

It's as if you swooned briefly before emerging from your body like a ghost.

You may actually *become* a ghost. It doesn't happen often, but according to Tibetan research, it does happen sometimes. If you're the sort of person who's formed deep attachments to the material world, you could decide you really don't want to leave it. In such circumstances, you'll set off in your ghost body trying to influence events. If you're particularly stubborn, you will keep trying to influence events even when experience shows you aren't succeeding very well. If your presence impinges on others—as it can do given the right combination of circumstances—a haunting results.

But most of the time no haunting occurs. While it's likely that your feelings will keep you hanging around for a little while, the worst that's likely to happen is that you drift into the dreams of friends or relatives before passing beyond the physical world altogether.

This is where Tibetan ideas of the afterlife become a little tricky for those of us familiar only with the Western way of thinking. In the West, we tend to view the physical world as real and the world of dreams—the dreams we experience each night when we fall asleep—as unreal; or, grudgingly, real only in the sense of something we create subjectively. Tibetan philosophy believes both are equally real. Dreams are not so much something we create as states we visit.[101] But from both Western and Tibetan viewpoints, it is reasonable to assume that the experience of death can be logically inferred from the experience of life.

On a regular twenty-four-hour cycle, your body loses touch with the physical world and you fall asleep. The natural response of your mind is to enter the dream state at intervals until you wake up again. (If you believe you never dream, you're wrong. Science has shown conclusively that each of us dreams every night. Those who think they don't have simply forgotten the experience.) Your body also loses touch with the physical world when you die. Tibetans would argue there is every reason to suppose a surviving mind will continue with its old habits and enter dream states just as it did throughout life.

While you dream at night, your environment seems solid and real. It's only when you wake up that you realize you were dreaming. The same thing happens after death. The experience is vivid and convincing, but it is as much driven by your mind as any sleeping dream. Tibetan texts chart a period of seven days after death during which your dreams are concerned largely with benevolent entities like the "Jesus" figure who met Maureen Cowan or the luminous beings who figure in so many other NDE reports. This is typically followed by a further five-day period during which your dreams become darker. The benevolent figures withdraw and are replaced by tougher deities of far more fearsome aspect.

There are graphic descriptions of both types of deity in the Tibetan texts,[102] but you would be well advised not to take them too seriously. The visions have no objective reality but represent projections of your hopes and fears. The appearance they take on is culturally conditioned so that while Tibetans might expect to see their traditional deities, Westerners will generate symbolic figures from our own cultural background. Tibetans believe that if you can accept this insight, there is a possibility of escaping the dream and returning to the clear light of primal consciousness. But as the experience continues liberation becomes more difficult, since the visions of the final five days are driven by negative patterns and emotions stored up during your lifetime.

During the final stages of your dream encounters, your

consciousness is moving further from its essence as the subtle body you are building grows stronger. Your thoughts naturally turn toward the pleasures of physical existence and your memories generate desire that draws you back to the world of matter. Tibetans believe your fantasies of sexual pleasure bring you into the proximity of couples who are making love, and when your spirit drifts too close to an act of conception it is drawn into the womb to begin your next life.

The electrical field "body" with its attached node of consciousness contributes to the cellular programming that permits the new fetus to develop. Although the field contains memory imprints from your previous existence, these are not readily accessible to consciousness, which, in any case, changes its nature as the physical brain develops. As Dr. Stevenson discovered, the traces of some high-level traumas or persistent peculiarities can be passed on to the new body, but by the time you are born any memory of earlier times will typically have disappeared. But not necessarily forever. Spontaneous recall may be triggered at a later date, and regression techniques can often access the data should the opportunity arise.

Tibetan religious beliefs are not, of course, shared by the majority of Westerners; nor, indeed, by Asians of other faiths. But the picture of the afterlife contained in Tibetan literature is not a matter of Buddhist doctrine. It was developed from a centuries-long investigation of the dream state using techniques closely akin to lucid dreaming. (A lucid dream is one during which you realize you are dreaming, but avoid awakening. This permits a direct conscious examination of the dream state itself, something quite impossible by any other means.)

If the picture stood alone, it would be little more than another of those interesting intellectual speculations about an afterlife that have arisen from time to time in various parts of the world. But it does not stand alone. Incredible though it must seem, this theory, developed in the isolation of the Himalayan fastness, weaves diverse threads of Western psychology and scientific research into a comprehensive, rational whole.

This doesn't make the theory true. But I suspect one day we'll both find it was pretty close.

Epilogue
Living With Death

The date of my death, preceded by the words, "Best Before."
British MP Clement Freud, when asked what wording he
would like on his headstone

A FEW YEARS AGO, my father-in-law attended a state banquet in
Europe. Among his fellow guests was an individual who had
earned himself a reputation as the Continent's top funeral
director. This man had buried emperors, princes, presidents, and
kings. He was at the pinnacle of his career and my father-in-law
was about to discover why.

Midway through the meal, an aide entered and whispered
discreetly in the undertaker's ear. The man listened solemnly,
then nodded once. The aide departed and, as my father-in-law
watched, Europe's leading funeral director did something quite
extraordinary. He reached forward, dipped two fingers into his
glass of wine, and stabbed himself fiercely in both eyes.

Then, tears streaming down his face, he rose and left the room
to offer his sympathetic condolences to the grieving widow.

It's an attitude many of us share, for death is something
almost impossible to take seriously. It frightens you, of course,
but only when it comes close. Health professionals recognize
the typical responses to news of impending death—disbelief,
shock, denial, numbness, sorrow, bargaining,[103] anger and
acceptance—but if your doctor hasn't told you you'll be dead

within the month, the chances are you don't really believe it will ever happen at all.

This is a pity. The Toltecs of ancient South America regarded Death as their spiritual teacher and those who did not heed its teaching as little better than living corpses. These are interesting insights. The Armenian philosopher G. I. Gurdjieff, so beloved of European intellectuals during the 1920s, taught much the same thing. He believed humanity lived in a state analogous to sleep and the necessary prelude to any spiritual progress was to wake up.

Ideas like these are difficult to accept on first encounter, but they make a lot of sense when you start to look into them. Most of us are prey to unconscious drives and urges that lead us to reproduce old patterns time and again. We pick the wrong partners, fight the old fights, repeat the same mistakes, then teach our faults to our children, blissfully unaware we are acting from anything other than free will. This is sleepwalking by any definition of the word.

But how to wake up? Gurdjieff tried it the hard way and imposed a regime on his pupils so harsh that it drove some of them to suicide. The Toltec way was better. Accepting Death as your teacher was the ultimate wake-up call.

So how do you accept Death as your teacher? The first step is to accept it's really going to happen to you. You know this, of course, but you don't feel it deep down where it counts. The next step is to realize it could happen to you before you close this book. That's the crucial step. It's not too hard to think of death as something nebulous that's lurking in the distant future. It's something else again to accept the absolute fact of your personal mortality, to understand the Reaper has been standing at your shoulder from the moment you were born, to grow conscious of the fact your next breath could really, truly be your last.

If this has begun to make you feel uneasy, take a moment to

consider the benefits. Once you recognize, deep down, that you could die at any second, a lot of things that hassle you don't seem important anymore. Every worry shrinks into perspective. You'll reorder your priorities, spend more time on things that really matter, set yourself goals that really count. Hard though it may be to believe, you'll have a lot more fun.

With Death as your teacher, you'll wake up to liberation.

Appendix

Recording Spirit Voices

DR. KONSTANTIN RAUDIVE outlined five different methods of generating the electronic voice phenomenon (EVP), four of which either require no specialized equipment at all or items easily obtainable from Radio Shack or similar outlets. These four are as follows:

1. Open Mike Recording

This is far and away the simplest of all the methods and requires nothing more than an ordinary tape recorder and microphone. (Most tape machines have a microphone built in nowadays and this works just as effectively as a detachable mike.)

Set up your equipment in a quiet room, switch on and record a brief preamble that should include the date and time of the recording, your identity, and the name(s) of anyone with you in the room. Dr. Raudive, who believed privately that there was a mediumistic aspect to the EVP, suggested that you might also call on any "unseen friends" in the vicinity and follow this by calling the names of dead friends or acquaintances.

After this preamble, leave the recorder running in silence for ten to fifteen minutes, then switch off, rewind, and listen for any electronic voice you may have picked up. Analysis of even a short fifteen-minute tape may well take several hours. Open-mike voices tend to be brief, fast, and very soft-spoken so that they can easily be missed altogether on the first few replays of the tape. (This is doubly true if the voices interrupt the recorded preamble, as sometimes happens.) Once a voice has been identified, several more replays are often needed in order to distinguish the individual words. Raudive discovered that the average listener had to train his or her ears over a period of time before the EVP became easily accessible. Musicians and other sound professionals often found it easier, however.

2. Radio Recording

The equipment needed for this form of EVP consists of a tape recorder and a radio. The broadcast recording may be made with an open microphone, but is better done by attaching radio and recorder via a direct jack plug. Since Raudive's original experiments, combined radio/cassette players have become commonplace. As the combination permits you to record radio programs, it is an ideal vehicle for EVP.

There are two possible approaches to the radio recording method. Friedrich Jürgenson, who first discovered the electronic voice phenomenon, firmly believed successful radio recording required a spirit mediator, an entity roughly equivalent to the "control" of a Spiritualist medium, who acts as a sort of gatekeeper, allowing some contacts, refusing others, and generally ensuring a smooth flow of "spirit communications."

To contact your personal mediator, you should switch on the radio, then slowly move the tuning dial from one end of the scale to the other. As you do so, listen carefully for a voice that will tell you to begin recording. (The message can be as terse as a single word like "Now" or "Begin.") Once you have the instruction, leave the radio tuned to the frequency at which you heard the voice and begin recording *even if normal radio broad-casting of music or speech is being transmitted.*

Analysis of tapes made in this way is particularly difficult, since you may have to learn to differentiate between the voice patterns of the phenomenon (typically speeded up and at a higher than normal pitch) and ordinary broadcast speech. Sound experts equipped with professional studio equipment may be able to filter out unwanted music or speech. For the rest of us, it is a matter of developing a very keen ear.

Should you decide against the mediator method—and despite Jürgenson's claim, it is not the only way to achieve results—you should simply tune the radio to an inter-frequency. That's to say, you should search out an area of the tuning scale at which no station is broadcasting and the radio consequently generates only white noise, an indeterminate rushing sound. Once you have found your white noise, begin recording.

As with open-mike recordings, you are unlikely to discern any voices while the recording is being made, and frequent playbacks may be necessary before your ear becomes attuned.

3. Combined Radio Jack and Microphone Recording

This variation on Method 2 was discovered accidentally by Dr. Raudive. It involves connecting a recorder to a radio via a jack, while simultaneously recording the radio broadcast through a microphone. In other words, the microphone of an attached recorder is left switched on. The actual recording session proceeds exactly as before, using either a mediator or white noise inter-frequency, but it was Dr. Raudive's experience that voices generated by this method were more distinctive.

4. Diode Recording

A diode is a small, inexpensive piece of specialist equipment that functions as a very primitive radio receiver—roughly equivalent to the "cat's whisker" crystal sets of radio pioneers. It cannot be tuned and will pull in signals on only one frequency. To generate perhaps the most effective EVP, the diode is attached to a short (6-8cm) aerial, then plugged via a jack into the recorder.

Raudive notes that recording sensitivity must be set to its highest level and some fine adjustments to the length of the aerial may have to be made to maximize results, but voices obtained in this way are easiest of all to hear and have characteristics closer to normal human speech.

End Notes

1 I was watching a television program the other night that ignored the lightning theory in favor of the claim that life arrived on earth on a meteorite or comet from space. This idea, delightfully known as the Panspermia Theory, fails to address the question of how life came about before it climbed onto the meteorite.

2 Maybe. As we shall see, cryonics, genetic engineering, and nanotechnology all hold out the tantalizing promise of defeating death permanently, perhaps even in your lifetime.

3 Apparently Russian soldiers on a nearby island used an army transport plane to rustle cattle. But the animals unbalanced the aircraft, so to avoid crashing, the crew drove them out of the loading bay at 20,000 ft.

4 A case that appears unrelated to the 26,000 chickens that exploded on Larry Mohler's ranch in Oregon since these birds were already dead.

5 Based on the latest available (1998) figures issued by the Office of Statistics.

6 370,962 women in 1998 as opposed to 353,897 men, a trend that had clearly been approaching for some time.

7 Unlikely, but not impossible. Ask your doctor.

8 They use healthy arteries cut from some other part of your body for this.

9 Or *ventricular arrhythmia* in their more obscure moods.

10 *The Chronicle of Este,* a Medieval history of Northern Italy.

11 June 24.

12 So it really does help to lick your wounds or, like a particularly repulsive friend of mine, have your dog lick them for you.

13 And indeed, the placebo effect, which allows some 30 percent of all conditions to be cured with wholly inert substances, meant dramatic results sometimes followed.

14 The other is Marburg, which was discovered in 1967.

15 After an early novel on the subject by Michael Crichton.

16 I'm being cautious here in case I've missed some, but the *only* commercially

available antiviral drug I'm aware of at the time of writing is something that helps cold sores. If you catch them early.

17 Readers of my less respectable books—*Martian Genesis, The Atlantis Enigma*, and *The Secret History of Ancient Egypt*—will be aware I have my doubts about the conventional theories of prehistory. But I'm determined to avoid controversy in the present work.

18 Or possibly the Arabs—nobody's quite sure.

19 Urine is high in nitrates. Later, it was discovered that the urine of heavy drinkers—beer or wine—was better still.

20 Proving yet again the old adage that the first casualty of war is truth.

21 Time of writing, spring 2001.

22 This total will increase. Earth's own gravitational influences on a near-Earth group called the Amors means that these asteroids too will eventually begin to intersect with the Earth's orbit. And since asteroids are so notoriously difficult to spot, the chances are that more intersectors are already in place and simply not yet discovered.

23 Unless you get a uranium-rich meteor, I suppose.

24 What I've just described is usually referred to by scientists as the "Tunguska Event" because nobody can say with absolute certainty whether it was caused by a comet fragment, a small comet, an asteroid, or a large meteor. I've even heard it argued that the antimatter drive of a flying saucer exploded over Siberia. Since I have no scientific reputation to protect, I feel free to select the theory I believe most likely, even though the evidence is circumstantial. But I would like to put on record that before I looked at the alternatives, I really wanted it to be the flying saucer.

25 One ghoulishly pointed out that my heart would stop if he put a bullet through it, but that didn't mean it was defective before the shot was fired.

26 Among my women friends at least.

27 I'm rather looking forward to this development. An optician once assured me that the presbyopia (farsightedness) of old age would cancel out the shortsightedness from which I've suffered since the age of twelve.

28 Stollery Director of Medicine, Dr. Alfred Conradi.

29 It transpired that it was all too easy to make mistakes after the invention of the stethoscope as well, but this took time to become clear.

30 The downside of such devices was that the rotting of the corpse—which tends to collapse in on itself—sometimes set them off.

31 Except for those small but pleasurable organs associated with reproduction.

32 Stiff but not sore—you're dead, remember.

33 If you're the type likely to die while jogging or taking some other form of vigorous exercise, you'll become a stiff noticeably faster than a couch potato like me. This is because the exercise will have increased the lactic acid content of your muscles before death occurred, thus giving *rigor mortis* a head start.

34 *The American Way of Death*, first published by Simon & Schuster, New York, in 1963 and reissued in a revised and updated edition in 2000.

35 The problem is by no means academic. In 1780, the largest cemetery in Paris, France, was closed down by official order and 20,000 bodies exhumed to be tastefully displayed in newly developed catacombs where you can view them to this day.

36 Or longer. I've been to wakes that seemed to last forever.

37 Which, of course, it doesn't. Even an embalmed corpse disintegrates eventually, and unless it's buried somewhere bone dry like the Artizona desert the process doesn't even take all that long.

38 Christians live in hope of (physical) resurrection on Judgment Day. Many theologians failed to see how God could manage this without a body, conveniently forgetting that by the time Judgment Day rolled around there would be little enough left whether you cremated it or not.

39 Utnapishtim was a survivor of the Universal Flood. What happened to his fellow-immortals—who should surely have survived as well if they were immune to death—is not made clear.

40 "The Jameson Satellite," by Neil R. Jones.

41 Our present knowledge of space flight suggests this would not actually be the case, but at time of publication, the idea seemed like good science.

42 "The Penultimate Trump," *Startling Stories*, March 1948.

43 *The Prospect of Immortality*, by Robert Ettinger, Doubleday, New York, 1964.

44 Mid-2001.

45 Assuming, that is, we're talking about freezing the whole body. Freezing only the head is based on the assumption that mind and personality reside exclusively in the brain. There have been suggestions from the field of organ transplants that this may not be the case.

46 Starfish and a few other creatures without backbones can be cloned in much the same way.

47 Biological jargon for a cell that's had its nucleus removed.

48 Now the Fox Chase Cancer Center.

49 This is exactly what it sounds like—a super-small version of the classical pipettes you and I once used in chemistry class.

50 Whose name I have been wholly unable to discover, although I suppose in the circumstances we might call her "Dolly" as well.

51 Whose name doesn't seem to be recorded anywhere either.

52 I regret to report Dolly didn't stay healthy. In the early days of 2002, it was reported she was suffering from arthritis.

53 This one I do know the name of—Bonny.

54 August 2001.

55 Easier to think of him or her as "it."

56 http://www.globalchange.com/.

57 Including the cloning of an ancient Pharaoh, an idea I explored in my novel *Resurrection*, which—publishers please take note—has yet to find a home.

58 One angstrom = 10^{-10} metre.

59 A substantial sum in 1959, as some of you may remember. I seem to recall I was earning the equivalent of forty dollars a month at the time.

60 Oddly enough, designs using more or less atoms than this specific figure didn't seem to work.

61 Celebrated annually in honor of Demeter the corn goddess.

62 Not that it did him much good. The shade of Samuel accurately prophesied that Isreal would fall to the Philistines, and some commentators believe the failure of Saul's kingship was actually due to his dabbling in sorcery.

63 Often described in Islam as "the little sleep."

64 As I propose to continue calling it in order to avoid bewildering you completely.

65 The term means "enlightened one." Westerners tend to think in terms of a single Buddha. Most Buddhists, however, believe there have been several.

66 The term "yourself" is tricky in that definition and I trust you'll take it with a pinch of salt.

67 Not the first, although he usually gets the credit.

68 "I think, therefore I am."

69 *In Natural and Supernatural*, Abacus, London, 1979.

70 Originally protected by the pseudonym Nelya Mikhailova.

71 Although Kulagina's mind did influence the biological field that moved the objects.

72 American readers will recognise the humorous reference to George and Martha Washington, the country's first presidential couple.

73 Carl Weschcke now heads Llewellyn Publications Inc., arguably the leading esoteric publisher in the United States.

74 Oddly enough, Griggs, the original builder, had been an army colonel before going into business.

75 The New Hanover County Public Library.

76 When I listened to the Gillhall tapes, this background noise sounded similar to that made by wind on an open microphone. Sheila St. Clair assured me, however, that the internal microphones were shielded from air currents.

77 The Society has declined to release precise details of the location in deference to the privacy of the owners.

78 Sir Shane had been sufficiently rash to publish a brief biographical sketch of Uncle Moreton headed *Sublime Failure*.

79 Regrettably without giving details.

80 The case is drawn from my personal files and the woman concerned asked me not to publish her name.

81 *Beyond the Occult* Bantam Press, 1988.

82 But I can't quite shake the feeling the two physicists may have based their findings on the spirit communications, a notoriously unreliable source.

83 Following an initial drop.

84 The acronym stands for Transcutaneous Electronic Nerve Stimulator.

85 Swaffer's findings were ignored by the makers of the movie *Mrs. Brown*, where the relationship between Queen Victoria (Judi Dench) and James Brown (Billy Connolly) was portrayed as one of simple friendship.

86 I wasn't a student at the time, but I suspect I looked like one.

87 The famous and flamboyant founder of Theosophy.

88 Interestingly, "Doctor" was identified as someone we've already met in chapter 14 of this book: Athenodorus, the Greek philosopher who rented the haunted house.

89 Science correspondent Robert Matthews in the online version of the *Sunday Telegraph*, March 4, 2001.

90 More detailed instructions on how to generate Electronic Voice Phenomena are given as an Appendix to this book.

91 Whom we've already met in the chapter on ghosts.

92 Source: a private letter to the present author.

93 *The Ghost of 29 Megacycles*, Grafton Books, London, 1987.

94 But he added that he was personally convinced of the validity of the experiments.

95 EVP = Electronic Voice Phenomenon, the neutral term used by researchers to describe "Raudive voices" in order to ensure that spirit communication is not automatically assumed.

96 See Macy's Web site at http://www.worlditc.org.

97 Dr. Stevenson considers a case "verified" if an individual's past life recall can be supported by historical evidence.

98 Frequently described to mediums by their spirit contacts.

99 She herself was Jewish, so the identification was interesting. But since she lived in Northern Ireland, a predominantly Christian culture, I suspect there may have been unconscious influences at work.

100 The most familiar exposition is the system of meridians familiar in Chinese acupuncture.

101 This is such a limited *précis* of a profound worldview that I'm almost ashamed to leave it without further expansion. But I'm fairly sure that to expand it here would only confuse us both and add surprisingly little to the matter at hand.

102 Notably in the *Tibetan Book of the Dead*.

103 If I survive this (God) I'll . . . never smoke again/go to church every day/always eat my greens/be a better person. . .

Bibliography

Ancient Spirit, J. H. Brennan, Little, Brown, London, 1992.

Beyond the Occult, Colin Wilson, Bantam Press, London, 1988.

Blueprint for Immortality, Harold Saxton Burr, Spearman, London, 1972.

Dictionary of Mind, Body and Spirit, Eileen Campbell and J. H. Brennan, Aquarian Press, London, 1994.

Discover Reincarnation, J. H. Brennan, Aquarian Press, London, 1992.

Dream Yoga and the Practice of Natural Light, Namkhai Norbu, Snow Lion, New York, 1992.

Exploring Reincarnation, Hans TenDam, Arkana, London, 1990.

Far Journeys, Robert A, Monroe, Souvenir Press, London, 1986.

Foundations of Tibetan Mysticism, Lama Anagarika Govinda, Samuel Weiser, Inc., Maine, 1969.

Ghosts of the Old West, Earl Murray, Contemporary Books, Chicago, 1988.

Harper's Encyclopedia of Mystical and Paranormal Experience Rosemary Ellen Guiley, HarperSanFrancisco, 1991.

Haunted Britain, Antony D. Hippisley Coxe, Pan Books, London, 1973.

Haunted Heartland, Beth Scott and Michael Norman, Warner Books, New York, 1985.

Haunted Ireland, John J. Dunne, Appletree Press, Belfast, 1989.

Hauntings and Apparitions, Andrew Mackenzie, Granada Publishing, St Albans, 1983.

Impact Earth, Austen Atkinson, Virgin Publishing, London, 2000.

In Search of Ghosts, Ian Wilson, Headline, London, 1996.

Jennet's Tale, Herbie Brennan, Mammoth Books, London, 2000.

Journeys Out of the Body, Robert A, Monroe, Souvenir Press, London, 1972.

Life After Life, Raymond A. Moody Jr., Bantam Books, New York, 1977.

Life Without Death? Nils O. Jacobson, Turnstone Books, London, 1974.

Life, Death and Psychical Research, ed. J. D. Pearce-Higgins and G. Stanley Whitby, Rider, London, 1973.

Living Magic, Ronald Rose, Rand McNally, New York, 1956.

More Lives Than One, Jeffrey Iverson, Pan Books, London, 1977.

Mysteries, Colin Wilson, Panther, London, 1979.

Nano, Ed Regis, Bantam Books, London, 1997.

Natural and Supernatural, Brian Inglis, Abacus, London, 1979.

Operation Trojan Horse, John A. Keel, Abacus, London, 1973.

Other Lives, Other Selves, Roger J. Woolger, Crucible, Wellingborough (England), 1990.

Poltergeist, Colin Wilson, New English Library, London, 1981.

Psychical Research Today, D. J. West, Pelican, London, 1962.

Reincarnation, Hans Stefan Santesson, Tandem, London, 1970.

Seriously Weird True Stories, Herbie Brennan, Scholastic Ltd., London, 1997.

Strange Deaths, Steve Moore, John Brown Publishing, London, 1997.

Techno Future, Herbie Brennan, Puffin Books, London, 2000.

The American Way of Death Revisited, Jessica Mitford, Virago Press, London, 2000.

The Belief in a Life After Death, C. J. Ducasse, Thomas, Springfield Ill., 1961.

The Black Death, Philip Ziegler, Penguin Books, London, 1982.

The Case for Reincarnation, Joe Fisher, Granada, London, 1985.

The Cathars and Reincarnation, Arthur Guirdham, Neville Spearman, London, 1970.

The Comedian Who Choked to Death on a Pie, editors of *Fortean Times*, Calder Books, New York, 1996.

The Coming Plague, Laurie Garrett, Penguin Books, London, 1995.

The Comte De Saint Germain, Jean Overton Fuller, East-West Publications, London, 1988.

The Encyclopedia of Parapsychology and Psychical Research, Arthur S. Berger and Joyce Berger, Paragon House, New York, 1991.

The Ghost of 29 Megacycles, John G. Fuller, Grafton, London, 1987.

The Ghostly Register, Arthur Myers, Contemporary Books, Chicago, 1986.

The Phenomena of Astral Projection, Sylvan Muldoon and Hereward Carrington, Rider, London, 1987.

The Projection of the Astral Body, Sylvan Muldoon and Hereward Carrington, Rider, London, 1989.

The Realm of Ghosts, Eric Maple, Pan Books, London, 1964.

The Step on the Stair, Sheila St Clair, Glendale Press, Dublin, 1989.

The Tibetan Book of the Dead, Robert A. F. Thurman, Aquarian Press, London, 1994.

The Tibetan Yogas of Dream and Sleep, Tenzin Wangyal Rinpoche, Snow Lion, New York, 1998.

The Trickster and the Paranormal, George P. Hansen, Xlibris, 2001.

Tibetan Buddhist Medicine and Psychiatry, Terry Clifford, Samuel Weiser, Inc., Maine, 1990.

Tibetan Yoga and Secret Doctrines, W.Y. Evans-Wentz, Oxford University Press, London, 1969.

What Doctors Don't Tell You, Lynne McTaggart, Thorsons, London, 1996.

When We Die, Cedric Mims, Robinson Publishing, London, 1998.

Acknowledgments

THIS HAS TO start with Maggie Phillips and Sophie Hicks of the Ed Victor Literary Agency. On the day I got back from a particularly depressing seminar in the West of Ireland, I received a letter from Maggie asking if I'd be interested in writing a book on death. It was an odd way of cheering me up, but proved to be the starting point of one of my most interesting projects. Sophie was the one who turned the idea into a reality by finding a suitable publisher—although she had to look further than the British Isles to do so.

Once the project got under way, lots of people made interesting suggestions, among them my father-in-law, Chris Burgess, who told me the marvelous anecdote about the European undertaker, and Gary Collins, who drew my attention to the Toltec way of death. Steve Peek found me a vital research source the day after I asked for it. Carl Weschcke was a prince when it came to information about the haunting of his former home. Jacks, as always, got me through the hard times.

You were all marvelous and I want to say so publicly.

Adios.

—last word of John Thanos, executed by lethal injection,
May 16, 1994

Index

About the Author

With books achieving international sales at the multi-million copy level, prolific Irish writer Herbie Brennan has charted a personal interest in spirituality, reincarnation, psychical research, comparative religion and transpersonal psychology that has culminated in this major examination of the mystery of death.

Brennan's intellectual journey began early with a childhood study of Yoga philosophy and expanded into a lifelong fascination for mysticism and the paranormal. In more recent times, an abiding interest in astronomy has led to two children's books on the subject, one specially commissioned for exclusive distribution in U.K. schools.

Over the past few years, his reappraisal of ancient history has stirred lively debate on TV and radio as well as in the press. He broadcasts and lectures regularly throughout the UK and Ireland. He lives in County Carlow, Ireland.